# Surry County Records

Surry County, Virginia,
1652-1684

# Surry County Records

Surry County, Virginia,
1652-1684

By *Eliza Timberlake Davis*

*Reprinted in an Improved Format*

With a New Index by
Robert Barnes

CLEARFIELD COMPANY

Originally published: [195?]
Reprinted in an improved format and with a new index by
Genealogical Publishing Co., Inc.
Baltimore, 1980
Copyright © 1980
Genealogical Publishing Co., Inc.
Baltimore, Maryland
All Rights Reserved
Library of Congress Catalogue Card Number 80-52582
International Standard Book Number 0-8063-0904-0
*Made in the United States of America*

Printed for Clearfield Company, Inc.
by Genealogical Publishing Co., Inc.
Baltimore, Maryland
1995

# NOTE

**S**URRY COUNTY, Virginia, located in southern Tidewater Virginia, was formed in 1652 from James City County. Bounded today by Charles City, Prince George, and Sussex counties, Surry was a parent to Brunswick and Sussex counties, formed in 1720 and 1753 respectively.

The records in this volume, originally abstracted by Eliza Timberlake Davis, derive from the first two volumes of Surry County court order books—those fascinating sources of genealogical, biographical, and sociological information pertaining to the people of colonial Virginia. The court order books comprise a detailed record of transactions relating to the transfer of land, the settling of estates, and the sale of property, and to all manner of personal contracts, legal depositions, and court inquests. In her abstracts Mrs. Davis has retained much of the spelling and phraseology of the original records, preserved, in turn, in this re-typed version.

SURRY COUNTY RECORDS


BOOK, I, 1652-1672


Page 3. 19 Oct. 1650-1651. This document, the first part illegible, concerns an indenture made of service between one Clarke and Richard Bland, merchant, for six years. Clarke stated before signing that he had promised Mr. John Bland, in London, he would serve six years and he would be as good as his word. This indenture was afterwards assigned to Mr. Edward Bland by the said Richard Bland and it seems had been lost or removed from amongst the writings of the said Mr. Edward Bland. As this was lost Clarke was to serve only that custom of the said county having no indenture. Signed, John Holmewood, Robt. Stanton.

Page 4. 7 Nov. 1652. Mr. John Dibdall did at a Court held in this place volunteer and made in open court a petition signed by himself, Robert Lancashear and seventy others, and John Collier without timely redress to Petition etc.

Page 5. 7 Nov. 1652. In Virginia: the petition of John Dibdall humbly showeth that Richard Colt, chyrurgeon, having sayed besyde their fear of God hath att divers tymes to divers persons, vowed ye death of ye petitioner and to have his blood yea his hart blood for ye plaint, hath bound ye sayd Colt to good behaviour...prevented Mr. Simpson, physician, repairing to ye sick wife though att the poynt of death...and disturbs ye peace of ye Commonwealth...Desires that Colt suffer penalty of the Law.

Page 6. 15 July 1652. Thos. Woodhouse and Richard Colt bind themselves on penalty of one hundred thousand pounds of tobacco to be payd unto ye Keepers of ye Liberties of England by Authority of Parliament...
    Wit.: Ben Sidway, Wm. Thomas, Geo. Jordan.
                                                     By order of Mr. Ben Sidway.
Richard Colt enjoyned to be upon good behaviour and keep the peace of ye keepers of the Liberty of England...John Dibdall, minister. This obligation to stand in full power and venture. John Corker, Deponent.

Page 6. 10 Sept. 1652. This bill bindes Mr. John Hix to pay unto Mr. Brasure or his assignor in full seven hundred pounds of tobacco and caskes on ye first day of November next, if not enough, made to seize for satisfaction.

Page 7. Coll. Thomas Swann, by himself and his Deputies or Deputers, will execute and perform the Office of High Sheriff for the County of Surry for the year 1652...to perform the Office of High Sheriff...in full force. Signed: Tho. Swann, Geo. Jordan, Ben. Sidway. Sealed and delivered in the Presence of; Barth. Kinpe, Sam Abbott, Robt. Stanton.

Page 8. 7 9'br 1652. Foulke Jones, planter, receives greetings from William Vaughan, whereas the latter oweth unto Fouke Jones, planter, 600 lbs. of tobacco and caskes, and said Foulke Jones stands indebted to Mr. Walter Chiles for 3000 lbs. of tobacco and casks...Wm. Vaughan binds over to sd. Foulke Jones all of his tobacco crop for the year, made on ground belonging to Mr. Carter, Sr. Wit.: Thos. Pittman, Sarah Brewster.

Page 9. 7 9'br 1652. Daniel Hutton bargained with Thomas Pittman to build him a house by a "certayne tyme," but conditions were altogether negelected, the petition states and desires damages. Wants jury to inquire how much.

SURRY COUNTY RECORDS

Depositions concerning the building of the house of Daniel Hutton by Thomas Pittman were made by Chr. Mitchell, aged four and thirty years; by John Hux, aged forty years, and Thomas Woodhouse. Thos. Gray, Jr., also testified. The jury found for the Defendant, and damages set at 20 lbs. of tobacco.

Jurrors:
- Mr. William Cockerham.
- Mr. John Spiltimber
- Mr. Wm. Carter
- Mr. Robt. Dunster
- Mr. Jno. Leake
- Mr. Jno. Barrow
- Mr. Jno. Senior.
- Mr. Jno. Holmeswoode
- Mr. Henry Emlin
- Mr. James Mason
- Mr. Jno. King
- Mr. Jno. Saynes?

Page 12. (no date). Capt. Pittman, by order from the Governor to send to the Constable these named to make their appearance at James Towne...with their arms fixed, Feb. 1651. They have replyed to Left. Ludwick.
- Jno. Rawlings
- Luke Mezel
- Chr. Baker
- Dan Hutton
- Mr. Ross
- Roger Hotten
- Mr. Hethe
- Mr. Barrow

Page 13. 19 April 1652. John Corker deed to Brady and Spiltimber. John Corker of the County of Surry, Gent., for a valuable consideration in hand paid by Jno. Brady and Jno. Spiltimber, sells land lying on the south side of Besse, adjoining Thomas Warringe, his land, John Braddie and Jno. Spiltimber...day of Aug. 1652. Wit.: Robt. Spenser.

Page 13. 19 April 1652. Deposition of Wm. Murrell, aged 40 years, or thereabouts, that coming from the river he asked Heiward whether he intended to stay at Mr. Ogbourne's.

Page 14. 5 br, 1652 (sic). Deposition of Thomas Cutler, aged 25 years or thereabouts sworn and sayeth that Michael Heiward told Eliza. Rookings that if he, Michael Heiward, died in this country she would be the better of what he had.

Page 14. 3 9br. 1652. Deposition of Stephen Yates, aged 46 or thereabouts, that Michael Heiward and the deponent were by the garden pales, deponent being bound for the...in Mr. Janney's vessel, and took his leave of the said Heiward, who answered him, "Well friend, I shall never see thee more, for here I shall leave my Yorkshire heels." Your deponent answered... does as I have done, give what thou hast to...meaning Eliza Rookings. He replied that he would not give her but half, the other half to put him into the ground...these words were said about a fortnight before the sd. Heiward dyed.    Robt. Stanton, Clk.           Signed, Stephen Yates.

Page 14. 3 9'br 1652. To the Right Worshupful, the Com's for Surry Countye, the Humble Petition of Phillis Cooper, Relict of Jno. Cooper. That her late husband bought of Marye Crafton a maidservant in Jan. 1650, which servant by bargaingoes to serve plaintif's husband until February next. Now so it is that the servant applied to the last Court for her freedom and obtained order for the same. Plaintif wants redress for loss sustained in clothes, care, etc. The Court decides against Mary Crafton, and ordered reparation for losses. Mary Crafton made petition against the decree of the Court.

Page 15. These presents testify that I, John Cawsey, of the Maine in James City County, Taylor, have sold unto David Hamey of the same Citty, a servant maide named Frances Jones for the full terme of five years and three quarters to be completed and ended and then this said Frances to be free, further the sd John Cawsey doe hereby bind myself and my exors. to make good and lawfule sale of the aforesaid servant and to warrant and defend the sd Hamey or his assignes forever...that may prevent or challenge my interests in the servant. 3 Feb. 1645. John Cawse. Wit.: Jnohn Corker, Edm. Mathewes.

The assignment on the back side of this condition as followeth viz.: I, Mary Crafton, Relict of Thomas Crafton, doe assign all my rights &

BOOK I, 1652-1672    3

interests that I have in the within named servant unto Jno. Cooper or his
assigns for the full terme that she hath to serve by assignment to my husband, deceased, witness my hand this 3 day of Feb. 1650.
  Test.: Geo. Jordan, Wm. Rose.    Signed Marye Crafton, her mark.
The assignment to Thos. Crafton, viz.: Memorandum that Edward Hamey doe
assign my right and title of the condition unto Tho. Crafton...this 26
March 1649.    Edw. Hamey.    Test.: the mark of Jno. Rawlin.

Page 15. 13 br 16-? (sic). Wm. Rose, aged 30 years or thereabouts, testified that Jno. Cooper bought the maid of the widdowe Crofton and was content to take all her rights and title, etc. Signed William Rose.

Page 16. 5 7br 1652. James Sowerby Deposeth that the maidservant which John
Cooper bought of the widdowe Crafton said, hearing that her oulde dame
sould her, that she was a foole if she serve soe longe as she was sould for,
she had not so long to serve. Whereupon the sd maidservant left her sd
master and went to the Court in the chiefest time of his croppe, it being
Whitson holydayes, etc. Signum, Ja. Sowerby.

Page 16. 3 9br 1652. Capt. Geo. Jordan testified regarding this servant.
Francis Norton also testified.

Page 17. 11 9br 1652. Recorded. Ind. between John Blackborne of the Parish
of Southwarke in Va., taylor, of the one part, and Jno. Dibdall, Blackbourne moving for four hundredweight of merchantable tobacco...all that
land withwoods, timber,...beg. at...a poplar at the head of Sunken Marsh
to a Pohickerye...in a small swamp, etc. Mark of John Blackbourne.
  Wit.: Morris Rose, Richard Dibdall, Anis Warde.

Page 18. 1 Feb. 1652. Be it known unto all men by these presents That
Thomas Felton, carpenter, for the consideration of the sume of one Thousand
fower hundred pounds of tob. in Leafe do hereby covenant to build Mr. John
Holmwood a Dwelling House fiftye foote Long, Twenty foote wide with a shedd
along the side of a shedd at one end, with a chimney at the inside at one
end and at the other end a chimney without, and a chimney at the side of
the house on the outside, to partition the house into three Roomes and to
lay the Lofte and also to build a Porch six foote wide and tenn foote long,
the timber to be brought in place and the said Felton to Rive, dubb, and
draw all bourds, the sd worke to be begunn between this and Christmas next,
and the sd Felton not to leave ths sd work untill all be finished and to
follow it with all convenient expedition. In consideration whereof the
sd Jno. Holmwood, his heirs, etc., are hereby obliged to pay the sd one
thousand fower hundred pounds of tobacco unto the said Thomas Felton or
his assigns first deduction what shall be lawfully due from the sd Felton
to the estate of Edward Bland, merchant, deceased. This work to be performed on the plantation of Berkeley. Signed, Jno. Holmwood; the mark of
Thos. Felton.

Page 18. 15 X'br 1652. Jno. Flood, aged thirtye years or thereabouts,
sworn sayeth that Wm. Haslewood, marriner, deceased, being at Richard
Bavin's, the said Bavin's wife gave sd Haslewood a Ring to carry home...
and tould him that shee hoped to see him in again, whereupon he said that
if he never came again they had enough in their hands to fortify themselves,
the sd Bavin's wife Replyed that shee would not take...the vallew of what
they owed him for the Ring He answered her that what they had in their
hands they might keep, if he never came again, and further sayeth not.
Signed, Jno. Flood.    Wit. Robert Stanton.

John Blackborne, aged thirtye years or thereabouts, sworn and ex. sayeth
That he bought a servant of Wm. Haslewood, marriner, deceased, for Richard
Bavin for which he was to give eleven hundred pounds of tobacco, and that
the sd Haslewood was to allowe the sd Bavin one hundred and forty pounds
of tobacco and casks and that this Deponent brought the servant from
aboard the Shippe to the sd Bavin's house and that the sd Bavin paid him
all of the tobacco except one hhd. That this Deponent heard Mrs. Bavin
say to Haslewood that she would venture a ring home by him, the sd Hasle-

wood said unto her that she would not make him, for her husband had enough in his hands to satisfie himself if he never came again and that he would leave the sd Bavin's bill in the hands of Coll. Browne but noe levye of Attorney...if he never brought the Ring again and further sayeth not.
Jno. Blackborne.

Page 19. 17 9br 1652. These are the names of the Keepers of the Libertye of England by Authority of Parliament: so will and require you to Empannell and Jurye to enquire if they can finde howe a man at Jno. Bishop's Creek, latelye found dead in the waters came by his Death, accordynge to Custome in the like Kinde thereof faile not. Ct. given this 17 9br 1652.
To the Constable at Smith's Fort, his Dept. or Depts.
The jurors named, vizt.:

  Mr. John Bishopp    Mr. John Hitchcock
  Mr. James Mason    Mr. Robert Mason
  Mr. Thos. Binns    Mr. Thos. Hadlye
  Mr. Jno. Phibbs    Mr. Edmond Howell   Jos.
  Mr. John Courtman    Mr. Robert Palmer
  Mr. John Leake

This is the Jury of Inquest appointed to give theire verdick uppon the bodye of Robt. Woodford, a Northamptonshire man. Sworne before me this 10 of 9ber 1652. Thomas Worrin. Jury's verdict that Robert Woodford servant to Mr. Eveline (or Eneline) desirous to go overboard wadynge over the Creeke was accidentally drowned.

Page 19. 16 Feb. 1651. Ind. between Richard Bavin of the Par. of Southwarke in Virginia, planter, of the one part and Jno. Flood, planter of the part. Richard Bavin, moving, sells to Jno. Flood for 800 weight of tobacco and caske a parcel of land, together with woods, timber, etc., being bounded upon ye land of Coll. Jno. Flood, southward upon the Springe Swamp...toward Sunken Marsh. Rec. 15 Xbris 1652. Wit.: Daniel Hutton, Jno. Dibdall, Jno. Dobbs, Rich. Dibdall.

Page 20. 4 Jan. 1652. Mr. Corker: I have received ye noate in which you certify by me that Mr. Joanes questes you for a debt due from me and Mr. Holdins for Burgesse charge the same being 2072 lbs. of tobacco, the debts were...to Mr. Joanes who obtained an order for it with a greater some amounting to 2997 lbs. of tobacco and caske is already taken for payment, nothing else at present but Rest this 9 ber 1646. Signed, Wm. Worlick.

Page 21. 26 Oct. 1652. Jno. Gibbings and Francis Howgoode bind themselves to pay unto Wm. Murrell the sume of eighteen hundred pounds of good tob. Wit.: Gregorye Rawlings, the mark of Jno. Heiward.

Page 21. 5 Jan. 1652. Robt. Shepard, of Lawnes Creek Parish, Gent., for a valuable sume of tobacco, have given unto Lieut. William Caufield a deed for 100 acres of land or thereabouts, lying at the mouth of Lawnes Creek, in James City Countye. Rec. 7 Jan. 1652. Wit.: James Baylor, Wm. Batt.

Page 22. 21 Feb. 1652. This bill bindeth me John Bruton, my heirs, etc., to pay to Jno. Holmswood, gentleman, the full and just sum of 1028 lbs of tobacco and caskes, ...and two milch cows. Signed John Bruton.

Page 22. Primo Martis 1652. Timothye Issell is to pay to Jno. Holmwood 450 lbs. of tobacco.

Page 23. 25 Feb. 1652. I, John Jennings, by virtue of Timothye Issell, his writing, doe give Mr. Jno. Orchard full power for me in my place and action in behalf of the whole right of a patent for land belonging unto me containing 211 acres as by the pattent appeared unto William Rose and what he shall doe in acknowledging thereof and bind myself heirs and administrators and confirms as if I were personally present.
 Assigns over to Wm. Rose all rights in 211 acres of land, in the patent expressed...in Surry County, bounding upon the land of Thomas Woodhouse, 4 Jan. 1652.

Page 23. 2 Aug. 1653. By the Governor of Virginia. Whereas Jonathan Newell and Edmond Potin are desirous to depart out of the Collonye in the shipp The Two Brother, whereof is Commander Richard Waters. These are therefore to lycense the sd Jonathan Newell and Edmond Potin to goe upon Board the sd shippe and a just Warrant for the sd Capt. Waters to give them their Transportation out of this country.
Dated at Kecoughten this 2nd August 1653. Signed, Rich: Bennett. Rec. 20 Aug. 1653. Ro: Stanton.

Page 24. 5 Feb. 1652. Thomas Warringe, Gentleman: James Mason, planter, and John Wattkins, cooper, are bound unto Jno. Spiltimber, planter, in the sum and penalty of 50,000 lbs of good tobacco. Whereas the above named Jno. Spiltimber and Thos. Warringe are bound for the credits, goods, chattells, etc. of Geo. Powell, planter, on behalfe of Marye Powell, now the orphant under the tuition of him the said Thos. Waringe, of the Bond in the surety's Office at James City in Va. etc. Signed Thos. Waringe, James Mason, Jno. Watkins. Wit.: Jno. Richards, Nicholas Perrye, Sack. Brewster.

Page 25. 16 Jan. 1652. Capt. Benj. Sidway...the Court Authorized to dispose of a piece of land...in Upper Chippoakes...belonging to Lester Harrison, the orphant of Benj. Harrison, gent., deceased....sell unto Mr. William Thomas, his heirs, etc.
Wit.: Wm. Batt, Robert Stanton.

Page 25. 9 April 1652. Daniel Barwicke doe confess to being arrested by Kirbye Riggan, atty. of Capt. Whittye of London, marriner, and doe binde myself to appear in person and answer the suit on the fifth day of April etc.
Teste: Martin Hammond, Wm. Marriott.

Page 25. 25 Feb, 1652. Robert Bateman of Smith's Fort in Va. pays a debt to Thos. Warringe wuth 575 lbs of tobacco.
Wit.: Jno. Courtman, Robt. Major.

Page 6. 6 April 1653. Jno. Garye, aged 50 years, testified that he, on the first day of April last, being at Goodman Woodhouse, sall Richard Bavin fall from a mare "upon a log Lyinge on the ground of so fall he dyed in three or fower hours or thereabouts," but that he was not hurt by the mare, and that his burial there were twenty people or thereabouts.
Signed: Jno. Garye.

Page 26. 6 April 1653. Henry Meddows assigns his Right & Title in a Patent to Robt. Spencer and Robert Attkins. Wit.: Jno. Holmwood, Robt. Morsley.

Page 27. 10 March 1652. Ind. between Coll. Henry Browne, Esq., of the one part and Coll. Geo. Ludlow, Esq., Capt. Geo. Jordan, and Mr. William Browne. Coll. Henry Browne for natural love and affection to his wife, Ann Browne, and his children, and for her and their maintenance to his creditors, goods, chattels, servants, in Virginia, this deed of gift, for maintenance of wife and children and education of children, etc.
Wit.: Law. Baker, Robt. Stanton, Sack Brewster.
"To deed made void, see page 163."

Page 28. 9 April 1653. Wm. Edwards...makes over to Mr. Walter Chiles, merchant, two men servants, one named Lewys Delonbatt, ye other Francis Ware, and cows and hogs ye Corker bought of Wm. Turner, and Wm. Edwards makes over on behalf of William Corker unto the aforesaid Mr. Chiles for the security of a certain sum of tobacco, bed, and furniture, being at Mr. Corker's house. Wit.: Jeames Jolly, Sarah Edwards.

Page 29. 3 June 1653. Wm. Lea, exor. of Gregorye Rawlings...Gregorye Rawlings indebted unto Robt. Fox, of Wappings in the county (page torn), marriner, in the sum of 4000 lbs of tobacco...for goods bought of the sd Fox several years yett, have sold to Robt. Fox 6 steers at the dwelling house of said Lee, situate in Upper Chippoaks Creek, etc.
Wit.: Steeven Yates, Jno. Heiward, Sack Brewster.

Wm. Lea makes Wm. Thomas his lawfuly attorney to acknowledge the bill of sale.

Page 29. 5 May 1653. This bill of sale Anthony Truett...to pay Wm. Murrell 355 lbs. of tobacco. Signed, Sack Brewster.

Page 30. 4 7br 1653. John Blackbourne assigns to Jno. Jennings his pattent (whole right and title) for 151 acres of land.

Page 30. 5 June 1653. John Johnson, of James Citty County, in Va., planter, ...sells to Robert Roberts...450 acres of land being the half of a moiety or patt. for 900 acres of land in Upper Chippokes, in Swann's Bay.
    Wit.: Hen.: Randolph, Sam Taylor.
Robert Roberts assigns to Geo. Stephens on 5 Jan. 1653. Wit.: Geo. Jordan, Thos. Warringe. Rec. 7 July 1755 (sic).

Page 30. 6 day of 7br 1653. Henerye Bannister of Lower Chippoakes in Surry County, planter, sells 275 acres of land by...Last Will & Test. of within named Wm. Shepard, deceased, sells to Wm. Batt of Lower Chippokes.
    Wit.: Jno. Board, Jno. Price, Sack Brewster.

Page 31. 10 July 1653. By the Grand Assemblye, Mr. William Edwards is added to the Commissioners of Surry County. Jno. Corker, Clk. to the Assembly.

Page 31. 2 9br 1653. Gentlemen: You that be the Jurye are to take notice that the cause of your meetings heere at present is to inquire and find how Jno. Briant, a boy and late servant to Jno. Spilltimber and Jno. Bradye came to his death, for when any man wooman or childe doe come to their death by any casualtye or untimelye meanes, enquirye is to be made thereof by the oaths of men. Now there hath been a former Inquest which did show the corpse and found certaine stripes on the back and bruises on the left thigh of the sd corpse, but forasmuch as they did not deliver in their presentment how the sd bruise and stripes might come, it was thought fitt that further Inquiry should be made...you are to inquire whether he came to his death by the hand of men, or the kick and tread of a horse, or by falling against a stump or tree, or by the informity of any disease. If by hands of men, then what weapon, and whether the wounds or blows of sd weapon were the immediate cause of his death, and whether there were formerly any ill will or malice to ye sd boy, or his master, and if this doth appeare then you are to inquire what goods, cattle, land, tenements and offender had at ye time, etc. Robt. Stanton, Cl. Ct.

    Wee whose names are hereafter subscribed called and commanded by the Worshipfull Court of the Countye of Surry the 2nd day of 9br, now instructed to Inquire and finde how Jno. Briant, the late servant of Jno. Spilltimber and Jno. Bradye came to his death and therefore by same doe find ye Jno. Briant died a natural death. Witness our hand and seale this 3 9br 1653.

| | |
|---|---|
| Signed: Wm. Agbbrorowe? | Jno. Bishoff |
| Hen. Bannister | Nich. Perrye |
| Thos. Binns | Jno. Board |
| Jno. King | Peter Greene |
| Jno. Price | Thos. Woodhouse |
| Rob. Warren | Thos. Dimeage |
| Jno. Hux | Rich. Shortland |
| Rich. Blunt | Jno. Raines |
| Wm. Marriott | Austine Hunnicutt |

Page 32. 2 Oct. 1653. Karbrye Kiggan, the atty. of Capt. Jno. Whittye, of London, Mariner, made complaint of some serious proceedings passed against him at a County Court in Surry...at the instigation of Left. Coll. Thos. Swann, Sheriffe of sd county, etc...concerning the appraisment of Daniel Barwicke. Signed: Richard Bennett.

Page 32. 2 day 9br 1653. Anthony Triuette?, planter, for the love and affection, deeds a sow to Richardina Field, wife of Jno. Gittings, planter, and she sells the sowe to John Frame, but if Richardina Field, alias

BOOK I, 1652-1672    7

Gittings, die without heir to return to Anthony Triuett. Wit.: Jno. Corker, Sack Brewster, Clk.

Page 32. 3 Oct. 1653. Edward Hurlstone, carpenter, binds over to Mr. Jno. Price a cowe, bought of Mr. Bannister, security for sd Hurlstone of the sd Mr. Price for the finishing of his house.

Page 33. 7 Jan. 1653. Jno. Cogan discharges and acquits Anthony Truett of all bills, etc.

Page 33. 15 June 1653. Eliza Simpson binds herself to pay to Thos. Welch of Portsmouth, chyrurgeon, the sum of 800 lbs. of tobacco, also to save Henry Jones and Jno. Saynes...where they stand bound to sd Welch.
Wit.: Thos. Hartlye.

Page 33. 25 9br 1653. Math. Battell, cooper, sells to Wm. Hemlocke, planter, one black cowe... Test.: Rob. Bloyse.

Page 33. 5 Dec. 1653. Indenture between Xpo. Vahan and Harme Scott all his right and title of land he did lease from Daniel Massingale, the title of the same land belonging to Xpo. Lawson, unto Francis Harrington, planter, on condition that the latter bind to Vahan his corn and tobacco crop that Harrington shall make in 1654, for the payment of 950 lbs. of tobacco yearly by terms of lease to Masingale, etc.

Page 33. 21 March 1653. Robt. Digby of Bristol, mariner, hast received of Wm. Batt 320 lbs. of tobacco that sd Batt adventured by him, and binds himself to pay same.
Wit.: Wm. Edwards, Thos. Culmer.

Page 34. 24 Oct. 1654. Christopher Boez (or Boaz) of Virginia, planter, sells to Nicholas Perrye, merchant, all his right and title for a term of years and in a plantation and lease for 50 acres in Tappahannock Marsh in the Parish of Wallingford in the County of James Citty in Virginia, and now in the tenure and possession of Xpo. Boaz for the same term of years by the assignment of Charles Magney with full warranty against sd Boez, etc., they pay Nicholas Perrye his heirs, etc. at the house of Boaz 929 lbs. of tobacco on the 24 day of Oct. 1654.
Wit.: Nich. Rennolds, Sack Brewster. Signed the mark of Xpo. Boaz.

Page 35. 17 May 1653. Henerye Randolph, merchant, sells to Richard Attkins of Chard in (illegible) in Somerset, Colony of Va., 5180 lbs. of tobacco.
Signed: Hen.: Randolphe
Wit.: Ab. Wood, Sack Brewster.

Page 36. 3 8br 1653. Geo. Raymond is bound for a bill to Mr. Peter Mackrell, merchant, 8 lbs of good English money to be paid in London for goods aboard the ship Hopewell that Mr. Mackrell shipped, and disposed of by Geo. Raymond in the West Indies, provided that the ship called Hopewell, of which Geo. Raymond is master, shall home safe the porte of London. Then this bond to stand in force, etc.
Signed: Geo. Raymond.
Wit.: Jno. Kent, Robert Stanton, Clk.

Page 36. 9 July 1654. To my knowledge Geo. Browne is lawfully Intrusted with the credits of Capt. Wm. Cox, deceased.
Howell Pryce, Clk. of Charles Cittye County.

Page 37. Edward Sanderson testified that when he came to Virginia, and meeting with his brother, Montagne Sanderson, the Latter being an associate and acquaintance of Mr. Daniel Coates, found that Mrs. Daniel Coates was married to Richard Esell.

Page 37. 22 March 1653. John Holmwood, Atty. of Mr. Theodorick Bland, assigns to John Barker all his patent rights, etc.
Wit.: Ben Sidwaye, Robt. Stanton.

Page 38. 9 Jan. 1653. Indenture between Theodorick Bland, merchant, and John Barker, planter, of the other part that the said Theo. Bland in the name of John Bland, by letter of Atty. from Theo. Bland to John Barker, and that John Bland & Co. at the plantation at Chippoaks Creek according to a patent in the name of Mrs. Jane Bland, wife of the aforesaid Edward Bland, deceased, dated 9 May 1652, same to John Barker, for 10,000 weight of tobacco, one-half on claim and one-half on 10 of Nov. next.
Signed: Theo. Bland, John Barker.
Wit.: Rich. Stevens, Jno. Holmwood.

Page 39. 5 May 1654, Petition of Randall Holt that he be reimbursed for the loss of his boat, that boat and men were for the County's service and the boat lost and was not allowed the value by 200 lbs. of tobacco at the least and was forced to sue for that too, and was at much expense and was not allowed any charge or cost of such and hath been not above 200 lbs.

Page 39. 22 March 1653. Thos. Woodhouse for a valuable consideration received of John Zaynes sold him an Indian boy.
Wit.: John Cogan.

Page 39. 30 March 1654. Wm. Rose, for himself and his heirs, etc., to Matthew Battell and Richard Tias, 211 acres of land.

Page 41. 22 March 1653. Richard Shortland, Atty. for Mrs. Cicely Dunston, discharges Roger Nicholson from all debts due formerly to the deceased Wm. Lea, his mother or father-in-law or any other claim to the estate of Wm. Lea, Deceased.
Signed: Richard Shortland.
Wit.: Wm. Marriott, Sam. Hubye.

Page 41. 7 March 1653. Deposition of Thos. Gray, Sr., aged 60 years or thereabouts, that Daniel Hutton did bequeath his whole estate to Rebeckah his wife. Wm. Rose, aged 30, testified to the same. 27 March 1653.

Page 41. 22 March 1653. Transaction about tobacco in which Martin Hammond, Jno. Billison, and Jno. Markham have a part.

Page 42. 2 May 1654. Deposition of Wm. Carter, Sr., aged 54 years or thereabouts. This deposition said that when Marye Powell died, the said Powell was near fifteen years old, and that Richard Powell, her father, gave her about fower head of cattle a little before the death of him.
Alice Carter, aged 55 years, or thereabouts, deposed and said that the week before Mr. Pitt's ship was burned, Mary Powell was born, and that to the best of the Deponent's knowledge, Mary Powell was neere fifteen years old when she died.

Page 42. 5 July 1654. John Dibdall, Capt. John Frame, and Richard Dibdall, Gent., are bound to the Court of Surry County for 20,000 lbs. of tobacco.

Page 42. 1 Xber 1653. And: Robbinson and Dorothy Kew are bound to Alex Mabrick in the sum of 40,000 lbs. of tobacco for keeping Dorothy and the child of the said Dorothy and other charges.
Wit.: Thos. Culmer, Charles Barham, Sack Brewster.
Dorothy Kew discharges Alex Mabrick from all debts. 9ber 1653.

Page 44. March 1654. Robert Morsley of Upper Chippoakes in Surry County, Southwark Par., Gent., sells to Thos. Holton 100 acres of land at the head of Chippoaks Creek,...adj. Wm. Lea, adj. to a patent of the said Holton.
Wit.: John Harvie, Masum? Curry.

Page 45. 14 Oct. 1650. Ind. between Martin Hammond of the one part and Wm. Hammond with consent of his said father doth to Martin Hammond and Jane his wife from the day of date, William to follow whatever employment Martin and his wife Employ him and find him lodging, washing, and apparel.
Wit.: John Hammond, Thomas ap Thomas, Law. Littleboy.

BOOK I, 1652-1672

Page 46. 1 July 1650. Indenture between Nicholas Reynolds, Gent., of the one part, and Edward Hurlston, carpenter, of the second part, a neck of land on Lawnes Creek in James City County for "Tenn yeares." For the first five years 100 lbs. of tobacco yearly, 10 Nov., and the last five years two capons a year.
  Wit.: Eustice Grimes, Jno. Gossall.
23 Feb. 1651. Edward Hurlston assignes to Thos. Covington.
  Wit.: Eustice Grimes, Eliza Hardinge.

Page 47. 1 May 1654. James Mason, of Mathews Mount, planter, sells to Richard Merydale certain possessions including stock, right, and claims in and to his servants and their services; viz., William Savage for seven years; William Pegler for his term; and Wm. Foreman for his term; and all to be paid at some convenient place or upon his own plantation called and known as Mathews Mount, within one quarter of a mile from James River where a ship, or Shallop or sloop may safely come and ride.
  Wit.: Sack Brewster, Edw. Petway.

Page 50. 4 July 1654. Wm. Gopeinge, he moving, sells to Jno. King all his right and title, etc., in 100 acres of land inheritane in his new plantation the Birchen Swamp, part of 250 acres lately given and granted from Sir William Berkeley, Gov. of Va., 6 9ber 1651. The 100 acres is on the south side of Upper Chipoaks Creek in Surry County, from Wm. Simmons land ...adj. the plantation of Jno. King.
  Wit.: Nich. Perry, Peter Adams.

Page 51. Jan. 1653. An article of agreement between John Saines (Zaines) and Jno. Berrye regarding some work. John Berrye's wife to work in the ground.
  Wit.: John Gorange.

Page 51. 1654. Wm. Rickett for himself and exors. binds over his crop of corn to Wm. Marriott.

Page 52. 6 7br 1654. Jno. Dibdall, Clerke; Richard Dibdall, planter; and Lieut. Coll. Thos. Swann, Esq., are bound to the Court for 30,000 lbs. tob. to be paid to the Commissioners of Surry County.

Page 52. 11 Aug. 1654. Obligations of John Fisher, deceased, and his children of what belongs and appertains to the rights and claims of Marye and Joseph Fisherm children of the said John Fisher, according to the meaning of the court.
  Wit.: Wm. Cockerham, Ro: Stanton, Sack: Brewster.

Page 52. 6 7br 1654. John Dibdall, Clerk; Richard Dibdall, planter, are bound to the Court for 30,000 lbs. of tob. for William Fisher, son of John Fisher. The above two men with Coll. Thos. Swann are bound for the same amount for Joseph and Marye Fisher, Children of John Fisher.

Page 53. 7 7bris 1654. The humble supplication of Jno. King, the suppliant, being informed by Mr. Price concerning the testimony of Capt. Jordan and Jno. Wattkins, confesses before the Bench that "I did say Capt. Jordan was perjured and am heartily sorry and ask the Court to accept and acknowledge in full."

Bro. Cockerham, Pray be pleased to confess a Judgment to Mr. Arthur Allen for 539 lbs. of tobacco. Your loving sister, Eliza: Shepherd. Recorded 7 7bris 1654.

Page 54. 7 7bris 1654. Ind. between Wm. Caufield, of Chippoaks in Surry County, planter, of the one part, (and) Henerye Bannister, of sd county, and Karby Kigan, of Isle of Wight County, planters. Wm. Caufield, for divers causes, he moving, and for tender love and care for future maintenance of his deare wife, Dorcas Caufield, and his children, Robert Caufield, and Eliza Caufield, makes over to Henerye Bannister, Karby Kigan and for use and behalf of his wife and children all movables and immovables belong-

ing to him with all plantation houses, grounds, cattles, hogs, etc.
Wit.: Jno. Board, Sack Brewster.

Page 55. 6 7br 1654. Thos. Culmer empowers Robt. Stanton to acknowledge a a judgment to Jno. Spiltimber and John Bradye for 1472 lbs. of tob. and caskes.

Page 55. 25 July 1654. John Sewell to appear at the next Court to answer such matters as shall be objected against him by Rich: Clarke, and that John Sewell shall be of good behaviour...
Signed: Jno. Sewell, Will. Burchell.

Page 55. 5 7br 1654. Jno. Dobbs builds himself a house of six length of boards with chimney on one side. To make three rooms, 20 ft. wide. Geo. Burcher to raise all the boards. John Dobbs confesses judgment.

Page 56. 25 Sept. 1654. Articles of agreement made & indented the 23rd of Sept. 1654 between Mr. Thos. Warren, Gent., of Smith's Fort in the County of Surry of the one part and Mrs. Elizabeth Sheapard, widdow, of Lower Chippoakes in the aforesaid County of Surry of the other part, before the solemnation of the right of matrimony betwist them.
First, that Mr. Thos. Warren to have and enjoy to his own proper use the estate of Maj. Robert Sheppard, deceased, that is now in possession of the aforesaid Mrs. Elizabeth Sheaperd, Relict of the said Maj. Robert Sheapard, deceased, debts being first paid. Mr. Thos. Warren to pay all debts due the estate. She to dispose of at her pleasure one gold ring, so also a ring with mark, D. S., onepair of silver tongs, with mark R. S., one silver milkhorne? with the mark I. S. She to appoint the overseer of her children's estate, specified in the following articles-Thomas Warren, 29 Sept. 1656, deliver to joint use of Ann Sheapard, John Sheapard, Robert Sheapard, and William Sheapard, certain stock, horse, cattle, etc.
Thos. Warren, 29 Sept. 1656, to give to the proper use of the orphant if orphant should die in nonage...to return to trustees. Thos. Warren to give Priscilla Sheapard and Susan Sheapard, the debt being paid, theire full share, and part of theire father's estate, Mr. Thos. Warren to keep small stocke of Robt. Sheapard given him by his godmother and are recorded, and give due account to the Orphant Ct. yearly. Mr. Thos. Warren to oblige himself to maintain all of the above named children; to give them sufficient education, bed. etc., until they choose guardians, or come to age.
Signed: Thos. Warrings.
Wit.: Edward Folliot (Halliot), Wm. Cockerham.
15 Sept. 1654.

Deposition of Will Gaping, aged 50 years or thereabouts, his wife being at the house of John Fisher, deceased, a little while after sd Fisher died, Thomas Reynolds being there, sd Reynolds demanded satisfaction of the children of sd Fisher for Physicke yt said Reynolds had administered to there father. Mr. Thomas Reinolds, demanding 710 lbs. but they agreed for 500 pounds and caskes, and further sayeth not.
8 die 9br 1654.
Mark of Will Gaping.

Page 57. Whereas Capt. Henerye Browne of the Four Mile Tree, hath let unto Peter Adams his house and 100 acres of land for ten years...to keep him from all suits, etc., and...to enjoy the same.
Will Harman, Geo. Jordan.

Page 57. 5 Oct. 1654. We whose names are subscribed by impanneling of ye Sheriffe, appointed by Mr. Law. Baker, Commissioned to view the corpse of Tobias Swann, servant to Mr. Richard Blunt. We...could not find any sign or impression of blow, of stroke, wrack or bruise, but according to the testimony of Mr. John Corker and Mr. Robt. Stanton, and sworne by Mr. Samuel Baker that the blow from the horse may have caused his death.
Wit.: Peter Greene   Tobias Cooke   Anthony -(?)-
Mark of Richard Dewe   Thos. Covington   Jno. Slaughter

BOOK I, 1652-1672    11

        Mark of John Claye      Mark of Jno. Benton
        Mark of Thomas ap Thomas Jno. Slaughter
        Mark of Ralph Slaughter

Page 60. 7 March 1654. Marriage of Alcie? Jones and Thos. Hart.

Page 60. 14 Sept. 1646. To his very approved kind friend, Capt. Ro: Shepard at his house at Chippoakes these present in Virginia.

                                            London, Sep. ye 14, 1646

Capt. Shepard

    And Lo: friend, my Kindest Love, Salute you and your good wife wt jopes these may find you in good health. Yours of the 22nd Feb. & of the 24 March last came to hand with twenty hogsheads of tobacco not yet sould. Shall allowe you ye best price for such goods that any man hath had this yeare. Doe see you desire to be just and honest and honest to pay your debts. I am glad & willinge to it & take it verye Kindlye as I also doe Lovinglye thanke you for your care and paynes about my Debt wtt the Executors of my Honnest friend Mr. Fowler, decd., Intreatinge you to putt an end to it this yeare in selling those cattle you have for present tol and likewise to gett Capt. Browne & Capt. Freeman to send me the remainder, they make me a answer to take interest wh I use not. But I have reason to take it of them whoe have been great gainers & myself a Looser my money being kept from me. The Acct. is here Inclosed. They sent me two Hogd. of tob. for interest this last yeare wh I accept & take Kindly that they are mindful of me, And doe not deserve (if may be) to suethem But that I may be honestlye pd for I am Confidente noe man in the Landdesireth more to pay their debts than Mr. Fowler did me for I have many letters of Deepe expressions to that purpose & effect & I doubt but he did expresse as much to his Executors.

    I pray Sr. gett them to make an end wth me this yeare. Touchinge your Bonde, if you had desired me to send it I would though there is £ 40:19:04 cominge to me. But you write for it Conditionally. If these 20 hogs. do pay the Debt, then God forbid I should have kept it. But you be assured it shall not ride up in Judgment and against you or your executors. Some of those twenty hogs. are good But yet not the right Sweetsentes and the most parte doe be sound good leafe but of the common sort and soe be your neighbors Mr. Webbs. Had they been Right I would have allowed you 5d per pound for them this yeare Though I cann and have bought as large sound well cured tob. for 2½ and cann buy 1000 hogs. at this time. But as I allwayes say noe more shall give you a better price than I will. If you can agree with Mr. Wilkinson upon Reasonable Termes get him what freight you cann. If the be like to be great Cropps agree betimes, if not be not too hastye. Besides the 17 Sayleof Dutch we have eight or more the Largest Shipps goeinge that ever went for Virginia. Thus havinge noe more at present But my prayers for your health & Prosperity I leave you to God and Remaine.

                                          Your assured Lo: friende,
                                          John White

Recorded 8 March 1654.

Page 61. 31 March 1655. Capt. Geo. Jordan Petitions to the Grand Assembly in regards to reports concerning his marriage with Eliza. Coates...and declares that it may be just lawful.
    Edw. Hill, speaker.
    Cha. Norwood, Clk. of Assembly, Rec. 20 Apr. 1655.

Page 62. At a Quarter Court held at James Cittye the 26th of March 1655. Present Rich. Bennett, Esq.; Gov.; Coll. Wm. Claiborne; Coll. Thomas Pettus; Coll. Bridg: Freemans Esq.; Mr. Edward Digges; Coll. Wm. Tayler.

Capt. Geo. Jordan produced certain papers to prove his case- that sd

SURRY COUNTY RECORDS

Eliza: Coates was formerly married to Daniel Coates...that sd Daniel Coates deceased on 13 April last in Ireland, wherefore it is now lawful for sd Eliza: to marry who she pleased...The Court did conceive that the last is so and that the marriage to Geo. Jordan is Judges Both by Civil and Common law of England and so Certified.
Rec. 20 April 1655.

Page 62. 1 May 1655. Jno. Gittings, impotent and destitute implores charitable benevolences for his livelihood, And he shall praise God.

Page 62. 1 May 1655. Thos. Stagge certifies that Wm. Morrell stood indebted in 1642 for 20 lbs. & paid on debt and shipped home 4 hogs. of tob. and afterwards 8 hogs. more paid in full. 16 Jan. 1645.

Page 63. 22 April 1655. These are to lycense and authorize you to celebrate the Act of Matrimony between Thomas alias Sackford Brewster to Sackford Hall in the County of Suffolk, Gent., on the one part & Elizabeth Watkins on the other part being noe knowne Impediment to the contrarie providded it be done between the hours of eight and twelve in the forenoon according to the Orders of the Church of England for which doeing this shall be sufficient Warrt.
Given this 22 of April 1655.
To ye well beloved in Christ Mr. Thomas Luke, Minister.
Signed: Nicho: Merriweather, Clk. Ct.

This is to Certify that on the 23 April 1655 Matrimonie between the persons within Subscribed was solemnized by mee in the presence of John Cocker that gave her. Robert Stanton, Clk. of Surry County.
Rec. 1 May 1655.

Page 63. 2 April 1655. Thomas Woodhouse of James Citty for value received sell to Mr. Robt. Hubbard of James Citty a divident of land in Surry County & adj. to the Church containing 400 acres granted to Thomas Woodhouse by patent from Sir Wm. Berkeley then Gov. of Virginia, all houses, gardens, etc. belonging to sd Plantation. Signed Thomas Woodhouse, 2 April 1655.
Wit.: John Flood, Geo. Jordan.
Rec.: 1 May 1655.

Page 66. 23 Jan. 1653. An assignment of a patent of Land 670 acres granted to Thos. Crafton and by Crafton assigned to Rich. Bavin & Daniel Hutton and said John Blackbourne and by Blackbourne to Will. Holmwood as Ct. by Relict of sd Blackbourne.
John Jennings; Will: Browne.

Page 66. 20 June 1655. Acct. of Est. of Mr. James Tayler, deceased, by Ja: Mason, Wm. Batt.
Payments to: Mr. Jno. Wood
    Maj. Geo. Fawden
    Mr. Francis Slaughter
    Mr. Humph. Allen
    Lt. Coll. Thos. Swann
    Wm. Marriott
    Law. Baker
    Maj. Wm. Butler
    Richard Harris, for wines and attendance on the Dr.
    Capt. Wombell, for sugar
    Mr. Jno. Batt
    Suit of Coll. Yardly
    Suit of Mr. Yarrett
    Mr. Holmwood
    Mr. Arthur Allen
    Many others
Payments to:
    Mr. Wiggen
    Maj. Hill
    Wm. Corker
    Fra. England
    Dr. Harrison, for physicke
    Karby Kigan, for Capt. Hardye
    Sam Hubye
    John Burgess, for a coffin
    Eustace Grymes for making a grave
    Coll. Jno. Gee
    Mr. Filmore, the orphants Dyett
Signed: Nich. Hill; Law. Baker.

Page 68. 13 July 1655. Wm. Collins, London merchant, Appt. fr. Robert Stanton, of Virginia, atty. Thomas Louder, Joseph Parker. Est. of John Collins discharges Daniel Williams of debt of Jno. Corker, Wm. Marriott.

Page 69. 9 June 1655. John Ivy sells 200 acres of land to Richard Tias and Henry White.
Wit.: Eliza: Jollye; Thos. Pittman.

Page 69. 3 July 1655. Henry Meddowes sells his patent of 300 acres of Land granted to him 20 7br 1649, in April 1653 to Robt. Spencer $ Robt. Atkins & now by Atkins to Spencer 6 May 1655.
Rec.: 3 July 1655.
Geo. Harrison; John Sewell.

Page 69. 3 July 1655. Deposition of Richard Warrener, aged 20 years, that Richard Gossage did depart this life in the home of Mr. Peter Greene...in the presence of him and Eliza. Sawyer heard him tell Mr. Greene that Gossage would give, and did give him, Peter Greene, compensation to satisfy Greene for "his diett and trouble."
Signed: Richard Warner.
Eliza Lawyer or Sawyer, aged 24 years, also swore.

Page 70. 4 July 1655. Petition to the Surry Court by Eliza. the admrx. of Jno. Watkins, Deceased, now wife of Thos. alias Sackford Brewster, stating certain grievances against Coll. Henry Browne and Capt. Geo. Hardye, a transaction to which Robert Mosely and James Rowell had made oath...all of which would appear in Chancery.

Page 70. April 1655. Coll. Richard Meridale acquitted Mr. Peter Greene of debt.
Wit.: Fra. Slaughter.

Page 70. Petition of Complaint by Thos. Binns against Mrs. Eliza. Mason, wife of Mr. James Mason, in defense of Binns' wife, Martha.

Page 70. 4 July 1655. Mr. John Bond testified that Mr. Bannister gave his daughter Clara her mother's clothing.

Page 71. 4 July 1655. Commissioners were appointed by Coll. Thos. Swann to ascertain the cause of the death of Elizabeth Burke.

Page 72. 2 April 1655. Giles Brent, Esq., Atty. for Wm. Bretton and Temperance his wife on 25 of March last sold to Thos. Binns and Jno. Bishop arrears upon a patent of Land in Surry Co. called Grindall's Old Forte, or Middle Plantation Ground, on an extent layed off upon the said land by deed now at large appears...to Anthony Sackford Brewster to act of sd deed.
Signed: Giles Brent.
Wit.: Nich. Meriweather.

Page 73. 4 7br 1655. Sam. Hubye, Planter, assigns to Wm. Batt 16 hd. of cattle...Wm. Batt bound to Adam Daniel for payment of 2000 lbs of Good tobacco and 3015 lbs. to Adam Daniel.

Page 74. 6 7br 1655. Ind. 1 Dec. 1654 between Robert Warren & Humohrye, the Indian, of the other part, the Indian to be in his employ for three years, Warren promising to furnish him meat, drink, apparel, lodging, washing, etc.
Wit.: Charles Barcroft; Geo. Seaborn.

Page 74. 30 Dec. 1654. Sam Hubye, planter, & an Indian boy belonging to the People, or Natuon of Seacocks, called in the Indian Language, Higham,... to serve four years,
Wit.: James Forbes; Wm. Batt.
Rec.: 1655.

Page 75. 20 9br 1655. Alice Carter, widdow, acknowledges that Edward Pettaway married the Relict of Wm. Carter, son-in-law to Mrs. Alice Carter, and that 500 acres of land was bequeathed to the sd William Carter, Jr., by his

father, Wm. Carter, Sr., husband to Alice Carter, and that Edward Pettaway for the life of Eliza Carter, Relict of Wm. Carter, Jr., have her plantation, 145 acres, but what is leased to Thos. Culmer and Mathew Hobson.
Wit.: Nich. Perry; Rich. Blunt.

Page 75. Robt. Webb, son of Stephen Webbs, was borne the 16th day of Nov. 1636. Wm. Webb was born the 15 day of Feb. 1645. Being formerly in an old Bible and subscribed by the father's own hand.

Page 76. 3 Jan. 1655. Ind. 24 Nov. 1655, between John Corker of Surry County and wife Dorothea & Capt. Richard Webster of James Citty, for valuable consideration in Tob. sell a water mill and land on each side, John Corker to build a mill house.
Wit.: Geo. Jordan; Hen: -(?)-

Page 77. 26 May 1655. Arthur Jordan, Southwarke Par., planter, and Robert Stanton, Clerke, in behalf of Elizabeth Hutton, orphant, now in tuition of Arthur Jordan, he being appointed guardian, a parcel of land 136 acres, formerly in the occupancy of Richard Harris, cooper, deceased, and by him sold to Daniel Ludwell, chyrurgion, and he to Daniel Hutton, father of sd orphant now in the care of sd Arthur Jordan by the Court 4 May 1655 to dispose of sd land adj. Coll. Henry Browne and Coll. Thos. Swann for 500 lbs. of tob. to Robert Stanton. Lease Arthur Jordan, to Robt. Stanton.
Wit.: Rich. Hill, Jno. Flood.

Page 79. 3 Jan. 1655. Debts due from John Spilltimber, Capt. Benj. Sidway, Capt. Jno. Fox, the Chirgion of Fox's shipp, Mrs. Corker, Daniel Masingale, to Mr. Baker for the use of Mr. Symmonds, Johanna Bradye.

Page 79. 22 Jan. 1655. John Dibdall, Clk, to Richard Hill, a piece of land in Surry County, except 500 acres due to Benj. Harrison, orphant, is made good by 500 acres...survey 25 9br 1650.

Page 80. A difference arose between Mr. Robert Stanton and Jno. Dibdall over the land which Mr. John Fisher by will gave to his children, which for nonpayment was repossessed by Dibdall & in settlement propose to give to the said children of sd Fisher (one of whom Robt. Stanton has married) 5500 lbs. of tobacco and absolve himself, Dibdall, of all claims, etc....870 lbs. pd. by Dibdall in settlement, 17 Jan. 1655.

Page 81. Feb. 1655. Eliza. Bannister, Robt. Hill, & Charles Borecraft upon petition of Robt. Webb were appointed his guardians. They desire to be released.
Wit.: Wm. Buttes, Thos. Dimmett, Rice Williams.

Page 82. Abraham Sheares, Jr., Lawful atty. for my mother, Mrs. Elizabeth Sheares, wants administration on the est. of Abraham Sheares, his father. 15 Jan. 1635.
Wit.: Thos. Taberer; Wm. Lewen; Wm. Bresse?

Page 82. Jno. Holmwood sells to Francis Slaughter, a negro boy 14 years old, called Peter, 13 March 1654.
Wit.: Edward Folliott, Arthur Allen.

Page 82. 7 May 1656. Received aboard the slope belonging to the Shippe Luke of Bristol, of Wm. Batt 9 hhd. of tob. to be laden aboard sd shipp for the use and acct. of Jeremie Holeway and Capt. Edward Fox; 10 May 1655.
Signed: Edward Cooke.

Page 83. 6 Nov. 1655. Francis Slaughter pays a certain amount to Thos. Culmer of Surry Co., Chyrurgion, his heirs, etc., all of Slaughter's right in and claim of Slaughter's wife in the house and plantation he now lives in.
Signed: Thos. Culmer.
Rich. Skinner; David Parnell.

BOOK I, 1652-1672                    15

Page 83.  30 Oct. 1656.  Thos. Hunt, assignee of Jonothan Parsons, appoints Robert Stanton atty.

Page 84.  Thomas Peeters authorizes Mr. Thos. Pittman atty. Peeters left a boat in Jno. Bishopp's Creek and the sail at his house to be sent to Mr. Walter Chiles at Jamestown, but Mr. Wm. Edwards came and received sd boat and made use of it for himself and sold the boat to Mr. Wood & More, of Pagan's Creek, etc.

(?) The balance of several accounts for goods sold by Wm. Thomas for the accts. of Henry and John Richards, vizt.:

| | |
|---|---|
| Xpher Greenfield | Joseph Whitmell |
| Francis Hogwood | Sam. Waterhouse |
| Jno. Ivy | John Rutherforde |
| Garrett Harrell | Thos. Peeters |
| Rich. Rogers | Jno. Fisher |
| Jno. King | Henry Bayle |
| Wm. Ogborne | Jno. Ludwell |
| Jno. Gittings | Mathew Edloe |
| Rich. Jones | Grego. Rawlings |
| Jno. Reaves | Rich. Hide |
| Jno. Blackborne | Seth Swaine |
| Rich. Braines (Barnes?) | John Wilkerson |
| Ro: Morsley | Capt. Marshall |
| Ro: Stanton | Wm. Craddocke |
| Wm. Hanatt | Wm. Jennings |
| Geo. Gibson | Jno. Spilltimber |
| Sam Paine | Edward Ellis |
| Anthony Faucett? | Thos. Dunnington |
| Thos. Biggs | Rich. Rix |
| Wm. Loweden | Jno. Corker |
| Ben Sidway | Luke Mizelle |
| Thos. Andrewes | Wm. Webb |
| Wm. Carter | Jno. Westorpe? |
| Nich. Perry | Wm. Marriott |
| Geo. Steevens | Jno. Sanders |
| Thos. Baylie | Wm. Rose |
| Wm. Shorte | Coll. Jno. Flood |
| Wm. Batt | Coll. Moulsworth? |
| Peter Garrett | Sackford Brewster |
| Edward Young | Andrew Cane? |
| Robert Dennett | Matthew Warriner |
| Hen. White | Thos. Woodhouse |
| Robt. Copcutt? | Robt. Medley |
| Jno. Harry | Thos. Gray |
| Thos. Swann | Roger Potter |
| Coll. Henry Browne | Jno. Barrow |
| Charles Forde | Jno. Hux |
| Jerom Ham. | Jno. Willson |
| Wm. Radway | Thos. Pittman |

(?).  May 1656.  These are the names of his highness sd to seg. so much of est. on behalf of Jno. Richards of London to the value of 60,000 lbs. of tob....in the Colony of Virginia  Debts being due from sd Thomas in Consideration of that estate of sd Thomas like to be conveyed out of the Collony to the great damage of the said Richards. Richards to present an account of what he shall sieze...
    To any Sheriff, or Sheriffs in the County.
    Signed: Bridges Freeman

Page 86.  14 April 1656.  Robert Atkins acknowledges debt to Wm. Marriott. Wit.: Jno. Courtman; Walter Rouse.

Page 86.  5 Jan. 1652.  Wm. Steevens, planter, sells to Nich. Williams, planter.
    Wit.: Geo. Jordan; Zach. Brewster.

SURRY COUNTY RECORDS

Page 86. 7 May 1656. The Court granted judgment to Jno. Richards, merchant, upon his attachment for 20 hhds. of tobacco shipped aboard the John & Katherine, Richard Dennis, commander,...is shipped by Wm. Thomas, deceased, the whereas the overseer in feoff interest pretends that fineness of the same was sweet scented and came above the common sort, the estate finding ...500 lbs. of tob. Judgment granted likewise against 16 hhds. tob. shipped by sd Thomas aboard the Pilgrime, James Wattkins, commander, marked "W" and the brand arrow with costs...
Vera: Robert Stanton.

Page 87. 24 May 1657. These presents bindeth me, Jno. Wilkinson, my heirs, etc. to pay or cause to be paid to Henry and John Richards, their Heirs etc., 634 lbs. of good tobacco without ground or seconds, with good caskes & caskes not to have Venders security 70 lbs. per caske to be paid at my now dwelling house before 10 of Oct. Next.
Signed: Jno. Wilkinson.
Wit.: Ben Sidway.

Page 87. 2 July 1657. The Declaration of Mr. Thomas Warren, taken the 2 July 1657 that being at James Cittye in June last in Company with several gentlemen, Mr. Randall Holt of Hogg Island comeinge into the Company and Hearing that the Quarter Court obtained a Reversion of an order passed in sd Courte, fell into a discourse of the proceedings of Courts, of the Difference of Opinions & much more to that effect and beinge agravated by one Thomas ap Thomas, who in complaint of some passages between them and Capt. Sidway this Deponent did reprove the sd Holt for speakinge somethinge to sarglye? of sd Company the sd Holt replied that he had sd nothing to the Deponent and asked whether he would stir setting doggs and sd further that there was none but owles and asses, knaves and rogues of a Commission, Whereupon this Deponent called Witnesses thereof and left the Companye and further sayeth not.
Signed: Thos. Warren.

Page 87. 2 July 1656-7. To the Worshippful Court of Surry County Ct. The Humble Petition of Randall Holt, Sheweth that ye Petitioner understanding yet hee is accused for aprobrious speeches that should be given out by the Petitioner against the Worshipful Court wh ye Petitioner calleth ye God of Heaven, the sd Accusee knoweth not of least evil toward the Worshipful Court, or Members, But if the Petitioner hath in the least kinde spoke abruptly to cause the Worshipful Court the be distreste by yet was & is utterlye unknown Through Ignorance done by the Pt. and is alsoe Heartilye sorrye & Doth Humblye Submitt to the Censure of the Worshipful Court & ever pray. Presented and recorded 2 July 1656-7. Book of Orders.

Page 88. 26 June 1656-7. The Ballance of the Bookes of Maj. Jno. Westhorpe, deceased, left in the hands of Capt. Wm. Thomas at his goinge for England and now deceased unto Mr. Charles Sparrow, administrator of the sd Westhorpe by Mr. Thomas Jones feoffe in trust of the sd Thomas, deceased:

Thos. Gray
Xpo. Greenfield
Coll. Moulsworth
W. Hanett
Thos. Clarke
Capt. Wm. Harris
Howell Pryse
Tho. Steevenson
Robt. Evens
Wm. Walthall
Wm. Gapinge
Mr. Cocke
Edward Fitsgarrett
Ben Cartwright
Capt. Bishopp
Jno. Corker
Geo. Varnam
Capt. Peebles
Capt. Epps
Capt. Marshall
Wm. Rogers
Coll. Hill
Antho. Freyette?
Da: Endicus
Geo. Carefoot
Capt. Sidway
Henry Dame?
Mr. Wyatt
Jno. Baylie
Wm. Radway
Jno. Dibdell
Jno. Garye
Rich: Carter
Griffeth Dickenson
Segg Hanero?
Mr. Richards

BOOK I, 1652-1672                  17

                Wm. Wood                    Ch. Sparrowe
                Jno. King                   James Warrendine
                Mark Averye                 Wm. **Shogh?**
                Wm. Agborowe                Jno. Graves by Morgan
                Wm. Sandes                  Jno. Bannister
                Edw. Richards               Jno. Huntley
                Garrett Howell              Wm. Webb
                Ralph Poole                 Mr. Reynolds
                Mr. Hamline                 Mr. Birde
                Francis Hogwood             Jno. Tayler

The balance of the Acct. above specified and leonginge to the est. of Jno. Westhorpe, I Charles Sparrow doe acknowledge to have received of Thomas Jones being left feoffe in Trust of the est. of Wm. Thomas, deceased. 26 June 1656
    Signed: Ch. Sparrowe.
    Wit. Jno. Richards, Ben Sidway.
In final settlement of this account Mr. Jno. Sadler and Mr. Richard Prime merchant were due rent received from Mr. Rice Hooe.

Page 89. 3 7br 1656. Martin Hammond sells Coll. Thos. Swann cows, etc.
    Wit.: Wm. Marriott.
Wm. Jennings sold John Blackborne a cow.

Page 89. 8 Sept. 1656. The mark of Wm. Jennings. The mark of John Flood.
    Test.: John Gittinge.

Page 87 (sic). 2 Sept. 1656. Jane Blackborne, Relict and Admr. of Mr. Jno. Blackborne, deceased, assigns to Robert Stanton her right & title to the bill of sale.
    Wit.: Wm. Hall, Thos. Jones.

Page 90. 5 Nov. 1656-7. These presents bindeth me, Job Beazley...to pay Jane Pamplin or her heirs etc. 1500...
    Signed: Job Bageley.
    Wit.: Nich. Hill, Robt. Stanton.

Page 90. 10 Xbr 1656. Rec. of Robert Stanton first year's rent of a plantation where he now lives, in behalf of the orphant of Daniel Hutton, dec., of which I am guardian.
    Signed: Ar. Jordan.
    Wit.: Geo. Jordan, Wm. Browne.

Page 91. 19 9br 1656. Wee whose names unto subscribed, chosen arbitors between Capt. Geo. Jordan atty. of James Jauncey, merchant, who is atty. of Mr. Thomas Marsh, admr. of Mr. Thos. Jauncey, deceased, and Marye Blunt, Relict of Richard Blunt, deceased,...that Mr. Geo. Jordan having been possessed with all the estate of Richard Blunt in Virginia, which now can be found, and be delivered up by sd Marye on her oath...Capt. Jordan out of same forthwith to deliver to her 2 cows, 2 heifers, 1 maid servant, 6 bbls. of Indian corn, her bed and its furnishings, her wearing clothes, linens, and what property of herself...before January next, and the crop next ensueing...and Capt. Jordan defend her from harm etc.

Memo. That Wee...admrs. doe finde the whole estate of Richard Blunt, deceased, which he dyed possessed of properly to belonge to Tho: Jauncey, deceased, the said Jauncey havinge disbursed abiut fower hundred pounds sterling upon that design of **pd Hasty?** And what awarde the Relict of Rich. Blunt, dceased, is done by the consent of the sd Capt. Jordan one of charitye & freelye toward her maintenance...having had that relation to the said Blunt and that latter payment above mentioned is likewise to be satisfied out of the est. that shall be sould by the saide Capt. Jordan But by him to be reserved to her. 19 9br 1656.
    Thos. Swann, Wm. Butler, Ben Sidway, Wm. Edwards.

Page 91.   3 June 1656.  John Richards, merchant, bought a plantation of 350 acres at outcry of the est. of Wm. Thomas, deceased, for 8100 lbs. of tobacco, and assigns same to Mr. Arthur Allen, all rights, etc.
  Signed: Jno. Richards.
  Wit.: Thos. Swann, Wm. Butler, Ben Sidway.

Page 92.          To Mr. John Fisher Ic (sic) This in Virginia
                  Graves End the 25th 9br 1653.

Mr. Fisher

  Lovinge friend, I rec'd yours of the 24th of Julye 1653 I am glad of your safe arrival I am sorrye that Capt. Reade did putt to soe much trouble I have writt unto Capt. Stagg Ic: your goodes I was forced to compound with Crosbe to goe forward in the suite it was but in vaine for your wittnesses was not in England & hee would not confess the debt hee pd mee sixtye pounds downe & I have taken his two bonds in your name for sixtye pounds more to be pd at six months & six months I question not but it will be pd when it is due: for ye Gentlemen I believe for your other two Bonds you will never recover one pennye.  You write that I should pay your sister 25 lbs.  I have not soe much in my hand but I never heard of her.  What civill curtesye I can doe for you ye may be confidant of it.  Not else at present but my love to you & your wife I rest Your lovinge friend.
                                                          James Jenkins

To Jno. Fisher Ic in Virginia whom God preserve.

Page 92.          Graves End, 10 Jan. 1653.

Mr. Fisher

  Lovinge friend I rec'd your letter & have pd your bill of exchange that you drew upon me.  I gave you an acct of it by Capt. Tulley - the other money is not yet due.  My love to you and your wife.  I rest
                                                  Your lovinge friend,
                                                          James Jenkins
  Rec. 4 9ber 1656.

Page 92.  10 March 1655.  John King in the County of Surry, Virginia, appoints his loving friend Jno. Flood his true and lawful attorney to pay recover... all debts due me...bonds, etc.  Matthew Battell; Wm. Simmons.

Page 92.  15 Jan. 1656.  Wm. Hukins his acct.  Five months diett for his wife. Charge of a buriall and a sheete.
Signed and sworne in Court by Geo. Woodward.

Page 93.  To all Xtian People to whom this Present Writing shall come:  Wee Wm. Powell of Southwarke in the Countye of Surrey England, Baker, administrator of the goodes & chattels, debts, rights & credits of Capt. Wm. Powell late of Chippoakes in the Collonye of Virginia his naturall Brother deceased, & heire to George Powell, late whilest he lives at Chippokes afforesd since alsoe deceased also Wm. Parke of Leadenhall Street in London, cheesemonger, & Ann my wife send greetings:  Know ye that whereas me the sd Wm. Powell...and Ann my wife have by writinge under ye hands & seales bearing date the day of the date heereof Bargained and sold unto Wm. Batt of Chippoakes in Virginia afforesd Gente., and his heirs eight hundred acres of Land be it more or less Lyinge in the county of Surrey in Virginia and all other plantations...wood houses...Now wee the sd Wm. Powell, Wm. Parke and Ann my wife doe hereby constitute ordaine and appoint Mr. Ralph Dunstan and Mr. Samuel Hubye and either of them atty...to acknowledge this Indenture... sett our hands & seale this first day of Julye in the year of our Lord according to the English account...Wm. Powell, Wm. Parke, Anne Parke,
  Written on Parchment & Witnessed on the back of the same by these following:
    Fra. Gillowe, Arthur Bailey, John White, Robert Fox, Fra. Mayo.
    Attested by Raph Dunstan & Sam Hubye.  Rec. ultimo Xber 1656.

Page 93. 1 July 1656. Indenture between William Powell, Southwarke Par., baker, admr. of Capt. William Powell, late of Chippoakes, his natural brother, deceased, and heir unto Geo. Powell, the natural sonne of the sd Capt. William Powell, since also deceased, and Wm. Parke of Leaden Hall St., London, and Ann his wife, Ann, grandchild of the sd William Powell, party to these presents of the one part, and Wm. Batt of Chippoakes Creek, Collonye of Va., of the other part. Wm. Powell...Wm. Parke and Ann his wife for a certain consideration sell all their rights to 800 acres of land, late of the sd Wm. Powell and Geo. Powell, his son, in Surry Co.; 600 acres in Lower Chippoakes on James River...and 200 acres on Little Creek, called Crouches Creek, etc. etc....
 Wm. Powell, Wm. Parke, Ann Parke, Ar. Bailey, John White, Rob. Fox, Fra. Mayo.

Page 95. 17 Jan. 1656. At a Court in Surry County, 13 Jan. 1656 It was ordered to audit and settle and deliver all accounts depending between Capt. George Jordan and Mr. Richard Hill, deceased...a bill in the hands of Mr. Jno. Dibdall, also Mr. Jennings, etc.
 Test: Peter Knight, John Flood, Benjamin Sidway.
 Rec.: 6 Feb. 1656.

Page 96. 30 Jan. 1655. This bill bindeth Mr. James Hugate to pay to Thos. Swann 200 pounds of good tobacco on 10 Xbr next.
 Signed Jasque Huguet.
 Wit.: Wm. Hill, Wm. Penn.

Page 96. 25 Jan. 1656. A covenant between Thos. Swann of the one part and James Hugate to build for Mr. Swann one small quartering house, 25, or 30 ft. and an outhouse to make up 90 ft. of housing, breadth between 15 and 25 ft. Hugate to find and Diett for himself...Hugate is to find nayles etc. Hugate and wife to live in the house.

Page 96. 6 Nov. 1656. Theodoricke Blande discharges Amaro de Sores? for all claims concerning the bill, 2500 pounds of tob. due to Edward Blande, deceased.
 Signed: Thos. Blande.
 Jno. Holmwood, Thos.

Page 96. 13 July 1656. Received of Wm. Aman? in full all accounts and debts.
 Signed: John Laine.
 John Leeke, Edward Barnsford.

Page 97. 6 Jan. 1656. Wm. Martin, Lower Chippoakes in the new county of Surry in Va., gentleman, attorney of Coll. Henerye Bishopp, now living in England on the one part, and John Grove, of Bristoll in the Realmes of England, seven hundred acres of land...called Lower Chippoakes, part of a dividert of land of Capt. Wm. Powell and afterward granted to Sir Wm. Berkeley, Knt., ny Order of Court 27 Nov. 1643, and afterward purchased by sd Coll. Bishopp from sd Wm. Berkeley...20 Aug. 1646, bounded as followes: Northerly on the James River, Easterly by Chippoakes Creek, West by Sunken Marsh, Southerly by the mainland,...from Coll. Henerye Bishopp date 29 April 1646 and sells to John Grove, merchant,...as by a former writing from said Martin 12 April 1656, may appear.
 John Jennings atty. for John Grove. 12 Jan. 1656.

Page 98. 13 Jan. 1656. Matthew Hill authorizes his friend Jno. Leade atty. to confess judgment for debts.

Page 98. To Coll. Jno. Flood and the rest of the Commissioners for Surry County Court, Gentlemen: It has pleased God to take my husband and having no Will I have considered that Capt. Geo. Jordan (besides his Relatives as a Brother-in-Law) hath the most knowledge and relations to his business and I therefore humbly desire the Court to grant him admr. of my husband's estate, for I have referred the whole business to his trust, love, and good sense soe I rest.    Your humble servant, Hannah Hill.
 Rec.: 14 Jan. 1656.

SURRY COUNTY RECORDS

Page 98. Xber 1656. At a Grand Assembly held at James Citty it was ordered that Mr. John Corker be added to the Commissioners of Surry County.
Rec.: 14 Jan. 1656.
Teste: Henry Randolph, Cl. Assembly.

Page 99. 14 Jan. 1656. To the Worshipful Court of Surry Co. The Humble Petition of Ralph Poole, admr. of John Sanders in the behalf of the mother of sd Sanders, Humbly sheweth that the estate of Wm. Thomas stands indebted to your Petitioner for a debt of 5550 lbs. of tob. now sues the administrators of Wm. Thomas, who have in use sums of Tobacco and shipped sums of tobacco for England, putting out the said Sanders, and his mark, and marks it for themselves, Deserves to be paid for loss, and acct. attached - for physick and looking after Westropes household; Pt. to Mr. Thomas by Mr. Mason from Sanders; pd salary of Mr. Agborowe, etc.

Page 99. Rec. 14 Jan. 1656. To Henerye Commes or Daniel Veale, My love to you remember these are onlye to Intreate you to pay to ye Bearer hearof the 6 hundred ct of tob. wh. is due me from you 300 weight of sugar The Bill I have lost else I would have sent it you. I have made the Bearer Phillip Elliott my attorney & what agreement hee makes with you I will stand to Soe this noate with his scribe shall be as your safe warrant discharge so I reste.
Your Lovinge friend till Deathe
Signed: Richard Tench
From Aboard The Bristoll Mercht.
25 June 1654

Page 99. 13 Jan. 1656. Know all men that wee Thos. Culmer of Lawnes Creek Par. Surry County, chrurgeon, and Wm. Marriott of same par. gent. are bound unto Jno. Cogan of Jordan's Parish in Charles Cittye County, chrurgeon, for 5200 lbs. tob. to be paid before 10 9br next.
Jos. Dunn, Thos. Hunt.
Rec.: 15 Jan. 1656.

Page 100. 3 Nov. 1656. Be it known that Wm. Marriott & Thomas Binns are bound to the Court of Surry County for 30,000 lbs. of tobacco discharge Eliza Bannister guardianesse of Robert Webb, orphant, of 10,000 lbs. of tob. which shee was to pay sd Webb, he being come of age.
Wm. Marriott, Thos. Binns.
Wit.: Wm. Batt, Karbye Kigan

Page 100. 3 March 1656. Richard Sharpe cannot attend Court, wants case referred to next Court.

Page 100. 2 March 1656. Henrye Jarrard authorizes his friend Thos. Busby his atty. Teste: Robert Morslay.

Page 100. 3 May 1656. Jno. Baldwin & Griffith Dickson have a suit, want Robert Stanton to defer it to next Court.
Signed: Charles Gregorye.

Page 100. 11 Oct. 1656. Robert Sneade, who married the Relict of Jno. Batt, authorizes his friend Jno. Orchard his atty.
Wit.: Nich. Perry, Wm. Willson.

Page 101. 25 Jan. 1652. Samuel Watterhouse sells Wm. Thomas his heirs, etc. 50 acres of land, where Watterhouse lives.
Rec.: 3 May 1656.
Wit.: Thos. Jones, Joseph Witmell.

Page 102. 20 March 1655. Matthew Battell makes friends, James & Thomas Sowerbye his Attys.
Wit.: Jno. King, Jr., Hen.: Lathard

Page 102. 4 May 1657. Nicholas Perry bound to Henry & John Richards with certain livestock. Wants deed recorded.
John Okeham, Wm. Jennings.

BOOK I, 1652-1672

Page 103. 9 April 1657. We whose names are subscribed & so sworn by Mr. Charles Ford, coroner, as to how ye body (torn off) Willcox found dead above high water mark at a place called ye Half Way Acre in Southwarke Parish in Surry County, came to his death from bleeding at the mouth.
Signed: Charles Flood, John King, Austin Hunnicutt, Wm. Brown, Arthur Jordan, Richard Case, Roger Potter, Francis Sowerbye, Wm. Simmons, Jno. Flood, Thos. Gray, Ro: Stanton, Arthur Jordan, Jno. Flood.

Page 103. 5 May 1657. Thos. Strong had a suit with Theodorick Bland, Merchant for 340 lbs. tobacco.
Wit.: Wm. Allen, Willyam Rookin, Samuel Cornell.

Page 104. 5 May 1657. Deposition of Anthony Redwood, aged 25 years or thereabouts. Said that all the corn...brought to the mill in ye name of Robert Warren ye last spring was all ground and delivered back again...and no corn unground.
Signed: Anthony Reedwood.

Page 104. 31 July 1657. Henry Meadows of Blackwater, planter, sells cows with definite markings, to Matthew Battell, cooper, of same county.

Page 104. 9 July 1657. Henry Meadows to pay the estate of Capt. Sparks 950 lbs. of tobacco in Battel's hands.
Wit.: Wm. Cockerham, Wm. Marriott.

Page 105. July 1657. Thomas Sowerby, aged 23 years or thereabouts, makes a Deposition about buying a Rundlett of powder whan aboard of one Rawlings with Col. John Jennings, from the gunner of the ship.

Page 105. 7 July 1657. Jno. Maive, servant to Mr. Charles Forde, aged 20, while servant to Wm. Jennings, went aboard Rawlings his ship, lying in Warwicksqueak Bay and carried a small parcell of boards and carried powder to Jno. Jennings' house, not knowing it was powder (in package).

Page 105. 7 July 1657. We, Wm. Jennings, John Kinge, and Arthur Jordan, are bound unto his Majesties Councill for 20,000 lbs. of Tob., or penalty. The condition that Col. Wm. Jennings personally appear at James Cittye on the third day of the Quarter Court to answer to ye Governor's Councill.

Page 105. 14 May 1657. Luke Deyney debt to Wm. Jeames his heirs etc. 344 lbs. of tobacco to be paid before the 10 of Oct. next.
Wit.: John Martine, P. Drinkwater.

Page 106. 1 May 1657. Ind. between Robert Warren and Sarah his wife of Lawnes Creek and Mrs. Elizabeth Hardye, widdowe, of the county of Isle of Wight, for a certain consideration sells to Mrs. Elizabeth Hardye a Mill House with all appurtenances belonging and all the land and houses on the land commonly called the Poplar Neck, this lands adjoins the old Plantation where the said Warren formerly lived, being divided by a run commonly called Deep Spring Run taking its course north west upon the land south and west and s.w. upon the land formerly held by Doctor Parolye, deceased, and now held by Wm. Ward, cooper, the outward bounds of sd land lying and being in the county of Surry...formerly belonging to Thomas Webb deceased, and by him purchased of Richard Attkins, deceased, and the other purchased by Warren of sd Webb, and now sold to Elizabeth Hardye.
Wit.: James Masonn, John Jennings.

Page 105. July 1657. Wm. Jennings and John King and Arthur Jordan are bound unto His Majesties Councill for 20,000 lbs. of tob. or penalty 7 July 1657 The Condition that Col. Wm. Jennings personally appear at James Cittye on the third day of the Quarter Court to answer to ye Governor & Councill.

Page 107. 3 Sept. 1657. Capt. Benjamin Sidway and Mary his wife owe Mr. John Blande of London, merchant, Theodoricke Blande and his employers and makes over land on the south side of James River in Charles Citty County called Jordans now in occupation of Capt. William Bothwell.
Signed: Ben Sidway, Mary Sidway.        Jno. Richards, Ro: Stanton.

Page 107. 11 Oct. 1647. Nathaniel Hunt of Martin's Plantation is bound to Wm. Jeames of London for 1148 lbs. of tob. for two years being 10 Oct. 1647.
    Recorded 29 7ber 1657.
    Wit.: Henerye Jackson, Jo: Parsons.

Page 107. 29 7ber 1657. Wm. Davis to pay to Dorothye Jeames, her heirs, etc., 278 lbs. of tob. 3 Feb. 1650.
    Signed: Wm. Davis.

Page 107. 29 7ber 1657. Tho. Loucringe of Martin's Hundred to pay to Jos. Vigore of London 200 lbs. of tob. 1 March 1652.
    Wit.: William Whitaker.

Page 107. 23 Feb. 1647. Jno. Fripps (C?) to pay to Wm. Jeames 200 lbs. of tob.
    Rec.: 29 7ber 1657.
    Wit.: Geo. Harwood.

Page 107. 7 March 1645. Samuel Sneade debt to Wm. Jeames 475 lbs. of tob.
    Wit.: John Friers.
    Recorded: 29 7ber 1657.

Page 108. 12 March 1647. David Mansell to Wm. Jeames and Jonathan Parsons debt of 450 lbs. of tob.
    Wit.: Henry Jackson.
    Rec.: 29 7ber 1657.

Page 108. 25 March 1649. Jno. Hutton to Charles Compton 1265 lbs. of tob.
    Wit.: Jno. Martine, Wm. Jeames.
    Rec.: 29 7ber 1657.

Page 108. 1 7ber 1649. Wm. Vincent to Mr. Wm. Jeames one hhd. tob.
    Wit.: Robert Churchman, Allex. Harwood.
    Rec.: 29 7ber 1657.

Page 108. 15 March 1657. Wm. Purnell to Wm. Jeames 90 lbs. of tob.
    Nath. Hunt; Jo. Parsons.
    Rec.: 29 7ber 1657.

Page 108. 16 Feb. 1645. Wm. Cocke to Wm. Jeames 357 lbs. of tob.
    Wit.: Robt. Jackson; Hen: Jackson.

Page 108. 27 March 1640. Thos. Broughton of Londo , merchant, to Wm. Jeames.
    Wit.: Geo. Harwood.

Page 108. July 1649. Andrew Kippinge, chyrurgion, to Wm. Jeams 600 lbs. of tobacco.
    Wit.: Barth. Knipe; Jno. Tully.
    Rec.: 29 7ber 1657.

Page 108. 17 April 1649. Robert Ellison, chyrurgion, to Wm. Jeames 750 lbs. tobacco.
    Hen. Jackson.
    Rec.: by Pat Drinkwater.

Page 108. 17 April 1649. Rudolph Spragan to Ch. Compton 809 lbs. tob.
    Wit.: Wm. George Harwood.
    Rec.: 29 7ber 1657.

Page 108. 15 Feb. 1649. Nich. Wattkins to Wm. Jeams 310 lbs. of tob.
    Wit.: George Harwood.
    Rec.: 29 7ber 1657.

Page 109. 14 (?) 1657. Charles Clay binds himself to Stephen Tichner, chyrurgion, seven years service in learning physick, and clothes, etc., to be furnished by Tichner.
Wit.: John Wall, Thos. Walters.
Rec. 10 (?) ber 1657.

Page 109. 9 ber 1657. John Grove, of the cittye of Bristol, merchant, makes Jno. Jennings of Isle of Wight County, Va., gent., his atty. to take possession of all his land and plantations in Virginia.
Wit.: Thos. Walters, Jno. Bond, David Warren, Edwd. Gibbs.

Page 110. 3 9ber 1657. Jo. Pauley received a patent on 10 June 1639 for 600 acres of land at the head of Lawnes Creek, and assigned by Pauley over to Thos. Webb 25 Aug. 1644, and purchased of Webb by George Stephens 15 Feb. 1644, and by George Stephens sold to George Hardye 21 May 1653, giving all his right and title with all profits, and all emoluments of fishing, fowling, hunting expressed in the patent.
Signed: George Stephens, Susannah Stephens.
Wit.: Robert Pitt, George Hardye, Jr.
By Nicholas Perry attorney for Hardye.

Page 110. 21 June 1645. This bill bindeth me, Nathaniel Littleton of Ackomack County, Esq., to Jno. Flower for 1625 lbs. of tobacco.
Abraham Read.
Rec.: 9ber 1657.

Page 110. Thos. Swann and Thos. Drue to John Flower.
Wit.: Rowland Sadler, Jno. Lotte?
Rec.: 9ber 1657.

Page 110. 2 Nov. 1642. Mathew Gough and John Flower, Marriner, of London, 2000 lbs. tob.
Wit.: Thos. Drewery, Jacob Mason.

Page 110. 4 July 1643. Capt. Mathew Gough to pay John Flower 1500 lbs. of tobacco.
Wit.: Jno. Potter.

Page 110. 1 March 1644. Daniel Tanner of Elizabeth Cittye, carpenter, and Cornelius Loide, of Elizabeth River, merchant, to John Flower, of London, 1200 lbs. tob.
John Knight, Ro: Wetherall.

Page 110. 25 Apr. 1646. Roger Booker to John Flower 160 lbs. tob.
Jno. Converse.

Page 110. March 1644. Daniel Tanner to Capt. Jno. Flower, a three year old steer.
Wit.: Peter Talbott; Jno. Converse.

Page 110. 6 Aug. 1643. Sam: Edwards to Jno. Flower 245 lbs. of tob.
Wit.: Jacob Masonn.

Page 110. 20 Oct. 1643. Barth. Hoskins of Elizabeth River, Va., to John Flower, or some of his owners of the shipp, Virginia Merct., 600 lbs. of tob.
Mathew Lynde; Wm. -(?)-.

Page 111. 2 March 1645. Wm. Newsome of Lower Chippoaks, planter, 300 lbs. tob.
Wit.: Thos. Yeoman.
9ber 1657.

Page 111. 8 April 1646. Jno. Stinger, Northampton County, Va., to John Flower, mariner, 650 lbs. tob.
Wit.: John Converse.      Rec.: 9ber 1657.

Page 112. 3 Jan. 1647. Jno. Senior 2000 lbs. of tob. pd in Jamestown Co.
Wit.: Edward Rudder.
9ber 1657.

Page 112. 31 Oct. 1643. Thos. Colner to Jno. Flower 4000 lbs. tob.
Wit.: Wm. Jennings, Jno. Clay.

Page 112. 21 April 1645. John Frame to Jno. Flower 300 lbs. tob.
Jere. Coote; Jno. Gibbs, atty.
Rec.: 9ber 1657.

Page 112. 7 Julye 1645. John Frame to Jno. Flower 300 lbs. of tob.
Wit.: Wm. **Lengor?**
Rec.: 9ber 1657.

Page 112. 20 Aug. 1643. Wm. Underwood and Wm. Burwell to pay Jno. Flower 7 lbs. money of England, or the rest of the owners of the shipp Virginia, merchant, for the passage of Wm. Underwood home for England to be paid 30 days after the ship Virginia Merchant arrived to London or any other port of discharge.
Wit.: Jacob Masonn; Geo. Preston.

Page 112. 10 Oct. 1643. Geo. Clarke and Wm. Parry (Perry) of Kegoughtan to pay Jno. Flower of Ratclif, Marriner, 900 lbs. of tob. for the use of the widdow Grant to ship the tob. and caskes aboard Mr. Thos. Varnell for England 16 day of 9ber next.
Wit.: Mathew Lynde, Jno. Potter.

Page 112. 30 June 1642. Wm. Barker of Kettle Creek in Va., planter, and Jno. Flower 900 lbs. tob.
Wit.: Thos. Drew, Robt. Elye.

Page 112. 19 Julye 1645. Richard Hamblett of Jno. Flower 225 lbs. tob.
Francis Sheppard.

Page 112. 17 Julye 1643. Richard Hamblett, living at Westopher, to Jno. Flower 200 weight of tob.
Wit.: Jacob Masonn, Robt. Wilson.

Page 113. 11 7ber 1643. Robt. Powis, clerk, & Henerye Hurd, Va. planter, to Jno. Flower of London, merchant, 1500 lbs. tobacco.
Rec. 9ber 1657.

Page 113. 11 7ber 1643. Robt. Powis, clerke, and Henery Hurd, of Va., planter, to Jno. Flower 1500 lbs. tob.
Wit.: Thos. Drew, Nich. Rennolds.

Page 113. 15 Xber 1645. James Stone to Jno. Flowers & Co. due 7 lbs. English money.
Wit.: Wm. Jeames, Robt. **Vause?**

Page 113. Jno. Gibbs, of Weinoke, certain heifers for the use of Jno. Flower.
Wit.: Adam Loftis.

Page 113. Aug. 1654. Thos. Baylie to Jno. Richards, Merchant, 704 lbs.

Page 113. 5 9ber 1657. Benj. Sidway to Jno. Richards, of London, How in Virginia, 14,376 lbs. of tob.

Page 113. 5 9ber 1657. Capt. Parke's Disbursements out of Mrs. Alice Parke's Est. Court allows her 600 lbs. of tob. 5 ber 1657, this for funerall expenses, fetchinge minnister, etc.

Page 113. 14 April 1651. Wm. Butts, of the City of Bristoll, merchant, his heirs, etc., are bound for 10 pounds of lawful money of England to Wm. Quarrell for the use of Charles Ford of Va., in James Cittye Countye. In case

sd Wm. Quarrell cometh not to receive the ten pounds, then return sd sum in goods unto Charles Ford.
 Signed: Wm. Butt.
 Wit.: Johanna Drew.

Page 114. Jan. 1656. Wm. Thomas received of Thomas Busby 450 lbs. tob.

Page 114. 7 Jan. 1657. Rob. Webb received of Wm. Marriott 10,000 lbs. of tob.

Page 114. 7 Jan. 1657. Absatt Concent of 790 lbs. of tobacco paid by Mr. Robt. King for use of Mr. Richard Woodward. On board Mary of Bristoll.

Page 114. 5 Jan. 1657. Alice Felton, widdow, for value received to Coll. Henry Browne my dwelling house & plantation adjoining, also stock, goods, furniture, etc.
 Wit.: Wm. Lea, Wm. Browne.

Page 115. 1 March 1657. Coll. Henry Browne and Ann, his wife, for sufficient compensation already received to Geo. Jordan, a parcell of land comprehended in a quatrant of a greater quantity in Surry County, on James River to the west end of Piper's Plantation to Coll. Jno. Flood's now in ye implement of Wm. Jennings, being sould from him to sd Jordan.
 Wm. Browne, Thos. Flood.
 Rec.: 3 March 1657.

Page 115. 4 Feb. 1654. Receipt from Dr. Thos. Rennolds for 1500 lbs. tob. & caske in part payment for 100 acres of land lying at the head of Smith's Fort bounding upon Mr. Corker west, and Spilltimber north. Rec. of Doctor Thos. Rennolds 100 acres of land at head of within fort, head of Mr. Corker's west and Spilltimber.
 Signed: Thos. Warren.
 Rec.: 10 May 1657.

Page 115. 3 March 1657. Jose Whotby and wife Mary petition the Court for postponement of their suit to the next Court.

Page 115. 11 Feb. 1657. Johannah Drew, the now wife of Thos. Steevenson, aged 20 years, testified that she saw Wm. Butte of Bristoll sign this writing a bill unto Charles Forde of Va., and to his wife for seven lbs. sterling, said bill was for two hogsheads of tob. rec. by Henry Butte of Charles Forde.
 Signed: Johannah Drew.
 Rec.: 10 March 1657.

Page 116. 1 March 1657. Deposition of John George that being at the house of Elizabeth Hardy in ye time of Ann Stanly her sister heard sd Stanley tell ye said Mrs. Hardy if she died she would give her all her cows in Hog Island, to whom Mrs. Hardy replied Alas, what shall I doe with thy cows whereupon I told Mrs. Hardy yt she may as well have them as another. To the truth of this I shall be ready to depose if situation shall require.
 Signed: John George.
 Rec.: 3 March 1657.

Page 116. 10 Jan. 1656. Robert Southerland (or Leatherland) assigns to Coll. Swann his heirs, etc., 3000 lbs. of tob. and 200 lbs. of tob. before 26 Oct. Next & 1000 lbs. of tob. next year following. 27 Sept. 1653.
 Thos. Drewe, Anthonye Bridges.
 Rec.: 10 Jan. 1656.

Page 116. 2 Aug. 1656. Thomas Smith bound to pay to Thos. Swann, or his assigns 300 lbs. of tob. etc.
 Rec.: 10 Jan. 1656.
 Wit.: Wm. Edwards.

Page 116. March 1657. Coll. Henry Browne and Ann his wife for valuable considerations sell to Samuel Paine of Chickahominy in James Cittye County,

Va., boatwright, one black mare, filly, etc.
Wit.: Wm. Browne, Wm. Fisher, Ro: Stanton.

Page 116.  21 Jan. 1655.  Know all men that I, Thos. Peirce, of Mulberry Island, in Va., send Greetings...me movinge make over to Wm. Peirce, my eldest sonne one cowe which Capt. Wm. Peirce and Mr. Wm. Spencer shall make choice of as to stock for sd Wm. & in case the cowe shall happen to dye within two years of the date thereof then sd. Capt. Peirce & Mr. Spencer to make choice of another for the use of sd Wm.and all increase until sd. Wm. is 21 years old to sd. Wm. Peirce the younger.  If he die before 21 years to return to me.
Signed: Thos. Peirce.
Wit.: Geo. Sugg.
Rec.: 30 May 1658.

Page 116.  22 April 1658.  Ralph Jones, admr. of Jno. Zaines, his est., has received just accounting from the hand of Lt. Coll. Thos. Swann.
Rec.: 30 May 1658.

Page 117.  7 April 1658.  By the Gov. & Capt. Gen'll of Va., Sam Mathews, Esq.,...send greetings whereas John Zaines, deceased, dying intestate and leaving an estate in diversgoods, rights & credits in case whereof Ralph Jones who married the Relict of Wm. Zanes, deceased, brother of the said Jno. Zaines, and in suit to a Court held at James Cittye on behalf of Wm. Zaines, sonne of Wm. Zaines, Deceased, heir at law to the est. of sd. Jno. Zaines, decd., on the descendant's est. , now know ye that the said Samuel Matthews, Esq., according to order of Ct., grant to Ralph Jones, admr. of all goods, rights, and credits of est., etc.
Rec.: May 1658.

Page 117.  25 May 1658.  Wm. Davis, aged 23 years, or thereabouts examined at Surry Court 27 ber 1657, sayeth that at his first comming into the Colonye with Mr. Haynes of Bristoll, the shipp riding before James Citty, Lt. Coll. Thos. Swann being aboard, that Davis of his own will offered to serve Coll. Thos. Swann ten yeares whereupon Coll. Swann bought the Deponent with whom he remained near upon two yeares & afterward was put off for 2000 pounds of live porke unto Robert Sorrell which...was paid that year in two payments, two years after, about a twelve month since, the sd Sorrell & Deponent being stripping tobacco and discoursing about obtaining the Deponent's freedom (had formerly discoursed upon the same) the sd Robt. Sorrell said unto the Deponent Wm. if thou will be ruled by me I will prescribe for thee that will pleade thy cause and aske thee nothing & shall nominate Major Morryson, but afterward the sd Sorrell sent the Deponent to Mr. Soane to request him in his name to be this Deponent's Attorney for to pleade for this Deponent's freedom which sd Soane undertook but after this sd Sorrell doubtinge the business would not fall out according to his expectations (the sd. Coll. Swann being noways bound to make good)...the sd Sorrell seemed to be then offended with sd Soane for meddling in it... whereupon a wager was laid between them and sd Deponent (Mr. Hampton, Minnister being present), Deponent declares that Sorrell lost the wager - a bottle of Dram and Sorrell came and called the Deponent Rouge and said that hee could finde in his heart to kick the Deponent up and down like a football, saying you Rogue, could you not say I did not send you, and further sayeth not.
Signed; Wm. Davis.
Rec.: 25 May 1658.

Page 117.  3 May 1658.  Ralph Creed, Security for Jno. Richards, for 548 lbs. tob. & caskes makes over all of his cropp.
Wit.: Benj. Sidway, James Masonne, Joseph Whitmell his Atty.

Page 117.  3 May 1658.  Henrye Meddowes, I pray you confess judgement for your friend, Henerye Clarke for a debt he owes Mr. Wm. Browne, this my note shall bear you harmless.
Your friende, Henerye Clarke.
Wit.: Thos. Culmer.

BOOK I, 1652-1672                                       27

Page 118. 10 Feb. 1657. Thos. Warren of Gray's Creek in Surry County, Gent.,
for a valuable consideration of 1500 lbs. of tob., sells to Thos. Rennolds
of Martin Brandon in Charles Cittye County, chyrurgion, his heirs, etc.,
100 acres of land at the head of Smith's Fort, bound west by the land of
Mr. John Corker, north by land of Anthonye Spilltimber, sonne of John Spilltimber,
  Signed: Thos. Warren..
  Wit.: Ben Sidway, Wm. Edwards, James Masonne, Ro. Stanton.
  Rec.: 3 May 1658.

Page 118. 20 March 1657. Sam Swaine hath released Anthonye Redwood out of
prison,...for 590 lbs. tob. so much by debt and charges now & Anthonye Redwood binds himself and exors. to pay Samuel Swann 595 lbs. of tob. at the
dwelling house of sd Swaine 10 Oct. next.
  Jno. Flood, Geo. Jordan.
  Rec.: 3 May 1658.

Page 118. 2 Aug. 1654. This is to certify to all that it may concern that I,
Christopher Lawson, assign to Thomas Andrews and to his wife so long as she
contains herself a widdowe the land that the said Thomas Andrews doth now
hold of the said Christopher Lawson Paying yearly two capons...if any Freeman cometh in with him to pay him 100 lbs. of tob. by the year.
  Wit.: John Courtman; Nich. Williams.
  Rec.: May 1658.

Page 119. 3 May 1658. Thos. Jarrell, aged 23 yeares or thereabouts. The
Deponent sayeth that his Master Marriott sent him from his house along with
John Bradye in March last unto Mr. Mason's house to carrye some parcells of
goods of sd Bradye & Deponent, went along with said Bradye & his wife & by
the way between his Master's and Mr. James Mason's house John Bradye asked
the Deponent when he was free & Deponent replied that he could not tell for
he the sd Bradye knew better than hee,  then said Bradye told the Deponent
if he would seek his freedom he believed he might get free and he would act
in court for him.
  Wit.: Wm. Batt, James Masonne.

Page 119. 3 May 1658. To the Surry County Court, Petition by Wm. Marriott
that on the sixth day of March last John Bradye came to the Petitioner's
house to go over unto a store at Goose Hill, the Petitioner went over with
him and he brought over goods with him and when he was come back to the
Petitioner's house the Petitioner asked him and his wife to stay all night,
but Bradye replied he had promised Mr. Mason to come thither and accordingly
did soe and desired the Petitioner to lend him a servant to carry his goods
along with him to Mr. Mason's house. The Petitioner did so which servant
the Petitioner formerly bought of Bradye and Spilltimber for 2650 lbs. of
tobacco and caskes, and by the way of goinge to Mr. Mason's house the said
Brady unworthilye asked the said servant how long he had to serve and told
him if he went over to the Gov. Councill that he might get free and told
him that he would assure him in this further to encourage him that John
Spilltimber's man Harry got free soe which conversation the servant very
well liked, but the Petitioner hearing of it asked the servant what business
he had at the Quarter Court. He replied that he had not thought to repair
thither before his countryman Bradye told him he might gett free if he would
seek for it.  Then the Petitioner tould his servant if he kept himself from
the gallowes hee would keep him from being free before the expiration of his
Indenture. Now may it please the court that since the time of Bradye's
tampering with the Petitioner's servant he lately behaved himself very stub-
bornly which before was otherwise and the Petitioner does very much doubt
when he finds his hope of freedom circumstanced that he will run away which
will be the overthrow of the Petitioner's crop and the damage of getting him
gain(?) which danger ariseth clearly through the seducements of evill coun-
cell of the sd Bradye...such abuses as these shall be suffered few men or
none will keep a servant and the Petitioner hereby prayeth that said Bradye
be compelled to secure the Petitioner the further safety of his servant from
running away and to pay costs of suite.
  Wm. Marriott.            Rec.: 3 May 1658.

Page 120. 27 June 1658. Lucas de Courtes desires that Thos Pittman Impleat Richard Tias in an action in Surry Co. Court, on the 6 July next to take a Deposition in the case.

Page 120. 12 Mar. 1657. Ind. between James Murray, planter of Surry Co., and Elizabeth Harris, (who) binds her son, John Phipps, as an apprentice to James Murray for one and twenty years, he being only four years old, but child to be free at 21 years, and give him a cow and calf and he to be edified in reading etc.
Rec.: July 1658.
Wit.: Jno. Gregorye, Ed. Pittway.

Page 120. July 1658. Richard Tias appoints his friend Jno. Rawlings his attorney.

Page 120. July 1658. Indenture between Thos. Andrews, Southwarke Par., Surry Co., and Robert Stanton, Councill Clerke. Thos. Andrews puts his daughter, Ann Andrews, an apprentice to Ro. Stanton and Mary his wife for a term of five years beginning 25 March 1658 to serve in such service as Stanton & wife shall employ her as fit for a woman and no other. If Mrs. Stanton die Thos. Andrews to be allowed to take away his daughter from sd R. Stanton. If Andrews die before his wife and the time not expired then Ann to serve full time and to find Ann meat and drink, apparell and lodging and teach her, or cause her to be taught to read, and instructed in the Christian religion and to sew and other things as women should know. At the expiration of her time to pay her 1000 lbs. of tobacco, certain live stock etc.
Rec.: 7 Aug. 1658.
Wit.: James Masonne, Jno. Corker.

Page 121. 15 May 1658. Jno. Newell, Atty. of Joseph Beaman of London, Merch't, appoints his friend Wm. Marriott to be in his place for sd Beaman to recover such goods, etc., in Surry Co., pay his debts, etc.
Wit.: Wm. Hosker, Rich. Jarrette.
Rec.: 1 9ber 1658.

Page 121. 12 Xber 1657. Wm. Lea sells to Thos. Wright a heifer.
Wit.: John Morecocke.
Rec.: 7 7ber 1658.

Page 121. May 1658. Wm. Lea sells two cows to Arthur Frenett (Trenett?).

Page 121. 3 June 1658. Court at Merchant's Hope.
    Mr. Thomas Drew  Mr. War. Horsemand
    Mr. Antho. Wyatt  Mr. James Parker
    Capt. Richard Tye  Mr. Stephen Hamelin
    Mr. Charles Sparrowe

Ordered that Mr. Nicholas Perrye deliver to Edward Ellis certain live stock belonging to Edward Greenwood, Thos. Ellis givinge caution to secure the sd Perrye for sd estate.
Hoel Fryse.
Rec.: 9ber 1658.

Page 121. 2 9ber 1658. Francis Gray, brother to Thos. Gray, both of Surry County, assign all right & title of this pattent over unto above sd Brother Thos. Gray to his use, etc. Rec.: 3 9ber 1658.
Wit.: Jno. Gittings, Sam. Swann.

"In this Booke stands recorded the Conveyances of the Land to which these following papers have relation."

Page 122. May 1654. Wm. Morslay I shall desire you by virtue of this note to give Mr. Jno. Barker Possession in my name of the Plantation I have at Upper Chippoakes which I have sould unto him as you will Ingage.
Your servant and lovinge friend, Thos. Blande. Rec.: 26 9ber 1658.

BOOK I, 1652-1672

Page 122. 13 Jan. 1653. Rec. of John Barker what he owes Mr. John Blande & Co., planter of Chippoakes, 5000 lbs. of tobacco.
Wit.: Francis Blande.
Rec.: July 1658.
Theodorick Blande.

Page 122. 15 9ber 1657. Order of Surry Court that we whose names are under written should value the damage of a parcell of work, which Thos. Bennett should have done for Thos. Binns, and Certify to the Clerke of the Court... damage worth 1350 lbs. of tob.
Rec.: 7 Aug. 1658.
James Masonne, Thos. Pittman.

Page 122. 5 9ber 1658. Peter Greene released of all debts to Edward Pettway. Wm. Michell; Hen. Soane.

Page 122. 24 10ber 1658. Anthony Whitman, 24 10ber 1658, examined sayeth that Roger Potter was one whom he always wanted to be with when he was free. He and said Potter planned to go away together to ye bay to hire the Potter furnished him with clothes, and planned to go by water, but what boat did not know. Potter promised to furnish him coat, drawers, shewes, stockings, and a shirt.

Page 123. James Hugate, examined, said that Roger Potter persuaded him to run away secretly to a remote part of the bay, and take Hugate's wife with them, she big with child, if she did otherwise than well they would throw her overboard. He told Col. Swann that Potter a second time importuned him to go, and would persuade Goodman Sine, his man, and Wm. Scarbrough and Thomas Maurice, also Wm. Rose his boy, and if Doll, at Thos. Andrews would not go, he would get her clothes, and lock them in his chest at the house of Thos. Gray, Jr., and go to Geo. Jordan's and take his sloop, if to big, take his wherry and if not in his way take Wm. Jennings, his boat, and carry her down to John Barroughe's plantation and there take in ye rest of ye company and so be gonne persuading Wm. Scarbrough and Thomas Morris, and calling ye sd Doll Potter's sister.
Jasque Hugate.

Page 124. John Alder, sent to the house of Mr. Stanton, met Roger Potter said James Hugate would speak with him, said he would get a suit of clothes from mad Ned Potter, said it would be upon Nedd's back perhaps at Col. Swann's boat.

Page 124. 2 Feb. 1658. A difference between Mr. Abraham Shears, Merchant, and Mr. Jno. Hawkins, Master of the Catch called The Adventure, concerning a voyage from Barbadoes to Virginia, met at the house of Mr. Corker.
Geo. Jordan, Thos. Adams, Jno. Jennings.

Page 124. Anthony Redwood to pay Maj. Crafton 400 lbs. of tob.
8 April 1658.

Page 125. 9 Jan. 1658. David Willyams appts. Robert Spencer to make acknowledgment of a small tract of land given by me to Nicholas Spencerand his wife during their life.
Rec. 3 Feb. 1658.
Wit.: Wm. Michell.

Page 125. 25 Jan. 1658. Richard Hide makes his loving friend, Jno. Gittings his atty. to Implead John Clark or Atty. of sd Clark.
Wit.: Isaac Tatem.

Page 125. Pet. to the Court of Jane King, widdowe, her husband John King deceased, to get possession of a legacy, and her husband's will to be discharged of the orphant's account.
Rec. 27 Jan. 1658.

Page 125.  29 Jan. 1658.  A difference between Bartholomew Owen and Thomas Gray.
    Wit.: Samuel Matthews.

Page 126.  15 9ber 1658.  A contract of Marriage agreed upon between Jno. Washington and Mary Foord, widow; John Washington delivers to Robert Stanton, Clerke, one mare to Thos. Plunt, sonne of Said Mary his heirs, etc. when Thomas is ten Years old.  As witness this deed 15 9ber 1658.
    Signed: Jno. Washington.
    In presence of: Jno. Flood, Edmund Shipman, Thos. Flood.

Page 24.  Wm. Scarbrough, examined, said 10 ber 1656 Potter said Mr. Delke would write him up a seat of land in the bay.

Page 126.  2 Jan. 1658.  John Bradye to pay Henery and John Richards, merchants, 3300 lbs. of tob. and make over to them one servant, Edward Fenn, who has to serve until 1669, & Household goods, cattle, etc.

Page 127.  27 Jan. 1658.  Wm. Batt, of Lower Cippoakes, Surry County, purchased of Henry Bannister 275 acres of land being part of the divident of the plantation formerly of Wm. Newsum by pattent bearing date 3 March 1636, commonly called Rich Neck, through which 275 acres runneth a swamp southward, being a branch of Sunken Marsh, so that on the Westward side of the Swamp lieth part of the 275 acres called Shepperd's Neck, also a tenement now in the possession of Burchell, now known that Wm. Batt for a valuable consideration in hand received, sold to Ralph Jones on the west side of the swamp except that sold to Wm. Burchell.

Page 127.  6 April 1659.  Nathaniel Silvester, merchant, a bond to Wm. Edwards of 16,000 lbs. of tobacco.  Wit.: Sam. Abbott.
    On the back of this Wm. Edwards assignes the bond to Abraham Shears, merchant.
    Wit.: Ben Sidway, Jno. Washington.

Page 127.  Dec. 1652.  Sir Wm. Berkeley discharged Wm. Edwards of a bond of 16,000 lbs. of tob.  Mr. Edwards security for Nathaniel Silvester, Apr. 1644, and by order of Court free from bond, Assigned to sd Shears 6 April 1659.
    Wit.: Walter Chiles.

Page 128.  Acct. of Jno. Zaines' Est. presented by Ralph Jones, Admr., Aprill 1659.  Ralph Jones makes Wm. Edwards Atty. for the estate of Jno. Zaines for all debts, more especially, from Wm. Scott & from Est. of Wm. Zaines, deceased.
    Wit.: Ann Watts, Jno. Dye.

Page 129.  16 March 1657.  Jeremiah Clements his pattent for 200 acres of land, 10 Jan. 1643.  On the back side assigned as followeth, viz.: Know all men that I, Capt. Henerye Berry, doe assigne over this pattent to Wm. Gapinge and his heirs.
    Teste: Thos. Brereton.
    Wm. Gapinge assignes to Anthonye French, 25 Jan. 1658.
    Wit.: Jno. Gittings, Robt. Spencer.
    Rec.: 26 Jan. 1658.

Page 129.  3 Oct. 1655.  Richard Hide of Chippoakes Creek, planter, sells to Christopher Greenfield all his rights in 50 acres of land, part of a divident of 450 acres, bounded by a poplar at the swamp side, divides this land from Edward Ellis.
    Wit.: Edward Ellis; Wm. Hill.

Page 129.  25 Jan. 1658.  Chris. Greenfield of Surry County sells 50 acres with housing etc. to Wm. Lea, payable 30 Dec. next 21 Aug. 1658.
    Wit.: Charles Gregorye, Matthew Hoggson.
    Wm. Lea assignes over to Henerye Comes on 1 Xber 1659.
    Wit.: Jno. Corker, John Modmore.

Page 130. 10 March 1659. The Plantation of Robt. Webb, by the decease of sd Webb, falls into the hands of Mr. Wm. Batt, and by lease was to be left in such condition and appoints Geo. Watkins, Edward Pettway and John Dollye and Peter Adams to see that the Plantation is so kept.
   Rec.: 16 May 1659.
   Law. Baker.

Page 130. 9 May 1659. Mrs. Dorothye Corker, aged 50 years, testified that Thos. Gates gave Thos. Gray, Sr., his sonne Thos. Gray, and Daughter Jane Gray, 50 acres of Land on Gray's Creek.

Page 131. 9 May 1659. John Hux, aged 46 years testified that Deponent married Jane Gray, daughter of Thos. Gray, Sr., and sister of Thos. Gray, Jr., at which time Thos. Gray, Sr., told the Deponent that he had 50 acres of land, given to his sons and daughters by Mr. Gates, which land was part of a divident where he lived at Gray's Creek, and that sd Gray, Sr., gave the Deponent satisfaction for his wife's part thereof and was 25 acres.
   Wit.: John Hux.
Luke Mizell, aged 45 years, testified that when Deponent was servant to Thos. Gray, Sr., Deceased, he did often hear sd Gray and his wife say that Gates had given 50 acres to their son Thomas and daughter, Jane.
   11 May 1659.
John Flood, aged 44 years, he living some ten years with Thos. Gray, Sr., when he lived at Gray's Creek, and heard the same.

Page 131. June 1659. Coll. Jno. Flood sold a red cow named Rose to Anthonye Holburt, formerly belonging to Eliza. Lather.

Page 131. 14 Nov. 1659. Wm. Jennings bound over to pay Mr. Thos. Flood, gent., 16,000 lbs. tob.

Page 132. 9 May 1659. Thos. Flood sells to Wm. Jennings all land in his occupation which he formerly held by lease from his father, Coll. John Flood, betwixt the land of John King and sd Jennings.
   Wit.: Thos. Pittman, Foulk Moulson.

Page 132. 1 May 1659. Wm. Jennings sells to Thos. Jones of Henrico Co., Va., an iron gray horse.
   Jno. Richards, James Sowerby.

Page 132. 6 July 1659. Martin Hamond sells James Mason cows.

Page 133. Depositions were made by the following people concerning certain matters:
      Wm. Lucas, aged 30 years.
      Ann Lucas, aged 29 yeares.
      Joseph Whitmoald, aged 20 yeares.
      Wm. Edwards, aged 43 yeares, said that Wm. Berkeley had desired the Deponent to demand a pair of cart wheels at the house of Harris, at Sunken Marsh, but Harris was dead. 25 Jan. 1659.

Page 137. 2 July 1659. The King of Wainokes sells to Eliza Short a boy of that Nation named Westophen from said day and date, in exchange for a young horse foal aged one year in full sale of said boy.
   Wit.: George Marshall, Thos. Bushby.

Page 138. 18 Aug. 1659. George Bussey, of Calvert County, Maryland, planter, appoints Francis Carpenter, his atty. in his behalf to receive by order of law of Mr. Law. Baker, or his atty. the full 1065 lbs. of tobacco and caskes due him for a bill under his name.
   Wit.: Samuel Hanes, Wm. Samsell.

Page 138. May 1660. Alice Parke for a valuable consideration, sells to Wm. Fisher one bay mare etc. 20 Xber 1659.
   Wit.: Wm. Marriott, Rob. Spencer.

Page 138. Wm. Fisher assigns to Robert Stanton.
   Rec.: 6 March 1659.
   Wit.: Joseph Fisher, Josephus Countenance.

Page 139. 14 July 1659. Tukesbury in the County of Gloucester. These are to certify that the bearer hereof, William Webb, was the younger brother of Stephen Webb, lately deceased, who heretofore lived and died in Virginia, as wee are credibly informed, and that the said Wm. Webb was an uncle to Robert Webb, sonne and heir apparent unto the said Stephen Webb, likewise deceased, and that the said Wm. Webb was the only brother of Stephen Webb, as to our knowledge, and we are informed by the Certificate annexed that Stephen Webb and Wm. Webb were borne in the countye of Bushlye in Worcester...of the Borough...and that Wm. Webb with his wife and family are now and for some years past have loved quietly in the town. Now at the request of the said Wm. Webb we are bold to so state.
   Rec.: 24 July 1659.
   John Liat, Bayliffe.
   Wit.: Thos. Clarke, Edward Philips, Jno. Batick & Jno. Carter, Andrew Hollams. Justices.

Page 139. 1659. Upon request made unto the minister & Churchwardens of the Parrish of Bushly in the County Worcester by Wm. Webb the bearer thereof to certifie under our hands that the said Wm. Webb was the Legitimate brother of Stephen Webb late deceased in Virginia, wee therefore the Minister and Churchwardens of the said Parrish of Bushley doe hereby that Stephen Webb was Baptized in our Parish Church of Bushly the fifth daie of September A. D. 1598, and that Wm. Webb, brother of the sd Stephen Webbs was Baptized the Tenth daie of May 1601, both being the sonnes of Steephen Webb and his wife.
   Thos. Cooke?, Minister of Bushley
   Longwoode
   Edward Dow-Church Wardens
   Walter Barnes
              also signed by:
              Thos. Lane                Rive Morris
              Rich. Biddle              Nich. Lane
              Jno. Mason                Jno. Granger
              Nicholas Morris           Edward Bilde

Page 140. I have examined the Books kept in the Parish of Bushly and doe hereby finde the abovesaid to be true and also I doe know that Steephen Webb was a freeholder of Cornwall Land...and lived there for many years till he sold his lands to severall persons who doe now enjoy the same.
   Richard Dowdeswell.
   Rec.: 24 July 1659.

Know that I, Wm. Webb of Tuksbury in the County of Gloucester...Brother unto Steepehn Webb late deceased in Va. and also to Robert Webb, alsoe deceased in Va., Appoints to Wm. Webb Webb and makes him Atty. for land that Stephen Webb and Robert Webb dyed seized & possessed in Va.
   Wm. Webb

Page 141. 24 Jan. 1659. Jno. & Peleg Dunstan, sonnes of John Dunstan, late of Lower Chippoakes in Surry County, Va., make over unto our Brother, Ralph Dunstan, all our rights etc. of land left our said brother by our father in his will.
   8 7ber 1659.

Page 142. 24 Jan. 1659. Tho. Steephens discharges John Barker from all debts.
   Tho. Steephen.

Page 142. George Jordan Discharges Martin Hammond of debt.

Page 143. 24 Jan. 1659. Discharge of Mrs. Alice Parke & Wr. Marriott, who married the Relict of Wm. Buttler of Giles Parke's Est.

Signed: William Fisher who married ye orphant of the deceased Capt. Giles Parke, Est.
Wit.: Wm. Lea, Geo. Carter.

Page 143. Arthur Jordan, aged 32 years, made deposition. 9ber 1659.
Edward Skelton, aged 22, made Deposition also.

George Steephens sells to Edward Follis land called Cabin Point, 700 acres.

Page 144. 25 Jan. 1659. John Cooper, aged 21 years, testified that Mr. Richard Hankins, atty. of Mrs. Francis Newton, upon his death bed desired that Wm. Batt & Thos. Binns take care of the est. of sd Newton untill they should further order out of England for his friends then Capt. Higgenford asked him whether he should have the management...etc.
Signed: Jno. Cooper.

Page 144. 8 9ber 1659. Henry Lea, aged 16 years, heard his Master, Richard Hopkins say before his death that Mr. Batt & Mr. Binns should have the ordering of his estate after his death and that Deponent might live with either of them.
Henry Lea.

Page 144. 9 8ber 1659. Ralph Dunstan, sonne of Jno. Dunstan, deceased, disclaims all right and title of land belonging to Jno. and Peleg Dunstan given them by my father in his will.
Wit.: John Corker, Rob. Spencer.

Page 145. May 1660. Mathew Battell sells to Francis Sowerby 105½ acres of land, houses, etc. conveyed to him in a joint deed between me, Matthew Battell and James Sowerby and formerly in possession of John Jennings, and then in Wm. Rose's and now set over unto Francis Sowerby his heirs, etc.
Mathew Battell. Ann Battell.

Page 147. 25 September 1659. Andrew Robinson, and Ann Shortland, widdowe, have contracted matrimony, and before solemnizing it, bequests to her sonne Ralph Shortland a mare.

Page 26 (sic). Dec. 1659. Jurah Hide makes Benj. Dawl her atty.

Page 148. 30 Jan. 1659. Alice Parke, widdowe, empowers her sonne Geo. Carter, to sell a mare.

Page 148. 1 May 1660. Wm. Edwards sells to Samuel Plowe one parcell of land a Patent if land I have on Sunken Marsh, near Sunken Marsh Mill which was once a patent of Mr. Thos. Browne's 350 acres and have received of Samuel Plow full satisfaction by a letter to Mrs. Mary Proctor to pay said Edwards. 20 April 1660.
James Mason, Wm. Marriott.

Page 149. 12 April 1654. A marriage about to be solemnized between Arthur Jordan & Elizabeth Bavinn, late of Southwark Parish, on certain conditions have mutually agreed that Arthur Jordan make sale of certain stock, live stock.
1 May 1660.

Page 149. 31 Oct. 1659. Susannah Stanhard to Mr. Robert Stanton, asks him to record a sale of land which her husband made to Edwin Colby.

Page 149. Thos. Harris, of Isle of Wight, appoints Thos. Dulmore his atty.
Samuel Haswell; Wm. Lewis?

Page 150. Col. Henry Browne found a dead body in the woods, servant to Wm. Rose, planter named Robert Story, who Left his master's service and hanged himself. 2 April 1660. Names of jury: Robt. Hamlin, John Marable, James Tatem, Rich. Case, Xpher Lewis, Tho. Andrews, John Hux, John Sawyer, Luke Mizell.

Page 150. 17 Oct. 1659. The body of Wm. Hawkes was viewed, he being the servant of Coll. Thos. Swann. He fell from an ox cart, the wheels of which passed over him. Robert Stanton, Wm. Rose, Thos. Andrews, Wm. Browne, Wm. Fisher, Thos. Wise, Fra. Sowerby, Hen. Browne, Barth. Owen, Rich. Case.

Page 151. 7 March 1659. Wm. Marriott bound to Coll. Thos. Swann 200 lbs. Condition by that Wm. Marriott by the Grace of God shall marry and take to Wife Susannah Swann, daughter to Capt. Thos. Swann, if ye sd. Wm. Marriott after ye marriage shall dye before ye sd Susannah that then sd Marriott shall by his Last Will & Test. give unto Susannah 100 lbs. sterling.
 Wit.: John Dibdall, Robt. Stanton.

Page 151. 20 May 1660. Ralph Creed in consideration of two good cows out of ye stock of Thos. Chiffers and 7000 lbs. of tob....sells to Chiffers 1100 acres of land at the head of Sunken Marsh near Chippoakes, late in possession of Richard Hill and sold to Robert Creed by George Jordan by Order of Court to be held by sd Thos. Chivers.

Page 152. 1 May 1660. Geo. Jordan relinquishes his right in land Ralph Creed sold to Thomas Chivers of 1100 acres by his purchase of sd land from Ralph Creed.

Page 152. 2 Jan. 1656. Indenture between Roger Delke and Michael Upchurch of a Plantation on Lawnes Creek lying between John Gregory and sd Michael Upchurch (Upshure) 40 acres of land, if less than the lease to Timothy Madmonker, for 21 years.
 Rec. May 1660.

Page 153. 1 Jan. 1656. Indenture between Roger Delke, of Lawnes Creek Parish, Gent., and Tobyas Cooke, Planter, taken upon the Creek betwixt Jno. Bruten and John Bancos, 100 acres, for 21 years, and one barrell of Indian corn paid to Roger Delke on the first of January.
 Rec.: 1 May 1660.

Page 154. 30 June 1660. Mrs. Mary Ewen gives power of attorney to Mr. Francis Newton, planter, of her affairs in Virginia, substitute for her well beloved brother, Nicholas Newton, since deceased and Richard Hopkins his lawful attorney 6 Dec. 1659. Mrs. Ewen had 1400 acres of land, belonging to the patent, 7 negroes, 50 head of cattle, 15 hoggs, etc.

Page 154. John Cooper, aged 20 years or thereabouts, testified on 25 Jan. 1659(60) that on the sixth of Dec. last Mr. Wm. Batte came to ye Plantation of Mr. Ewin in Virginia and did deliver to Mr. Richard Hopkins Attorney for Francis Newton, the Plantation, together with 7 negroes and Michael (a negro man since dead) was then alive, 50 head of cattle, etc.

Page 155. 27 June 1660. Whereas Ralph Dunstan sold 300 acres of land belonging to my husband, John Dunstan, unto Thomas Clarie with 300 acres Peleg Dunstan, my sonne, might pretend to some title, I, Cecilye Dunstan, doe bind myself and heirs to save and keep harmless the sd Thos. Clarie and his heirs from any claim, Peleg Dunstan after six months comes of age to relinquish his claim.
 Rec.: 3 July 1660.

Page 155. 15 May 1660-7. (sic). Jas. Sowerby is bound to Matthew Battell for 764 lbs. of tob.

Page 155. 12 Oct. 1657. Cecilye Dunstan gives to her eldest son, Ralph Dunstan, 300 acres.

Page 156. 3 July 1660. The corpse of Benjamin Watkins, viewed by the Jury, he being the late servant of Jno. Suggs, the said Benjamin Watkins (voide of the fear of God) did desparately & wilfully hang himself.

| | |
|---|---|
| Austin Hunnicutt | Daniel Webster |
| Henry Braderton | Rich. Skinner |
| Edmund Wilkins | Richard Smith |

BOOK I, 1652-1672                                     35

                Robt. Whittle?              Thos. Clarye
                Rich. Drew                  Rob. Hunt

Page 156.  26 March 1657.  Arthur Jordan, with consent of wife Elizabeth, sells
  to John Barker one colt.  Elizabeth Jordan desires that her brother-in-law
  Geo. Jordan acknowledge for her in Court.

Page 156.  15 Jan. 1659.  Jno. Lea, Surry County, Va., sells to Thos. Morgaine,
  planter, of Charles City County, a horse.
    Wit.: John Gittings, Geo. Duglas.
    Signed: William Lea.    Alse Lea.
    Rec.: July 1659.

Page 157.  3 July 1660.  Matthew Battell, cooper, of Surry County, sells to
  Thos. Busby, planter, in Surry County, one young horse.
    Wit.: Thos. Pittman, Barth. Owen.

Page 157.  20 7ber 1660-1.  By his Majestyes Governor and Captain Generall
  of Virginia it is thought fitt & accordingly ordered for the Speedy & better
  dispatch of all affaires tending to the peace and welfare of this Collony
  and the Inhabitants thereof that all officers whatsoever within this Country
  doe remaine and continue in their several offices untill further order to
  the contrary and forasmuch as it hath pleased Almighty God to invest our
  most gracious Soveraigne Charles the Second King of England, Scottland,
  France & Ireland & in the Dominion and just rights of his Royall father of
  ever sacred memorye - These are therefore in his Majestyes name strictly
  to charge & command you & every (one) of you forthwith to cause the sd
  King to be proclaimed in every of your Respective Contryes and that all
  writts warrants from henceforth issue in his Majestyes name - Here and fayle
  not as you will Answer the Contrarye at your uttmost Perille.  Given at
  James Cittye under my hand this 20th 7ber 1660-1.
    Signed: Wm. Berkeley.
  To the Sherriffe and all other Chiefs of Officers of Surry County.

                              The Proclamation

We the freemen & Inhabitants of the County now present doe According to
our Dutye & Allegeances Heartily Joyfully & Unanimously Acknowledge & Pro-
claim That Immediately upon the decease of ye late Sovereign Lord King
Charles the Imperiall Crowne of the Realme of England & of all the Kingdomes
Dominions & Rights belonging to the same did by Inherent Birthright & lawful
& undoubted succession descend & come to his most excellent Majestye Charles
the Second being Lineally Justly & Lawfully next heire of the Blood Royall
of the Realme and that by the goodnesse & Providence of Almighty God Hee
is of England, Scottland, France & Ireland, the most potent, mighty undoubted
King--and thereunto wee most humbly & faithfully doe submitt & oblige Our-
selves, our Heires & Posteritye forever.

                            God Save the King.

These Proclamations were Proclaimed at Southwarke in the Countye of Surry
in Virginia with the Acclamation of a great part of the county there Present
& Recorded the leventh day of 8ber being Thursday Anno 1660-1.
    Per: Ro: Stanton, Cl. of ye Countye.

Page 158.  4 7ber 1660.  Henry Artillerye sick and weak cannot attend Court
  to answer the complaint of Mr. Robert Spenser but will attend next Court.
    Dated: Hogg Island.
    Rec.: 5 7ber 1660.

Page 158.  4 7ber 1660.  Thomas Masonne binds over his whole crop to Mr.
  Thomas Culmer for debt of 350 lbs. of tobacco.
    Wit.: Anthony Spilltimber, John King.

Page 158.  19 July 1660.  Wm. Lea and wife, Alice Lea, acknowledge a debt to
  Wm. Heath of a sale of land, 250 acres, which was Thomas Felton's deceased.
    Wit.: John Morecocke, Ben. Dolly?

Page 158.  4 7ber 1660.  Wm. Jennings, cooper, sold a mare to Mr. Thos. Flood & he now assigns the same to Wm. Lea and wife, Alice.
   Wit.: Wm. Cockerham, Ro. Stanton.

Page 158.  1 Sept. 1660.  Indenture between Ralph Dunstan of Lower Chippoakes Surry Co., planter, & Hester his wife of the one part & Thomas Clarie, same Parish & County, cooper, of the other part; 300 acres in Lower Chippoakes Lawnes Cr. Parish, left Mr. Ralph Dunstan by his father, Mr. John Dunstan in his Last Will, he late of Chippoakes.  Thos. Clarie acknowledges the same to Arthur Long.
   14 Jan. 1661.
   Written on back: Judith Clarie, Arthur Allen, Wm. Cockerham.

Page 159.  10 Nov. 1660.  John Corker sells to Christopher Waldan? and Henry Cradock a parcel of land, 50 acres, bound by marked trees & Mr. Thomas Rolfe & from thence...up a swamp called the Devills Woodyard Swamp on the same side adjoining to the said line of marked trees...and pay the King's Rent when it is demanded.
   Wit.: Jno. Gittings, Fra. Mason.

Page 159.  5 Nov. 1660.  John Gregorye employs his friend Lieut. Coll. Caufield to crave to allow him to come to next Court as being lame & sick and wife also very sick, to ascertain what Mr. Pittway shall allege against him.

Page 159.  5 Nov. 1660.  Know all men present that I, Naomi Minter, of Bedingfield, confirm the sale of land that lyeth between Mr. Benjamin Sidway & Mr. Matthew Battell's house...unto Mr. Mathew Battell
   Wit.: Fran. Gray, Wm. Rollinson, Elias -(?)-

Page 160.  7 Feb. 1658.  Indenture between Henry Comes of the County of Isle of Wight, planter, & John Clarke of Surry County, Planter, land formerly possessed by Christopher Greenfield & sold by him to Mr. Wm. Lea, and sold by sd Lea to sd Henry & confirmed by sd Court of Surry County, etc.
   Wit.: John Jennings, Richard Clarke.
   Rec.: 10 Nov. 1660.

Page 160.  17 March 1657.  Indenture of Capt. Henry Perry, Esq., who intermarried with the executrix of Jeremiah Clements, of Upper Chippoakes, Gent., now sells 250 acres of land to Edward Oliver in Upper Chippoakes southward to the outmost end of the Patent of 350 acres formerly being to the abovesaid Clements, bordering upon the land of Wm. Gawine, westward & Wm. Thomas eastward.  If Oliver is deceased in his minority the land to return to said Perry.
   Wit.: Worsham Howsmanden, Wm. Drummond.
   Rec.: 10 Nov. 1660.

(This page very beautifully decorated at left corner top, and down left side in basketry, done with pen and ink, the script also very beautiful - E. T. D.)

Page 161.  10 Nov. 1660.  Indenture between Wm. Lea & his wife Alice, and Wm. Heath, planter, of Southwarke Par., Surry Co., for a parcel of land, 150 acres, formerly Thos. Felton's deceased...called Upper Chippoakes in the woods adj. the land which was John Harrye's unto the Plantation formerly Robert Moseley's adj. a great Swamp which divides Surry Co. and Charles Cittye County, which land was given by sd Thos. Felton in last Will & Test. to his wife Alice who is now the wife of sd William Lea.  Memo: 150 acres lies in Charles Cittye County, adjoining the rest of the divident, which lies in Surry County.
   Wit.: Robert Spenser, John Gittings.

Page 162.  10 Nov. 1660.  James Busby's agreement with Peter Gray to have Tob. house for one year.

Page 162.  6 June 1660.  Thos. Busby, planter, sells to Peter Gray his house and 300 acres of land on Chippoakes Creek, Surry Co., adj. land and Possession of John Barker.
   Wit.: Francis Gray, Anthony Allen.

BOOK I, 1652-1672    37

Page 162. May 1661. A list of cattle, etc., of Thos. Swann and Henry Cobb bound to Roger Potter for the Est. of John Willyam's orphant.
Wit.: Wm. Tuke.

Page 162. 30 March 1661. Jno. Richards acquits John Oakham from all demands of service.
Rec.: Jan. 1661.

Page 163. 8 May 1661. Henry Browne and Ann Browne to Capt. Jordan; they make null and void a gift to the County.

Page 163. 3 9ber 1660. Wm. Strong acquits Mr. Na. Stanton, of all debt.
Jan. 1661.

Page 164. 3 9ber 1660. Jno. Clay sells to Mr. Thos. Hunt, for a debt, one woman servant (Three years service) for which he receives satisfaction.
Wit.: Wm. Marriott.

Page 164. 8 May 1661. Mathew Battell sells to Theophilus Bedinfield 1080 lbs. of tob. and gives as bond a horse & two cows.

Page 164. 13 May 1661. Thos. Swann Reports a boat washed up on his shore on March last, 40 or 50 paces long, with 18 ft. keel, no ropes or sails.

Page 164. 14 Jan. 1660. Matthew Hoggson by marrying Mary, the daughter of George Burcher, sometime of Surry, deceased, confirmed with Morris, the only son of the said Burcher, in all and singular on the estate and whereas Maurice Williams was former partner with the decedent, and godfather... 2430 lbs. tob. due sd Hoggson.
Morris Williams and Burcher's Est. to be presented at Court 14 Jan. 1661. Maurice Williams was godfather to Morris Burcher, and left certain lands, cattle, and swine to his godchild, which remains in the sd decedent's hands for said Morris Burcher, and under Capt. Jordan.
Rec.: May 1661.

Page 165. 7 May 1661. George Cooke, planter, sells two cows to Geo. Blow and is bound for to sd Pittway for sd Geo. Cooke.
Wit.: Ed. Bushell, Thos. Culmer.

Page 165. 5 May 1661. Goods intended by me for Thos. Culmer for security for the estate of James Taylor, orphant. (Inventory follows).
3 March 1660.

Page 166. 16 April 1660. Robert Spensor, aged 30 years or thereabouts, said that Barth. Owen of Surry County, spoke scandalous words against the Commissioners of Surry County, saying he would never have justice in that county; and at James Cittye & several times highly reviled Capt. Geo. Jordan, calling him Roge Raskell... and several other base terms. Capt. Jordan rebuked the sd Owen for his scandalous & Mallitious words, and Owen replied...said Capt. Jordan would not live a month in the county, etc.
Signed: Robert Spensor.
Thomas Breweton.

Page 166. 19 Aug. 1660. Mrs. Fortune Mills examined at James Cittye Deposeth that Bartholomew Owen of Surry County, several times in the presence of the Deponent spoke disparingly and Scandalously of Capt. Jordan...and Maliciously against the Court.
Ed. Hill.

Page 166. 19 Aug. 1660. Roger Rawlings, aged 26 or thereabouts, Deposeth about the same things that Mrs. Fortune Mills had stated.

Page 167. 5 7bris 1660. At a Court in Southwarke Parish for the County:
Commissioners:  Capt. Geo. Jordan        Capt. Wm. Coskerham
                Mr. Arthur Allen         Mr. John Corker

The Court having received information yt Bartholomew Owen hath of late in divers places in ye sd Countye & Elsewhere Scandalized & Defamed them in Generall by taxing them with Injustice...by several Malicious words against their members, appoint Capt. Geo. Jordan to sue & prosecute sd Owen at next Court.
10 7ber 1660.
Ro: Stanton

Page 167. 31 Jan. 1661. In the year 1649, June 6th, Sir Wm. Berkeley... Capt. Gen. of Va. granted by Pattent to George Burcher 300 acres of land at the head of Upper Chippoakes Creek & Geo. Burcher deceasing in Jan. 1656, left sd land in Last Will & Testament to his son Maurice Burcher and daughter Mary Burcher, which sd Mary Burcher married Matthew Hoggson, and said Maurice on the back side of sd Pattent assigned to Matthew Hoggson all his right and title to sd Hoggson 15 Jan. 1660.
Teste: Matthew Yates, Jno. Burcher, the mark of Maurice Burcher.
And below that Maurice Burcher, Matthew & Mary Hoggson assign over to Mathew Yates or his heirs, all their rights etc. of the pattent on the other side. 30 Jan. 1660.
Maurice Burcher, Fra. Gray, Geo. Marshall, Matthew Hoggson, Mary Hoggson, appoint John Barker to act to sell the 300 acres to Matthew Yates, Sen., of Charles Cittye County.

Page 168. 24 May 1661. At a meeting of the Vestry of Southwarke Parish and Lawnes Creek Parish, present wereL Capt. Henry Browne, Esq.; Col. Thos. Swann; Mr. Thos. Warren; Mr. James Masonne; Mr. Jno. Corker; Capt. William Marriott; Mr. John Hux; Vestrymen.
Ro: Stanton, Barth. Owen, Church Wardens.
Lawnes Creek Parish: Mr. Arthur Allen; Lt. Coll. Wm. Caufield; Mr. Randall Holt; Mr. Austin Hunnicutt; Mr. Charles Barham; Mr. Edward Pettway; Mr. Andrew Robbinson; Mr. Richard Drew; Mr. Jno. Clay.
The purpose of meeting was an Act of Assembly enjoyning the erection of tann? houses in each county, Wee the majority of two vestrys...have agreed with Mr. Thos. Warren and Capt. Wm. Marriott to cause to be built on the east side of the Mill Run on Coll. Thos. Swann, his land (He gave land) etc.
Ro: Stanton by order of Vestry.

Page 169. 21 May 1661. Wm. Lea to pay to Henry & John Richards...730 lbs. of tob.
Wit.: Jno. Rawlings, Thos. Allcocke.

Page 169. 3 May 1661. Deposition of Lawrence Biggins aged 27 or thereabouts that he paid Mr. Charles Sparrow deceased about three years since, 13,300 lbs. of Tob. and two barrells of corn for the use of Marmaduke Beckwith.

Page 169. 3 May 1661. Deposition of Thos. Warren, aged 40 or thereabouts, that Lawrence Biggins about three years since paid Mr. Charles Sparrow, deceased, 13530 lbs. of tob. & cash for use of Mr. Beckwith.

Page 169. 30 Aug. 1661. Robert Attkins binds his son, Wm. Attkins, unto Roger Potter for ten years. If Toger Potter die before the ten years is out he is to live with the now wife of Potter as long as she is a widow.
Wit.: John Lookell.

Page 170. 25 June 1661. Fortune Mills & Roger Rawlings acknowledge a receipt from Capt. Francis Gray for the use of James Mills.

Page 170. 11 Oct. 1660. We, Cecylia Dunstan & Jno. Dunstan & Pheleg Dunstan bequeath to Andrew Robinson and his wife, Ann Robinson, etc., 50 acres of land, part of a dividend of 550 acres at the head of Chippoakes Creek, adj. Major Shepard. 11 Oct. 1660.
Wit.: Charles Barham, Ralph Dunstan, Tho. Whetthowe.

Page 171. 3 7ber 1661. Jno. Sidwell and wife Ann of Charles Cittye County sell to Richard Steevens of Surry County, a neck of land, 50 acres, on the

BOOK I, 1652-1672    39

west side of Lawnes Creek, part of which land Capt. Wm. Pearse formerly gave to Robert Lathacot and his heirs, which Lathacot was the father of the above Ann Sidwell, wife to John Sidwell, and warrant deed to Rich. Steevens.

Page 171. 3 7ber 1661. To the Hon. Coll. Brown the Humble Remonstrance of Peter Green in protest of the oath administered, especially upon the commanders of the Colony of which I was then one of the number, in behalf of my King & Countrye the which oath seemes soe Detestable & soe irrilegious to me that I not only Refuse to take it but do utterly detest the thoughts of it, being the most Damnable - imposition contrary to the fundamentall laws of the Kingdom, etc.

Page 172. 14 Jan. 1661. Indenture made 20 Aug. 1661 between Thomas Flood, Surry County, Gent., and Ralph Creed, carpenter, for 6700 lbs. of tob., 150 acres of land lately in possession of Wm. Jennings at the river side adj. Geo. Jordan to the creek that divides it from where Thos. Flood now lives.
Wit.: Geo. Jordan; Charles Muilley?

Page 174. 6 Oct. 1661. Indenture of Jno. & Peleg Dunstan, of Lower Chippaokes, planter, & Arthur Allen, Gent., planter, 500 acres of land of Lower Chippoakes formerly belonging to John Dunstan, their father, deceased, and given by him to Cicely Dunstan, his wife, by his last Will & Testament and to John & Peleg Dunstan, etc.

Page 175. 16 Nov. 1661. Capt. Francis Gray acknowledges receipt from Nath. Stanton of all debts.
Rec.: 23 9ber 1661.
Wit.: Will Fisher.

Page 175. 1 Jan. 1661. Indenture between Thomas Clarie, cooper, and Judith his wife, Lower Chippoakes, and Arthur Long, planter, for 300 acres, which Thos. Clarie Purchased of Ralph Dunstan 1 Sept. 1660.
Wit.: Capt. Law Barker, Capt. Wm. Corker, Mr. Arthur Allen.

Page 176. 15 Jan. 1661. Edward Curtis of Ratcliff, near London, England, Marriner, appoints his friend Walter Houlsworth, of Martin's Brandon in Charles Cittye County, his atty. to attend to his business in Va.
Wit.: Wm. Dowling, Rob. Cobicutt, Charles Gregory.

Page 176. Indenture 18 Feb. 1642 between Geo. Powell of Lower Chippoakes, James Cittye County, Va., Gent., and Steephen Webb of Lower Chippoakes, planter, for 40 lbs. English money, sell him 300 acres of land on the Creek, Chippoakes. and north to James River, south to the mainland, west to George Powell's land and Dame Clare his wife & Robert Webb, sonne of Stephen Webb,, building a house 45 by 20 ft., with two chimneys, glass windows, etc.
Wit.: Hamball Fletcher, Wm. Drummond.
Rec.: 15 Jan. 1661.

Page 178. 1 March 1661. Ind. Christopher Lewis, Lower Par., Surry Co., and Bartholomew Owen 200 acres of land on the west side of Gray's Creek, named the Great Level, adjoining Jno. Wattkins, orphant son of John Wattkins, deceased, eastward to land that Thos. Andrews holds of sd Lewis, and north to Lewis himself, west to Coll. Browne's orphants, being a part of division Christopher Lewis bought of Christopher Lawson.
Wit.: Geo. Jordan, Thos. Warren, Ro: Stanton, Chris. Lewis, Jane Lewis.

Page 179. 2 Jan. 1661. Thos. Pittman sells to Maj. Wm. Marriott all his rights etc. in a water mill jointly belonging to sd Pittman & John Rawlings, sells his one-half of sd mill.
Thos. Pittman; Francis Pittman.
Wit.: Geo. Jordan, John Rawlings.

Page 180. 20 Jan. 1661. John Leake & Wm. Lee sell to Wm. Marriott beds and other household furniture - for 3083 lbs. tob.
Wit.: John Morecocke, Theophilus Flere?

Page 181.  30 Nov. 1661.  Est. of the orphans of John Wattkins, cooper, deceased, to be presented by Mr. James Mason unto Eliza Brewster, the natural mother of sd orphants and finding the account not pleasing to Mrs. Brewster, to be turned over to Mr. Mason and further examined.
  Wit.: Geo. Jordan, Thos. Warren.

Page 181.  13 Aug. 1653.  Wm. Simmons sells to Robert Howse land on the west of Burchen Swamp for 21 years.
  Wit.: Anthony Bridges, Richard Nicholas.

Page 182.  1 March 1661.  To all to whom these presents letter shall come: Mr. James Mills, of Surry County, Va., 8 ber last signified his intent then to repair into Virginia, and now six months since he was expected but neither himself nor letter from him are arrived soe and now doubting whether he be living or dead his affairs to be unmanaged, his business and estate suffering etc.  Now whereas by the laws of England a man and wife may lawfully buy sell and bargain etc...Fortune Mills, his lawful wife, resolves to manage these affairs.
  Fortune Mills.
  Rec.: 4 March 1661.
  Wit.: Na. Knight, Charles Waitley?

Page 184.  11 June 1661.  A marriage about to be celebrated between Thomas Lane of Surry County, planter, and Eliza Jones, widdowe of the same county, for avoiding future trouble, that daughter, Elizabeth, shall have out of her deceased father's estate, ye said Thos. Lane binds himself to pay to Elizabeth Jones, daughter to the widow, when she comes of age or marries, the Plantation which was her deceased father's called Sheepheards worth 1000 lbs. tob. with cowes, etc.
  Geo. Harrison, Wm. Howse.

Page 184.  2 March 1661.  Thos. Allcocke, received payment of Luke Mizelle for a bill, formerly assigned to Mr. Wm. Edwards in 1660 of 1000 lbs. tob. which Edwards assigned to Allcocke.

Page 184.  16 Oct. 1661.  Geo. Blow sells to Walter Bartlett 50 acres of land, that he bought of Andrew Robinson, for 1500 lbs. tob.
  Wit.: Charles Jotham, Edward Petway, John Clay.
  Walter Bartlett assigns it to John Clay, 10 June 1661.
  Wit.: David Beechinoe, Sp... Rand.

Page 186.  25 March 1662.  Indenture between Christopher Lewis and Jane his wife, of Southwarke Parish, and Wm. Foreman for 60 acres of land, part of a divident bought of Christopher Lawson, north to Barth. Owen, west to Ann Browne's, and south where Lewis now lives.
  Wit.: John Corker.

Page 187.  6 May 1662.  Barth. Owen, of Gray's Creek, Southwarke Par., Surry Co., Gent., to Chris. Lewis, winecooper, certain livestock.

Page 187.  4 June 1662.  Thos. Hart says that Jno. Dye is indebted to him.

Page 187.  8 July 1662.  James Mills, Pipscoe Bay, in Va., appoints Robert Spenser his Atty. and in his place.
  Wit.: Jno. Collier, Hezekiah Binnell (or Bunnell).

Page 188.  25 Nov. 1659.  Indenture between Roger Delke and Capt. Thomas Adams for 200 acres of land at Lawnes Creek now in tenure of Jno. Bruton.
  Wit.: John Gregorye, John Beattie.

Page 190.  25 Nov. 1659.  Alice Gregorye, Relict of Roger Delke, deceased, and natural mother of Roger Delke, gives consent to the sale of land.

Page 190.  2 June 1662.  John Hux, planter, sells to Xpher Lewis a mare.

Page 190.  16 June 1662.  Elizabeth Short, of Moseley's Choice, Surry Co.,

BOOK I, 1652-1672                                                        41

widdow, makes her friend Hezachiah Bridgers, of the same county, her attorney, to recover debts.
Wit.: John Drewry, Peter Mason.

Page 191. Wm. Burshell and Sabian Burshell, his wife, to Geo. Watkins all goods, movable and unmovable; to Wm. Clarke, sonne of Richard Clarke.

Page 191. 1 July 1662. Jno. Rawlings, ye sonne of Gregory Rawlings, acknowledges he has received full satisfaction of Wm. Lea of all his rights and title in his father's estate, and acquits Jno. Rawlings of the account.
Wit.: John Lookes, John Billings.

Page 191. 4 July 1662. James Mills sells to Ellis Else all his rights etc. in the barke Supply with all appurtenances, <u>ankers</u>, cables, rigging, and other things and keep Else from being molested on this bill of sale according to law etc. In consideration Ellis Else promises to engage himself and heirs to pay 5000 lbs. of Tobacco (being Dutch weight)...to be delivered at the Manhattan according to custon: 2500 weight of beef before next 10 Nov.,... 2500 in the year 1663 and what goods sd James Mills...shall at any time betwixt the day of date hereof & last day of payment, be shipped aboard sd Barke from Virginia to New England or Manhattans and return to Virginia the freight...further that sd Else shall sayle with the Barke to New Haven and residue of Joanna Allerton's bill of sale, some sheep left in her hands to Va. for sd Mills & to be Accompanied to New England by Sd. Mills.
Wit.: Deliverance Samberton, Edward Heith.

Page 192. 20 June 1662. Jury's verdict of case between Barth. Owen, and Jno. Corker concerning trespass done upon the land of the orphans of Thos. Gray. They found some timber had been cut.

    Edward North     John Hux
    Thos. Andrews    Roger Potter
    Luke Mizelle     Anthony Spilltimber
    John Luke (or Looke)  Jno. Morecocke
    Jno. Rawlings     Wm. Bresse

Page 192. July 1663. Wm. Dennis complained to the Court that he had received a letter of invitation from Mrs. Fortune Mills to come to see her and do some work, being very urgent. He went and was by her and others anointed with a stinking <u>oyle</u> all over his body.

Page 193. 7th 7ber 1662. Mr. Culmer: My respects to you with my wive's: these are to lett you understand that it is not my long absence, nor being afar off, shall satisfye you for God willing I shall by some meanes either come in and satisfye you or cause my friend Mr. Steephens to do it for me.
 Sr. I am very sorry that it hath fallen out soe crosse that you have been played the knave withall as I am informed. Sr. I heare yt you had an intent to have served the Governor's Warrant upon me wh. caused me to absent myself as I did: And likewise I heare yt you can finde but thirty acres of land out of three hundred. Therefore I would intreat you to demand of Arthur Jordan the pattent and the platt & that will informe you where the rest is. I have sent you divers Letters but could never heare any answer of one- Therefore I would desire you to send me word herewith your proceedings are by Mr. Sam'll Steevens which lives in Warricksquiock Bay and hath a plantation at the Southward, soe having noe more at the present but hoping that you will send me an answer as soone as you can I remaine,
 Your Friend to Serve you, Wm. Jennings.
 Sr. John Dye presents his respects to you.

Page 193. 3 Sept. 1662. Indenture between John Thompson of Martin's Brandon in Virginia of the one part and John Freebourne of Surry County of the other for a parcell of land, 150 acres, the upper half of a parcell which "my Wife's father had in exchange with Charles Foard" & lying in Surry County next adjoining a parcell of land in possession of Matthew Battle.
 John Thompson, Sarah Thompson.
 Wit.: Mathew Edloe, Thos. Drinker, Samuel Duglas.

Page 194. 3 Sept. 1662. Jury asked to inquire into the death of a servant belonging to Mr. Peter Greene, whether by blow or bruise. The jury brought in a verdict of natural death.

  Mr. Geo. Watkins    Mr. Charles Baugham
  Jno. Bruton    Mr. Aust. Hunnicutt
  Allen Muggett    Mr. Richard Drew
  Mr. And. Robinson    Mr. A. Long
  Michael -(?)-    Henry Braderton
  Geo. Carter    Richard Jarrett
  Wm. Tuke    Jno. Mason

Page 194. 20 July 1662. Evaginus Christian (Quilstan) aged 26 years, testified that Katherine, servant to Peter Greene had told him that Mr. & Mrs. Greene had beatten her so terribly that she thought she would surely die, with kicks and blows that Mrs. Greene had given her. Had told this the Sunday night before her death, she dying the Sunday night following, and told Deponent to declare this after her death for the Lord's sake.

Page 195. 24 July 1662. Anne Dawson testified that she coming accidentally to the house of Mr. Peter Greene, was asked by Mrs. Greene to dress the corpse of Catton, a maid servant, and saw no blood or bruises except one spot on the breast of her shift.

Page 195. 3 Sept. 1662. Lawrence Baker & Wm. Cockerham ordered a Jury of twelve men to be at the house of Peter Greene "tomorrow morning by eight o'clock and fail not at your utmost peril."
Mr. John Clay, Constable.

Page 195. 20 April 1662. Thos. Allecocke discharges Peter Harrison of all debts.
Wit.: Wm. Rookins, Matthew Battle.
Rec.: 3 Sept. 1662.

Page 196. 9 9ber 1662. Wm. Phillips, of Southwarke Par., carpenter, for valuable considerations already received, to Lt. Coll. Ro. Spencer, certain livestock.
Wm. Leake.

Page 196. Nov. 1662. Whereas John Die presently departed this country & was indebted to Robert Spenser for 40 lbs. tob. Enough of his Est. to be used to pay said debt.
29 Oct. 1662.

Page 197. Nov. 1662. Mr. Stanton is urged by Walter Chiles to bring Roger Rawlings to account for some boards that belonged to Mr. Mills, would settle for some at the common rate.

Page 197. 5th 7ber 1662. Coll. Thos. Swann is bound to Berkeley Browne, son of Coll. Henry Browne, sq., deceased, 200 lbs. sterling to be paid on demand 20 Oct. 1662. Conditions are that Coll. Thos. Swann by God's Grace about to marry and take to his wife Mrs. Ann Browne, widdowe, late wife of Coll. Henry Browne, deceased, Coll. Swann shall pay to sd Berkeley Browne 100 lbs. sterling money of England, he not yet of lawful age, the other when he is twenty-one years old. If he die before that time, obligation to be null and void.

Page 197. 1662. Thos. Lillycrop departed this country, owes Mr. Wm. Marriott. Enough of his estate to be used to pay debt.

Page 198. Maj. Wm. Marriott complains that Thos. Wattson has departed this county owing him 259 lbs. of tob. and caskes.

Page 198. 6 Nov. 1662. Thomas Culmer, of Surry County, chrurgion, for love and affection gives to his daughter Hannah, now wife to Robert Lane, and to Robert Lane, 300 acres of land at Upper Sunken Marsh, Southwarke Par., formerly belonging to Wm. Jennings, cooper, and now belonging to sd Thos.

BOOK I, 1652-1672      43

Culmer. If daughter, Hannah, die, the land to go tosaid Robert Lane.
Wit.: Amos? Mason, Wm. Marriott, Geo. Wattkins, Ro: Spenser, Ro: Stanton.

Page 198. 4 Nov. 1662. John Bason (Mason) sells to Richard Skiner a parcell
of land at the head of Lawnes Creek on the west side of a dividant of land...
to Pawley's land, formerly belonged to Robert Parke.
Wit.: Geo. Wattkins, Michael Upchurch (Upshure).
Rec.: 5th 7ber 1662.

Page 199. 5th 9ber 1662. A Jury impanneled to find out the cause of the
death of Wm. Billingsley, who went out into the woods to keepe his master's
cattle last 29 July, and Jury found the place where his bones and a few
clothes were, the Jury found that having been sick and weak from distemper,
and not recovered, being there day and night and too weak to return fell
into the swamp, had no food or succor and died and wild beasts devoured his
flesh because he could not resist.

     Henry Briggs    Wm. Norwood
     Ar. Jordan     Mat. Battle
     Mat. Hoggson    Peter Harrison
     Jno. Gittings    Thos. Bentley
     Samuel Swann    Wm. Jordan
     Fra. Gray     Thos. Webster
     Wm. Knott

Page 199. 4 Oct. 1662. Thomas Adams, indebted to Thomas Hunt of James Citty
for 8200 lbs. tob. had negro Mallaka appraised at 6000 lbs. tob. and delivered
by the Sherriff of Isle of Wight County to sd Hunt by instruction of sd
Adams; also mentions a table at the house of Francis Kirkman (Richman?).
Wit.: Ro: Stanton.

Page 201. 17 Feb. 1662. Morris Burcher, Upper Chippoakes, to Capt. Thomas
Adams, of Isle of Wight, Va., 150 acres of land at Upper Chippoakes adj.
the land of Martin Brandon in the County of Charles Citty, bounded on the
S. W. by Fra. Harker...between John Harker & Wm. Pilkington, land given to
Morris Burcher by Morris Williams in his last Will & Test., which land was
assigned to Morris Williams by Burcher's deceased father, Geo. Burcher, out
of a patent said eorge took up in his own name, being for 300 acres in
rights of six servants purchased between the said Geo. Burcher & Morris
Williams...unto me my just rights as son to Geo. Burcher.
Wit.: Henry Briggs, John Knowles.

Page 203. 13 Oct. 1662. James Mills, bound for Roanoke River, receives a
note from Col. Thos. Swann to receive of Mr. Fortescue, Master of the Mary,
lately arrived from the Barbadoes, and now riding between Jamestown and
Newport News, a punshon of molasses and one of rum, to pay Swann for molasses
at 10 pounds of good sweet pork per gallon, and for rum at 25 lbs. per
gallon to be paid in Surry County some good place for delivery of same.
Wit.: Ro. Stanton, Wm. Spring.

Page 203. 13 April 1662. Thos. Allcock being arrested by Robert House,
Allcock having made an idiot boy drunk on a boat going to James Citty and
afterwards left him locked in his store, where there was some fire, and
became so burned that he became a public charge. The Court paid House
200 lbs. of tob. for care and aid of sd idiot boy.
Signed: Geo. Jordan.

Page 204. 18 Feb. 1662. Richard Ties appts. John Rawlings his Atty.

Page 204. 5 Jan. 1662. Thomas Webster appoints his friend Matthew Battell
his atty. in a judgment to Ro: Stanton, atty. of Henry & John Richards.
Thos. Coneson?

Page 204. 13 Jan. 1662. Wm. Strong makes Jno. Tooke his Atty.

Page 204. 16 December 1662. Jno. Clements 380 lbs. of tobacco in settlement of a bill due from Clements to Thomas Shorte for 517 lbs. tob. paid Mr. Jno. North & Richard Newell.

Page 205. 9 Jan. 1662. Christopher Michell sells to Francis Tombs certain livestock.
Wit.: Theophilus Flood.

Page 205. 20 Feb. 1662. A survey of the land Capt. Thos. Adams and Roger Delk, deceased, according to Delk's conveyance a survey by Geo. Watkins as witt. 27 Dec. 1662.
Wit.: Thos. Culmer, Austin Hunnicutt, Richard Harris, Jno. Bruton, Rich. Drew, Rich. Jarrott, Jno. Hodge, Jno. -(?), Thos. Lane, Jno. Phillips, John Mason, Humphrey Brame.

Page 204. 8 Jan. 1662. Judah Huby gives her daughter Sarah Houby two cows, household goods, etc., (which) was Judah Huby's in her widdowhood. Deed of gift.
Wit.: Wm. Darby, Edward Pettway.

Page 206. 18 Dec. 1662. John Looke makes over certain household goods to Thos. Woodhouse, with the latter is to satisfy Wm. Edwards for a debt of 2795 lbs. of tob.
Wit.: Nicholas Meriweather, Edward Hulin.

Page 206. 28 Feb. 1662. A deed from the widow of Henry Meddow, she moving, to John Binham, 100 acres...lately in possession of Maj. Robert Sheperd and by him given to Henry Meddow, late husband. She now confirms the sale made by her late husband to John Bingham.

Page 207. 20 Feb. 1662. Richard Steevens, sick and weak, failed to pay a debt due from James Mills to Robert Loudlow, merchant of London, part of which should have been paid to Wm. Thompson, atty. for Loudlow. Now James Mills mortgages all his boats etc. to Wm. Thompson for sd payment.
Arthur Jordan, Jane Flood.

Page 208. 22 Feb. 1662. John Rawlings, miller, has bought of Wm. Marriott his part of a water mill, and agrees to pay 1500 lbs. of tob. on 10 Oct. each year to Wm. Marriott.
Wit.: Law. Baker, James Mason, Ro. Stanton.

Page 209. 4 July 1662. The citation of a land patent to Jno. Rawlings, son of Gregory Rawlings, for 326 acres of land at Upper Chippoakes Creek is given when Jno. Rawlings assigns his patent to Wm. Boulding on 31 July 1662.
Wit.: Robert House, Jno. King.
This same patent is assigned by Wm. Boulding unto John Tatem 20 Jan. 1662. These two assignments acknowledged in Surry Court by Jno. Rawlings and Wm. Boulding.
Rec.: 21 Jan. 1662.
Wit.: Robert Spenser, Nath. Stanton.

Page 210. 25 Feb. 1662. 13 Feb. 1662. Capt. Thos. Adams sells a negro servant named Malott, we Wm. Marriott, the weighing to be recorded in next Courte, 3 March next, the price being 2560 lbs. of tob. & caskes.
Rec.: 13 Feb. 1662.
Wit.: Edward Bushell, James -(?)-

Page 210. 31 Jan. 1662. Inventory of goods and debts, which is bound over to Robert Spenser, who is security for James Mills unto Robert Stanton, atty. for Mr. Jno. Richards for 2360 lbs. tob., Thos. Hunt, of James Citty, 1400 lbs. tob., 20 gal. copper kettle; 22 gal. brass kettle; long table and frame two forms, one square table; small tester bed; old curtains; 2 court cupboards; one pr. brass andirons; 4 brass shovels; pewter dishes; pewter bason; iron andirons; etc. Debts due from Thos. Hunt & Arthur Jordan; Capt. Thos. Flood; and Mr. London; from the Duchman; from Watt Aston; Coll. Hill; Capt. Adams; damage received from Nicholas Cobb & Thos. Cullmer. Total, 23,045 lbs. tob. These debts thought to be recoverable, etc.

Page 211. 5 May 1663. Thos. Woodhouse had a patent for 200 acres of land on east side of Gray's Creek dated 4 7ber 1651, he assigns this patent to John Zaines 22 April 1652, who being deceased, the land belongs to Thos. Zaines of Southampton, who made Coll. Thos. Swann his atty., and Thos Swann on 5 May 1663, in open Court at Surry Co., assigned to Thos. Underwood.
Wit.: Law. Baker, Thos. Warren.

Page 211. 7 July 1663. John Looke binds over to Thos. Busby one horse bought of Ro. Stanton for 1050 lbs. of tobacco.
Wit.: Wm. Lea, Wm. Mathews.

Page 212. 13 July 1662. Capt. Thos. Swann obtained Judgment against the Est. of Richard Stanton in the Quarter Court, upon an attachment formerly served upon sd Richard Stanton, his estate in the Hands of Robert Stanton, and the latter to give an account of the est. of Richard Stanton, satisfying judgments, etc.

| Coll. Swann | Lt. Coll. Geo. Jordan |
| Thos. Bentley | James Mills |
| Wm. Phillips | Capt. Thomas Pittman |
| Francis Newsom, Est. | John Leeke |
| Roger Potter | Ralph Creed |
| Arthur Jordan | Wm. Rose |
| Henry Briggs | Capt. Thos. Flood |
| Jno. Barker | Jno. Rawlings |
| Richard Case | Anthony Spilltimber |
| Mr. Jno. Corker | Nathaniel King |
| Capt. Will Browne | Ann Pinhorne |
| Thos. Busby | Thos. Andrews |
| Henry Briggs | Robert Stanton |

Wit.: Thomas Flood, Joseph Trafton

Page 212. 26 Jan. 1662. Francis Gray sells to John Tatem 100 acres of land in Lawnes Creek Parish, adj. sd Tatem, he lately purchased of Jno. Rawlings on Chipnoakes Creek near Swann Bay, and warrant the sale.
Wit.: Ilias Osborne, Selby Sparrow.
Rec.: 10 May 1663

Page 212. 5 May 1663. James Mills assigns to widow Eliza Sgort, on order of Court, which he had obtained against Ar. Jordan for so much tob.
Wm. Thomson, Jno. Gittings.

Page 213. 24 March 1662. Anthony Spilltimber sells to John Brady the neck of land purchased of Jno. Corker, called Besse's Neck, a patent between "my father, deceased," and Jno. Brady.
Wit.: Jno. Corker.

Page 213. 5 May 1663. Roger Delke and wife Rebecka to loving brother Francis and Robert Rennells, born of my natural mother Alice Gregory, wife of Jno. Gregory, sonnes of the deceased Nicholas Rennells, of Lawnes Creek of Surry; now Roger Delk has given & Granted unto Jno. Gregory & Alice Gregory his natural mother for the use of brothers, Francis & Robert Rennells and unto their heirs, etc., one patent or tract of land...upon now part of land in the occupation of Thomas ap Thomas by lease beginning from Bennett's at a gutt which goeth out of thecreek up a swamp which parteth the land betwixt sd Thomas ap Thomas and John Burgess...to plantation called Mr. William Bartletts...to Francis and Robert Rennells...if they die without heirs, to return to Robert Delk and wife; but either son or daughter lawfully begotten, shall be heir to the guifte. 23 Aug. 1661.
Rec.: 5 May 1663
Wit.: James Griswold, Humph. Barnes, Aman de Jores, John Charles.

Page 214. 1 May 1663. Chris. Vahan to Thos. Andrews one cow, three years old, a chest, a gun, for security of a bill of 955 lbs. of tob.
John Leake, Wm. Corker.

Page 214. 9 April 1663. Wm. Norwood & Arthur Jordan define Spring Swamp Run as boundary, all relating to discussion including John Blackburn and Richard Bavin. Wit.: Geo. Watkin.

SURRY COUNTY RECORDS

Page 214. 1 April 1663. Indenture between Geo. Foster, planter, & Jno. Clemmens, both of Southwarke Parish, to Jno. Clemmens a parcel of land of 50 acres on the east side of Gray's Creek, bounding upon Reedy Branch to merked trees, formerly belonging to John Ivey, deceased.
Wit.: Nathaniel Stanton, Geo. Blow.

Page 215. 8 May 1663. Whereas Cecillye Dunstan, Widdow, late of the County of Surry, in her last Will & Test. ordered that a mare colt should be purchased for Susannah Robbinson, daughter of Andrew Robbinson, know all that I, Robert Carter, have sold to Peleg Dunstan and Ralph Dunstan exors, of sd Cecillye Dunstan, for the use of Susannah Robbinson, one mare etc.
Wit.: Alice Parke, Roger Potter.

Page 216. 30 June 1663. Wm. Mills covenants with Francis Jones, to serve him two years, he to be taught the trade of cooper and to find him good just Diett, washing, Lodging and cloathing, and all else necessary for him.
Wit.: John Leeke, Thos. Andrews, William Lea.

Page 216. The following bound to the Court for their good behaviour:
Jno. Gittings, Thos. Hunt Security. Wit.: Hoel Pryse, Nath. Stanton.
John LeGrade, Arthur Jordan & Robert Spenser Securities.
Wm. Scarboro, Arthur Jordan & Robert Spenser.
Eleanor, wife of John Rawlings, bound for appearance at the next Court.
Anne & Robt. Dennis, bond for good behaviour; sec. Jno. Gittings, Hoel Pryse.

Page 216. 2 7ber 1663. John Jennings' Petition to the Court that he has been accused of being uncivil to the Court, is heartily sorry and beseecheth pardon of the Court.

Page 217. 4 Oct. 1663. Robert Stanton reports the finding of a large canoe, good and sound.

Page 217. 4 9ber 1663. Robert Stanton Gives to Sarah Sparks one Red Heifer ...to first sonne of a husband she shall, or may marry, and her husband not to dispose of this gift; but after such a sonne is born, to give yearly an account of sd heifer & increase with the Court, and give bond accordingly to act for them & if sd first sonne should dye before he comes of age then to return to the second, or third, in age therefrom; and if she never have any sonne then to her eldest daughter, and soe to the second & third in age therefrom; the same as for above sonnes, and this my act and deed.
Robert Stanton.
Wit.: Mary Stanton, Joseph Fisher.

Page 217. 1 August 1663. Mr. Thos. Marston give Security to the Court for the Estate he shall recive of Mr. Robert Stanton, belonging to Joseph Fisher & to deliver to him when he comes to age, without charges.
Signed: Jno. Okeham.

Page 217. 6 July 1659. Mr. Robert Stanton, Guardian of Joseph Fisher, orphant, agt. Richard Dibdell for 8000 Lbs. tob. & cash to give acct. in James Citty, the orphant being removed thither, and bond given by sd Robert Stanton, stands fully charged by himself of sd estate and made satisfactory to the orphant.
Signed: Thomas Marsten, 24 7ber 1663.

Page 218. 5 Jan. 1663. Ro: Stanton, late Clerke of Surry County, he moving, makes Capt. Wm. Browne, atty. and Deputy for goods, debts, etc. due to Surry County to him, and dispose to his best interest.
Thos. Swann, Nath. Stanton.

Page 218. 3 Nov. 1663. John Okeham had three letters, giving him power of Attorney, delivery to him by Coll. Flood, Mr. Rennolds and Wm. Stanton to Implead Tho. Newhouse at the Court and that they are in James Citty County recorded.

BOOK I, 1652-1672                                           47

Page 218.  5 9ber 1663.  Thos. Hurt cannot appear in Court at the suit of
Thos. Robinson, requests Wm. Cockerham to act for him.
    Wit.: Thos. Smith.

Page 219.  3 day 9ber 1663.  Execution being this day served upon my boddye in
ye suite of Henry & John Richards for 2129 lbs. tob. etc.
    Signed: Barth. Owen.
    Wit.: Geo. Watkin, Nath. Stanton.

Page 219.  6 9ber 1663.  Bond of Wm. Strong & Thos. King, 5000 lbs. tob. to
behave themselves to all his Majesties people and especially towards Edward
Bushell.
    Wit.: Ro¥ Stanton.

Page 219.  Robert Hunt, cooper, petitions the Court on June 1662 for satisfaction of a debt due to him from Thos. Wynne's Est. Robert Hunt made
barrells and caskes for Wynne, and was to have received compensation in
Tob. and corn. Thos. Wynne died...(illegible)...and Robert Hunt desires
that his estate make settlement.

Page 220.  15 Jan. 1663.  Court of Surry County, present:
                Coll. Thos. Swann         Coll. Geo. Jordan
                Capt. Law. Baker          Mr. Thos. Warren
                Mr. Jas. Mason

John Smith, servant to Mr. Wm. Norwood, having run away several times, his
master desires that he be made to serve two months after the expiration of
his time, and pay 200 lbs. Tob. Estimates cost of finding him to be about
250 lbs. tob.

Page 221.  5 9ber 1663.  Said John Smith, desiring to live with Capt. Flood,
and having run away several times, there is 8 months service due, and 18
months by indenture - in all 26 months. Wm. Norwood, at the earnest request of John Smith, sells ye servant to Capt. Thos. Flood, 16 8ber 1663.
    Wit.: Geo. Jordan.

Page 221.  20 June 1663.  Mr. John Corker sold land to Xpher Vahan and Henry
Chaddock. Christopher Vahan assigns to Wm. Warrolow on 20 June 1663.
    Wit.: John Corker, John More.

Page 222.  24 Oct. 1663.  A jury was impannelled to inquire into the death of
a body washed ashore at Mr. James Mason's. It was found that the death came
by drowning, in what manner, not known.
                Peter Adams              Rich. Clarke
                Daniel Sturdivant        George Denigon
                Jno. Phillips            Thos. Lane
                Robt. Spenser            Geo. Harrison
                Jno. Dolly               Jno. Birchell
                Jno. Hancock?

Page 223.  17 Nov. 1663.  A difficulty between Mr. Robert Spenser, and Edward
Petway, Pettway kept unlawful dogs that attacked Spencer's hogs, killed
some, and others not found. Demands settlement in next Court.

Page 223.  7 Dec. 1663.  A bill of 300 lbs. tob. due to Jno. King.
    Wit. Geo. Manfield, Geo. Jordan, Edward Sanderson.

Page 223.  2 Jan. 1663.  Robt. sold Luke Mizle certain household goods to
bind an obligation for which he is indebted.

Page 223.  5 Dec. 1663.  Thos. Harte appoints his friend Robert Spenser to
confess judgment to Coll. Thos. Swann amt. due him by bill, at suit of
Capt. Law. Baker from Wm. Hare.
    Signed: Thos. Hartt.
    Wit.: John Shepperd.

Page 223. 12 Jan. 1663. Robert Spenser sells to his friend Capt. Grove certain cattle for debt of 400 lbs. tob.

Page 224. 12 Jan. 1663. John Tooke makes his wife Rebekah his Atty.

Page 223. 6 Jan. 1663. Richard Tius binds his son Thos. Tius to John Brady and his wife Elleno Brady from this day until he be of age - 17 years. If Brady and wife should die in the mean time, then sd Thos. Tias to return to his father...John Brady and wife to treat Richard. (sic) as their own child in allrespects.
  Signed: John Brady, Ellenor Brady, Rich. Tias.
  Wit.: Richard Ponderton, Barth. Owen.

age 224. 6 Jan. 1663. Richard Tias binds his son Rich. Tias to Anthony Spilltimber and his wife Mary, until the child is 21 years old. Spilltimber to treat the child as his own. If Spilltimber and wife die before the child is 21 years old, (he is) to return to his father, Richard Tias.
  Wit.: John Leeke?, Francis Tennis?

Page 224. 21 September 1663. Ind. between Ellinor Gilbert, widdow, and Edward Fen, some woodland for 18 years paying 7 days work yearly.

Page 225. 21 Feb. 1663. Jas. Sowerby makes his brother, Thos. Sowerby, his Atty. of his plantation and all there, etc.
  Wit.: Geo. Jordan, John Dawkes?

Page 225. (Omitted by E. T. D., but included as the last entry in Book I.)

Page 226. 7 March 1663. About three years since, Mathew Yates came out of the Island of Barbadoes, had tobacco due him for certain debts; but not heard of in two years, his goods and property should go to his children without trouble of law. Certain amounts due from Geo: Marshall; Thos. Morgan; Maylon Hogson. The Court is asked to appraise his goods, and make Inventory of goods left in the hands of John Barker by Mathew Yates.

Page 226. William Mason and Luke Mizell bound for 10,000 lbs. tob. to the High Sheriff of Surry County, for their good behaviour.

Page 227. 7 March 1663. Jas. Sowerby, late of Surry County, planter, possessed that formerly belonged to Mathew Battle and Daniel Massingale, 207 acres, and now Thos. Sowerby, his brother, has power of attorney to sell to whom he sees fit, and sells this land to Wm. Thompson, Clarke, 105 acres, with houses, orchards, etc.
  Wit.: Geo. Jordan, Jane Flood.

Page 228. 22 Feb. 1663. Thos. Smith, yeoman, Par. of Dorson in the County of Hereford in the Realmes of England, atty. of Richard James, yeoman, and wife Margery; Richard Watkins, yoeman, and Jane his wife; John Meredith, par. of Whitton, County of Radnor, and Mary his wife; have given over to Mr. Charles Barham, Gent., of the Par. of Lawnes Creek, Surry Co., Va., a tract of land which was formerly John Modmore's of aforesaid Modmore unto the aforenamed Margery, Jane, and Mary, the natural surviving sisters of the aforesaid Modmore, lying and being on Hog Island, Maine, and bounded by ye pattent...Mr. Charles Barham has paid bills of exchange upon his brother Mr. Richard Barham of London, England.
  Signed: Thos. Smith.
  Wit.: Andrew Robinson, David Williams.

Page 229. 26 Feb. 1663. I, Thomas Smith, atty. for the surviving sisters of John Modmore late of the Par. of Lawnes Creek in Surry Co., Va., have given Mr. Charles Barham possession houses and land, 300 acres, given to his sisters, after the decease of his children, by his will doth appear.
  Wit.: Wm. Cockerham, Thos. Clary.

Page 229. 1 March 1663. John Rawlings of Surry County, he moving, sells to Wm. Svarbrow of the same county, a parcel of land situated upon the ast

BOOK I, 1652-1672 49

side of Burchen Swamp on Chippoakes Creek, with negroes, etc., bounding upon Mr. Simons on one side and Burchen Swamp the other.

Page 230. Feb. 1663. Thomas Wall owes debt to Mr. Edward Sugg, of Bristoll, wherein Ralph Creed stands engaged with me; and do, for his better security, bind over to Ralph Creed his whole estate in Virginia, to satisfy until it is paid.
Signed: Thomas Wall.
Wit.: Francis Hogwood, Thos. Cary.

Page 231. 16 Feb. 1663. Inventory of the goods of Thos. Wall, 16 Feb. 1663, at the request of Ralph Creed, and presented to Court, debt due for Ralph Creed, himself, and Rob. Carterage for five days and a half to bring said Wall and his cheste from Newport News att 20 lbs. tob. a day, and two-thirds boat hire for yr voyage, and three and a half days going to pay Mr. Sugg, also for Wif's attendance upon him in his sickness, with the comfortablest things that a man in his condition could expect, to washing his linning from the time he arrived until he dyed, being newly come from sea very nasty, to entertaining those that came to bury him with three volleys of shott and digging his grave with the trouble of his funerall to paid appraisers according to law etc.

Page 231. 7 Feb. 1663/4. John Hilyard bound for debt unto John Looke or his heirs with certain Household goods.
Wit.: Wm. Lea, Elizabeth Ripley.
Signed: John Hilliard.

Page 232. 6 Dec. 1663. Indenture between Geo. Blow and John Bynam of ye Upper Parish, Geo. Blow moving, sells a parcell of land on the Southwest branch of Blackwater Swamp, all land on that side of the Swamp belonging to Blow, part of a divident of 600 acres.
Signed: Geo. Blow, Margery Blow, Richard Smith, Wm. Marriott.

Page 232. 24 Dec. 1660. Between John Gregory & Roger Delk with John Burges, sell a small divident of land according to an old lease made by the father of John Gregory & Mr. Nicholas Rennolds, now from John Gregory, with consent of Roger Delke, sold to Joh. Burgess for 12 years.
Wit.: Martyn Grimes, Susannah Gregory.

Page 232. 2 Nov. 1661. Edward Upchurch, he moving, made Mr. John Peed and Peleg Dunstan to pay out some sums of tob. by him indebted.
Wit.: John Ashton, Henry Tillary.

Page 233. May 1664. Edward Bushell & Barth. Owen to the King a bond for 10,000 lbs. tob. security for Thos. Lillicrop for abuse of Mr. Marriott.
Wit.: Wm. Corker, John Gregory.

Page 234. 10 May 1664. A Jury, summoned to determine how Robt. Wytell came to his death, found that he was riding in a cart, fell forward, and his brains were crushed out, whereof he dyed.

| Charles Barham | John Gregory |
| John Clary | Mr. Long |
| Thomas Lissison | James Reddick |
| Andrew Robinson | Richard Harris |
| Allen Magett | Walter Bartlett |
| Richard Drew | Samuell Cornell |

Wit.: Ar. Allen, Wm. Cockerham.

Page 234. 13 April 1664. Robt. Cartwright, carpenter, owes Capt. Flood & Mr. Benjamin Harrison for ye Elizabeth Chivers, a daughter of Thomas Chivers, dec'd., 5000 lbs. good tob., and to buy a mare when she is of age.
Wit.: Samuel Cocke, Thos. Salter.

Page 234. 2 May 1664. Thos. Pittman Appoints John Rawlings to confess judgment to Anthony Spilltimber and John Looke amt. due by bill.

Page 235. 14 April 1661. Wm. Butler, planter, indenture with Richard Drew, planter, land on southwest of Swamp between John Drew and where Butler now lives, formerly belonging to "my father, Wm. Butler, deceased," Est., 29 Aug. 1643, adjoining Mr. Wm. Laurence.
Rec.: 3 May 1664.
Wit.: Geo. Watkin, Joane Fones.

Page 235. 1 Aug. 1664. John Looke received of Mr. Geo. Jordan 1700 lbs. tob. for the future benefit of Rebecca Popham, and John Looke to record for said use of said Rebecca, my wife's daughter.
Rec.: 1 July 1664.
Wit.: Geo. Watkins.

Page 236. 17 April 1664. Mary Sparrow's boy was drowned 11 May 1664. Sarah Sparrow, aged 17 years, sworn said that one and a half hours before sunrise saw a sloop laden with tobacco belonging to the Batchelor of Bristoll, Mr. David Warren being Commander of ye sloope, therewent in a small boat out from the sloop, two men belonging to ye sloop and one boy to carry out ye anchor One of the men going to heave ye anchor fell over board into ye water, they put an oar unto him...but the man never rose again. The man in the small boat called to Mr. David Warren who was in the Cabin on board the sloope and told him he was lost, he answered, How so? Did you not seek means to save him? They made the small boat fast, but he never came to give any account. Arthur Allen, Will Cockerham, Dorothy Sparrow, Geo. Watkin.

Page 236. 11 May 1664. Wm. Strong and Henry Briggs are bound over to Court for good behavior.
Ed. Bushell, John Gittings.

Page 237. 4 Oct. 1662. Geo. Mansfield acquits Thos. Cullmer of all debts to Mr. Wm. Allen.
Rowland Flayce.

Page 237. 1 July 1664. Wm. Morton of New England, of New London, Gent., have sold to Wm. Thompson of Surry County, Va., Minister of God's Word, for a considerable sum of money, a neck of land sittuate in New London, aforesaid disjoyning upon ye Great River and was formerly in ye occupation of Richard Blondmore?, Minnister of ye Parrish and from him purchased by me ye sd Morton and from me to Wm. Thompson.
Wit.: Geo. Jordan, John Gittings.

Page 237. 17 April 1664. John Hilliard declares that the cattle in his possession & est. of my wife Jane Hilliard has no power to sell, or separate from a deed of gift from Wm. Thomas for the cow, the cattle are the increase, which remains in the custody of my brother, Thos. Hilliard.
Wit.: Geo. Jordan, Will Mays.

Page 240. 30 Sept. 1664. Wm. Marriott goes on the bond of Thos. Lillicrop, the latter being allowed to carry no rapier, or weapon during the pleasure of the Court, and his good behavior.

Page 238. 20 June 1664. John Rawlings, of Martin's Brandon, for himself and Wm. Scarbrough hath surveyed and assigned all rights to Mr. Humphrey Allen in a certain patent of land.

Page 238. July 1664. Wm. Annam appoints his friend Wm. Caufield his atty. in all affairs pertaining to sd Annam (or Aynam?).
Wit.: John Bookmaster, Robt. Caufield.

Page 240. 30 Sept. 1664. Walter Houlsworth, atty. for Edward Curtis, appts. friend Robert Dennis in a bill due from John Gittings.

Page 240. 30 Sept. 1664. Robert Dinnis put on good behaviour, asks for release.

BOOK I, 1652-1672                                                          51

Page 240. 30 September 1664. Gentlemen: This is to certify that Robert
Castle hath put in sufficient Security in this County for what estate he
shall receive belonging to Wm. Gray, orphant, of any person that shall deliver same.
    Signed: John Cockerham.

Page 241. 1 Aug. 1664. Wm. Thompson, of Surry County, Minnister of God's
Word, orders his loving friend, Geo. Jordan, to receive, sue, and execute
all business in Court or otherwise.
    Wit.: James Mills, Jane Flood.

Page 241. 9 8ber 1664. Bartholomew Owen sells to John Morecock a filly foale
of one year, and has received satisfaction.

Page 241. 9 8ber 1664. Capt. Thos. Flood, and Benj. Harrison sells a grey
mare to Nathaniel Stanton.
    Ed Bushell.

Page 242. 4 Oct. 1664. Petition of Robert Dinnis to the Court, stating that
for a long time he has had hinderances and disturbances in Court of Coll.
Jordan and that Jordan would not let him be put in Sec. for his predecessors
Est., and demands reparation.

Page 242. 5 Sept. 1664. John Ludwell appoints Simon Simons atty. for him.
    Wit.: Wm. Cogill, John Bull.

Page 242. Sept. 1664. James Mills arrested by Mr. Jones of Jamestown, atty.
at the suit of B. Faris? of Kickotan about a boat of negroes. Mr. Robert
Spenser of Surry County to be bondsman for his Security, and makes over a
certain parcell of goods to Spenser.
    Wit.: Geo. Jordan, Geo. Watkins.

Page 243. 4 October 1664. An audit is made of what Mr. Parker has apid
W. Yates, sold to him at his going to sea.

Page 243. 4 July 1664. The corpse of an unknown young man was found at the
Landing of Mr. Benjamin Harrison, and it was necessary to bury him immediately. Jury saw the body. Foreman, Mr. Henry Brigs.
            Mr. Mathew Battle              Mr. Mathew Mason
            Thos. Webster                  Richard Attkin
            Wm. Pettypole                  Sam Cary
            Mr. Benj. Harrison             Robert Cartwright
            Thos. Harker                   Mr. Wm. Norwood
            Maurice Burches?               Frentris Hogwood, constable

Page 245. 2 Nov. 1664. John Corker, Gent., & Capt. Wm. Corker, sonne and
heir of ye sd John Corker, assign all right and title in a Patent of Land...
except 50 acres formerly sold to Christopher Vaughan, between Spilltimber
and Mill Swamp, and 40 acres more between se Swamp and Blande, unto Maj.
Wm. Marriott.
    Wit.: Roger Preston, John Rawlings, Geo. Watkin.

Page 245. 10 9ber 1664. Richard Norman of Charles Cittye County, Martin's
Brandon, planter, makes friend, Francis -(?)-, atty. to sue Marmaduke Baskwitz.
    Wit.: Thos. Mudgett, Charles Gregory.

Page 244. 6 Sept. 1664. Thos. Wall, the sonne of Thos. Wall, of Southwarke
Parish, Surry County, hath putt himself to Ralph Creed, carpenter, for
five years.
    Wit.: Francis Hogwood, Thos. Cary.

Page 246. George Blow, he moving, sells to Rowland Hudson William Handcocke
land on east and southeast of Blackwater Swamp being at John Baison's
marked trees to a bridge...to Mr. Thos. Warren's cart path.
    Wit.:Geo. Carter.    Signed: Geo. Blow, Margritt Blow.

Page 247. 20 Jan. 1664. Richard Skinner appoints Mr. Edward Wilkins his atty.; Geo. Mansfield does the same.
Wit.: Francis England.

Page 248. 31 Dec. 1664. Thos. Bemis appts. Mr. Robert Spenser his atty.

Page 248. 11 Jan. 1664. Francis Hogwood acknowledges receipt of all debts and obligations from Wm. Rookings.
Wit.: Geo. Watkin

Page 248. 4 Jan. 1664. Ed. Bushell sells to Capt. Wm. Corker a mare.
Wit.: Richard Davis, Mary Bushell.

Page 248. 11 Jan. 1664. Samuel Plow sells to Wm. Marriott a parcell of land 350 acres. Plow bought it of Wm. Edwards and it was formerly Mr. Thos. Binn's land.
Wit.: Edward Pettway, Arthur Long, Aug. Hunnicutt.

Page 247. 20 Sept. 1664. James Mills gives bond to his wife, and Geo. Jordan.

Page 249. 11 Sept. 1664. Francis Mills, late of Surry County, Va., acknowledges a debt to the estate of his wife, Fortune Mills & Lt. Coll. Geo. Jordan, 500 lbs. sterling money of England, given as bond.
Whereas continued strife has arisen between James Mills and his wife, Fortune Mills, and also betwixt Geo. Jordan and James Mills all aforesaid relation to the house and land formerly belonging to Coll. John Flood situate in Surry County, Va. It is thought meete by the aforesaid as conducive to future peace and tranquillity of all...it is agreed...mutually that James Mills relinquish all right and interest he hath or may lawfully claim in any part of any parcell of land etc. formerly belonging to Coll. John Flood...and any goods, chattels etc. that his wife shall hereafter possess, during her life relinquishing all claim and title in furniture in said house by consent...the deed extends not to...houses and land given by said Coll. John Flood in his will.
Wit.: Mary Briggs, James Flood, Nath. Knight.
Mrs. Fortune Mills desired no maintenance out of James Mill's estate. Mills made over to her what she received from Coll. John Flood.
Wit.: Nath. Knight, Jane Flood.

Page 251. 3 Jan. 1664. Goods of Mr. Rowland Place were damaged in the ship Planters Adventure this present year. (List followed).

Page 251. 24 Feb. 1664. Wm. Corker to pay to Mr. John Corker in a friendly sale 1000 acres in possession of his father Mr. John Corker, and to be delivered to Maj. Marriott as his assignee 1500 lbs. Tob. etc.

Page 251. 6 May 1664. Thos. Reynolds appoints his wife, Jane, his atty. in a bill of sale to Peter Deberry.
Wit.: Geo. Marshall, Robert Dennis.

Page 251. 6 May 1664. Thos. Reynolds, and wife Jane, assigns all their rights and title in a bill of sale to Peter Deberry.
Wit.: Geo. Marshall, Robt. Dennis, Isaac Tatum.

Page 252. 9 May 1664. These presents witness that we Henry Latyard and Hen: Chaddocke sell to John Brady a parcell of land and Coll. Swann as soon as this land is confirmed to us, ye sd Latyard & Chaddock, from Doctor Reynolds.

Page 252. 16 Dec. 1664. Pet. of Griffith Dickinson entreats friend Capt. Thos. Pittman to petition the Ct. in his behalf and grant and order against John <u>Dollyes?</u> Est.

Page 252. 14 March 1664. John Newman, of the Parish of Stobunheath in ye County of Middlesex, Marriner, makes friend Henry Brigs his Atty. to receive of Andrew Robinson of Chipoaks Parish 940 pounds of tobacco.

Page 252. 14 March 1664. Lott Richards of the Citty of Bristoll, mcht. having transported in ye ship called ye Rain Bow one servant named William Freeman about eleven years old, having no indenture for him, now assign him to John Barnes of Lower Chippoakes for full term of eight years from ye arrival of ship - to be free from Barnes 10 Feb. 1664, ye Barnes to pay ye servant expenses for eight years, clothes and other things according to custom of ye country.
Wit.: William Cockerham.

Page 253. 15 March 1664. Ind. 1 March 1661, between Thos. Harte, Surry County, and Edward Petway, 250 acres at the head of a Creek called Moole Neck.
Rec.: 15 March 1664.
Wit.: Will Corker, Robt. Spenser.

Page 253. Aug. 1664. Wm. Reenes, Marriner, Boath Island, New England, sells to Wm. Thompson, Minnister, a Barke of which he has been master.
Wit.: Geo. Jordan, James Mills.

Page 254. 26 Xber 1664. Wm. Jordan sells to Hen. Briggs 2750 lbs. tob.
Wit.: Nath. Knight, Foulk Moulson.

Page 254. 8 Aug. 1664. Richard James & Margery his wife of Cussoff in the County of Hereford, Yeoman; Richard Watkin of Dorson, County of Harroford & Jane his wife; John Meredith, County of Radnor, and Mary his wife, did appoint Thomas Smith, of Dawson in the County of Herreford, aforesaid, yeoman, to be our lawful attorney in our names...an estate of land bequeathed unto us by John Modmore of Lyons Creek aforesaid, deceased, and by his Last will & Test., and whereas the sd Thos. Smith had made sail of sd land unto Mr. Charles Barham of Lynes Creek by certain deed of writing 2 Feb. 1663 & wee the sd Richard, James and Margery his wife; Richard Watkin & Jane his wife; John Meredith and Mary his wife by deed of writing 8 day of August 1664, Ratified and confirmed the sale.
Richard James, Mergery James, John Meredith, Mary Meredith, Thomas Smith.
Wit.: Wm. Irvin, Wm. Phillips, John Jannsey?

Page 254. 2 May 1665. I, Wm. Strong, substitute and appoint Luke Missell... to sell unto Ellis Vantor a Mill and appurtenances...
Wit.: Henry Sands.

Page 256. 1 May 1665. Henry Clarke, Senior, Planter, of Hog Island, security of Henry Clarke, Junior, sells to Randall Holt a cow and cattle.
Wit.: Thos. Amry, Ralph Dunstan.
Thos. Clarke Assigns all rights in the patent to Jno. Rawlings.
2 Jan. 1665.

Page 256. 15 March 1663. Sir Wm. Berkeley granted unto Thos. Clarke 50 acres of land being on the south side of James River on Upper Chippoakes Creek, formerly called Swan's Bay, N. W., on Main Creeke...to Capt. Bishop...to Mary Emmett land, being formerly granted to Wm. Gapin, deceased, now in possession of Thos. Clarke by marriage with the widow of Thos. Gapin.

Page 257. 1 May 1665. Edward Webb, of Hog Island, Lawnes Creek Parish, sells to Capt. Wm. Brown certain livestock, the condition being that this is a security for a debt to Capt. Wm. Browne, attu. for Robert Stanton, for the sum of 3039 lbs. tob. snd caskes.
Rec.: May 1665 by Randall Holt, Atty., for sd Webb.
Wit.: Geo. Watkin, Nath. Stanton.

Page 267. 25 April 1665. A Jury Summoned to investigate the death of a servant boy who lived with Ralph Coats, found he died a natural death.
          Daniel Upsheau      Rob. Spenser
          Math. Marriott      Aug. Spilltimber

SURRY COUNTY RECORDS

     John Looke     Jno. Brady
     Wm. Seaward    Ellis Vantor
     Daniel Sturdivant  John Hardye
     Francis Murray

Page 260. 30 Feb. 1663. Edward Bushell, trustee & Admr. of Est. of Thos. Adams, deceased, sells and delivers to Mr. Thos. Gwaltmey one sorrel mare ...tenn years.
 Rec.: 29 Sept. 1665.
 Wit.: James Attkins.

Page 260. 10 Aug. 1665. All these presents shall know that William Thompson purchased of Francis Sowerby of Surry County 105½ acres of land, being a patent to Mr. John Jennings dated April 1649. Now Wm. Thompson for 300 lbs. tob. sells to Francis Sowerby.
 Rec.: 5 Sept. 1665.
 Wit.: Geo. Jordan, Joshua Adams.

Page 260. 4 Sept. 1665. A warrant from Mr. Tho. Warrine, one of His Majesties Justices to impanel a jury and view the corpse of James Hugate, the jury has found bruised about hishead and face, also on hand and brow, left side of nose and his ear. Unable to find out "How he came to it," refer themselves to the court.
    Ellis Vantor    Edward Petway
    William Hie?    John Brady
    Geo. Foster    Wm. Foreman
    Francis Sowerby  Chris. Michell
    Edward Purify   Tobias Axleford
    Thos. Freeman

Page 261. 7 7ber 1665. A jury impanneled to ascertaine the cause of death of a servant maid belonging to Mr. Phillip Limbry, find that she "being sick and having no fear of God before her eyes, got out of her bed drown herself in the river, privately, early in the morning."
    Hen. Briggs    Thos. Clarke
    Wm. Norwood   Robert Laine
    Matthew Battle  John Thompson
    John Kippin    Wm. Carpenter
    Robert Cartwright Thos. Webster
    Thos. Sowerby
This verdict presented at the house of Mr. Hen. Briggs, 7 Sept. 1665.
 Signed: Geo. Jordan.

Page 261. 7 Jan. 1664. Indenture between Wm. Skinner, son to Anthony Skinner, deceased, and Geo. Watkin; bind himself to serve Watkin until 1667, with certain obligationsupon both parties.
 Rec.: 5 Sept. 1665.

Page 262. 5 Sept. 1660. I, William Lee, with the consent of my wife, sell all rights and title in a Plantation first sold by Richard Hide of Surry County to Christopher Greenfield, purchased by me from sd Greenfield and now sold to Thomas Adams of ye Isle of Wight County, for valuable consideration in hand paid.
 Signed: William Lea, Alice Lea.
 Wit.: Thos. Busby, Wm. Copeland.
Account by Wm. Lea to Ed. Burchell, administrator of Adams, and by Burchell assigned in Court to Ed. Elliss. 5 Sept. 1665.
 Geo. Watkin, Teste.

Page 262. 26 June 1665. Wm. Hare, of Lawnes Creek Parish, sells to Geo. Watkin and Edward Warren, Hare moving, certain cattle and household goods
 Rec.: 5 Sept. 1665.
 Wit.: Garrett Greenwalt, John Coffer.

Page 263. 7 Sept. 1665. Wm. Corker of James Citty County, Gent., in behalf of his father Mr. John Corker, sells to Mr. Wm. Marriott 50 acres of land,

and has received full satisfaction.
Rec.: 23 Oct. 1665.
Wit.: Thos. Busby, Nath. Stanton.

Page 263. 16 Aug. 1665. Will Corker Sells to Martin Gardiner 60 acres of land lying on a swamp on the south side of James River, Surry County, but if sd Gardner decease, then said Corker must have first chance to buy back, and Corker oblige himself to build at half charge a 20 ft. house.
Wit.: John Corker, Eliza. Whitt.

Page 263. 5 Nov. 1665. John Looke gives power of atty. to his wife, Rebecca Looke, to confess judgment to Wm. Heath for a debt.
Wit.: Thomas Roberts, Wm. Lea.

Page 264. 26 Oct. 1665. Humphre Barnes and Ann Barnes bind themselves as security for the presence in the next court of Katheryne Greene.
Signed: Humphre Barnes, H. Muggett.
Wit.: Amaro Delores.

Page 264. 3 Jan. 1665. Be it known by these presents that Gyles Linscott, of Warrencock, Surry County, shoemaker, sells to Xpher Lewis, winecooper, of the same county, certain livestock.
Rec.: 6 Jan. 1665.
Wit.: Geo. Watkin, Steph. Storeman?

Page 264. 4 Oct. 1665. By his Majesties Royal command, ordered that the last of Aug. 1664, there be a general audit of all public credits in his Majesties Collony of Va. in full power and authority, and all sheriffs and constables to appear at James Citty at such time as all disbursement of public Loans from the twentieth to the twenty-fifth of March and Twenty-third of May, annually.
Signature blotted, not legible.
Rec.: 6 Jan. 1665.

Page 265. 2 June 1665. George Jordan sells to Thos. Hunt, in Virginia, my dwelling house in Surry County and 400 acres of land thereto belonging, with all housing etc., cows, mare, beds, in a list under my hand, this said house and land, cattle and bedding to be enjoyed by sd Thomas Hunt, and his heires borne of Fortune his wife, ye naturall daughter of Mr. George Jordan, without any molestation by me ye sd Geo. Jordan or any person whatsoever; and warrant this deed to Thomas Hunt, who married ye said daughter of Geo. Jordan.
Wit.: Jno. Cary, Thos. Flood.

Page 265. 1 Jan. 1665. Edward Bushell sells to Coll. Thos. Swann one negro girl, Elizabeth, in payment of a debt of 1000 lbs. of tob.
Wit.: Geo. Jordan, Geo. Watkin.

Page 266. 6 March 1665. Roger Potter sells to Morbria? Markina a red heifer.
Wit.: Ed. Bushell.

Page 267. 26 Jan. 1665. A jury impaneled to ascertain how Jacob Garrett, servant to Mr. Richard Davis, came to his death, He being sent to his Master's plantation lost his way, and by extremity of cold, being out all night, was the cause of his death.

Rich. Briggs          Rich. Skinner
Corn. Wallett?        Rich. Jarrett
John Beaseley         Harmen Hill
John Walton           Wm. Butler
Roger Delk            James Griswold
Martin Johnson        Peter Greene, Foreman

Page 267. 6 May 1665. John Foreman, boateswain, of the good ship called William Sarey, John Konder, Commander, sould a man servant named John Chalker to Mrs. Mary Knott, six years.
Wit.: Tompson Boone, John Walker.

Page 267. 29 May 1665. Edward Wyatt, of the County of Gloucester, is indebted to James Mills, of Surry County and John Scott of Ashford, Long Island, 1000 weight of tob., and binds himself for this debt. The conditions are that Capt. John Scott, Esq., sold to James Mills two years of Edward Conquest, his time, to serve said Mills, and Mills to be instructed in the rudiments of navigation...Wyatt at his earnest request received of James Mills...not to let Conquest depart from Virginia.
Signed: Edward Wyatt.
Wit.: Cuthbert Potter, John Vinson.

Page 268. 20 July 1663. Indenture between Andrew Robinson, Surry County, and Ann, his wife, and William Cockerham and Charles Barham, Gent., for valuable consideration, 350 acres of land, patent to sd Robinson and Peleg Dunstan.
Rec.: 19 Nov. 1666.
Wit.: Geo. Watkins, Rich. Foanes.

Page 269. 27 April 1666. John Tatem, of Martin's Brandon, appoints Wm. Thompson, minister, of Surry County, atty. for bill of sale by me to Francis Gray for 100 acres at the next court of Surry Co.
Wit.: Wm. Rawlinson, Geo. Watkin.
John Tatem assigns all rights to Jno. Rawlings and Thos. Evans Jointly.
Signed: John Tatem.

Page 269. 24 May 1666. John Burgess, of Lawnes Creek, Surry County, sick & weak, appoints his wife, Mary Burgess, atty., in a suit depending against him.
Wit.: John Gregory; Richard B...?

Page 269. 8 Jan. 1666. Francis Mason, of James City, appoints his friend Richard Long? his atty.
Wit.: Andrew Robinson, John Hayward.

Page 270. 3 May 1666. Wm. Seward to Nicholas Meriweather, James City Island in Virginia, 300 acres of land in Surry County commonly called the Indian Spring, being part of a greater quantity taken up by Thomas Swann, Junior, beginning at White Marsh and Indian Spring to Coll. Jordan's corner tree... to Ready Branch issuing out of the Main Branch granted to Wm. Seward by patent 29 September 1664, to him the sd Wm. Seward and by sd Wm. Seward to Nicholas Meriwether, and Wm. Seward's wife Elizabeth, in right of her one-third, etc.
Wit.: Roger Rawlings, Thos. Hart.

Page 271. 7 May 1666. John Clarke and Katherine his wife sell to Edward Browne 200 acres of land in Isle of Wight County, being one-half of a patent for 400 acres. 4 May 1665.
Wit.: Thomas Gualtney, Elizabeth Browne, Geo. Watkin.

Page 271. 3 July 1666. Bartholomew Owen sells cattle of Wm. Rose, Senior, and Ann Rose his wife for the benefit of Jane, William, Ann and Mary Rose, son and daughters of Wm. Rose & his wife Ann.
Rec.: 1666.
Wit.: Luke Mizelle, John Morecocke.

Page 273. 30 June 1666. Marye Gualtney, aged 48 years or thereabouts, saith that today five weeks or soe about, Goodman Bartly came unto her and said that his wife were not well, but when she came found that Ann Simpson had a female child, etc. Katherine Clarke, aged 36 years, also testified, and said that Goody Gualtney came to her before she was up, to tell her that Goody Bartlett's daughter had this child. Dorothy Bartlett, aged 50 years testified about this matter.

Page 275. 3 Feb. 1661. Court Met at Merchant's Hope. Present were:
        Coll. Edward Hill        Maj. Gen. Manwaring Hamond
        Mr. Anthony Wyatt       Capt. Jno. Epps
        Capt. Robert Winne       Mr. John Holmwood
        Mr. Stephen Hamlin

Ordered that John Steevens pay within tenn days to Mason Battle 294 lbs. of tob. cash.
Test: Howell Pryce.

Page 274. 1 Nov. 1665. Indenture between John Corker, Gent., & Capt. Wm. Cockerham now living in James City County, and Mr. Wm. Marriott, of the other part, Surry County, for 24,5000 lbs. tob. all that land known as Ware Neck, or Southward houses, gardens, etc....upon Rolph's land...to the Creek...to Divall's Woodyard Swamp, S. by E. to Woods cart path to Mr. Warren's path, to Ware Neck path, to the Spilltimbers, west up Mill Swamp ...along Besse's Swamp...1120 acres; 500 acres purchased by John Casey by Pat. Oct. 1639 & 650 acres pat. to John Corker 2 Dec. 1640.
Signed: John Corker.
Wit.: Rand. Holte, Charles Barham, Geo. Watkin, Wm. Corker.

Page 275. 4 Sept. 1666. Roger Potter to Thos. Pitman for the use of Joseph Wall, his son-in-law, one black heifer, delivered to Thos. Pitman.
Wit.: Will Corker, Chris. Mizell.

Page 275. 4 Sept. 1666. Mary Hill, orphant hath due her...when she came to age or married, five cows, if Daniell Roome, Marrying, to said Mary Hill doe acknowledge to have received of Mr. Henry Brigs the five cows.
Daniell Roome.
Wit.: John Looke, Edmond Howell.

Page 275. 4 Sept. 1666. I, Francis Gray, did lett out ye Plantation that Hillyars live on, all right and title to Brother, Thomas Gray, as Thomas Gray lett it t Thos. Dickinson.
Wit.: Geo. Watkin.

Page 276. 4 Sept. 1666. Mr. Peter Greene of Surry County, Va., and Wm. Cockin, of sle of Wight County, a parcell of wood land ground in the Lower Parish of Surry County, 100 acres, from the cart path to the saw mill which belongs to Ed. Bushell, west along the swamp to Mr. Green's line, to the Great Swamp, commonly called Capt. Law. Baker's Swamp, to Mr. Barker's cart pathn to Wm. Cookin.
Signed: Peter Greene, Kathering Greene, William Cookin (Cockin).

Page 276. 2 May 1666. Robert Laine and Hannah his wife, sell to Thos. Taylor, Martin's Brandon, Charles City County, marriner, land, garden, etc. patent 15 March 1662, reserving to Nathaniel Knight one-half of the land purchased by him of the heirs of Coll. Flood, patent called Broad Neck, and assigned to Robert Laine, etc.
Rec.: 4 Sept. 1666.

Page 277. 4 Sept. 1666. John Clarke, aged 30 years, or thereabout, sayeth that about the latter part of July, being at the house of Thos. Gualtney, two days before his death, and desiring said Gualtney to make a Will, and sett all things in order, ye sd Gualtney answered ye Deponent I give to my sonne William Gualtney, ye horse, fole and bed I now lye upon & my land I know nobody can take it from him & all ye rest of my goods I give to my wife and leave att her Disposal and further sayeth not.
John Clarke.
Patrick Bartley age about 40 yeares, sworn said that being at the house of Thos. Gualtney ye Saturday before his decease Deponent said to him Now that Capt. Corker is here it is good for you to sett things to right and relieve your wife of a great deal of trouble, and Gualtney answered I leave to my wife's disposal, for her and her children, for I know she will be careful of hers as well as mine.
4 Sept. 1666.
Thos. Colt swore that he made a bequest to William and said wife should have the rest.

Page 277. 10 Nov. 1666, Roger Delk, of Surry County, and wife Rebecca, sell to Robert Kee of Isle of Wight a Parcell of land in Surry County adj. land sold to Thos. Adams, along creek to gum...to creek called Lawnes Creek,

to valley between John Burgess, lately deceased, and John Black...to Thos. Ward...to Myles End.
Rec.: 13 Nov. 1666.
Wit.: John Jennings, Trystam Easton.

Page 277. 13 Nov. 1666. Francis Hogwood brought his servant before Geo. Jordan. This servant being James Norman saying that he had run away several times in two years.
13 Nov. 1666.

Page 278. 16 Nov. 1666. Ind. Dorothy Meddows, widdow, of Blackwater in Surry County, Va., and John Clarke, for a parcell of land in Blackwater, 100 acres - house and land - one year's rent 50 lbs. good tob., if not paid to reenter land.
Wit.: Martha Luther, Thos. Adkins.

Page 279. 13 Nov. 1666. Ind. Peter Greene & Katheryne his wife and Wm. Cockin or Cocker for 3600 lbs. tob. woodland ground in the lower Par. of Surry County, 100 acres to mill of Mr. Ed. Burshell, west to Greene's line, to Capt. Law. Baker's Swamp.
Wit.: Thos. Swann, Will Browne.

Page 279. 15 Nov. 1666. Thos. Harris of Isle of Wight makes Robt. Spenser his atty. to impleat Capt. Wm. Corker in a debt.

Page 280. 15 Jan. 1666. Ind. 6 Jan. 1666 Between Peter Greene of Surry County and Nicholas Hill, senior, of ye Isle of Wight of the other part for 3500 lbs. of tobacco, a parcell of land, 70 acres, in Surry County on the south side of James River, west side head of Lawnes Creek, beginning at Maj. Wm. Butler's cor. tree, running up to gead of creek to a swamp, N. E. side of Peter Green's dwelling house adj. sd Greene's old field, part of 150 acres granted to Peter Green, 21 Feb. 1663.
Wit.: John Salway, Robt. Spenser.

Page 281. Benj. Harrison, of Surry County, makes over to John Taylor, 50 acres of land on Round Island.
Wit.: Thos. Salter, Morris Burcher.

Page 281. 4 Jan. 1666. Nath. Stanton sells to Thos. Swann a gray mare for debt.
Wit.: Geo. Hall, Wm. Batt.

Page 281. 4 Oct. 1666. Conditions agreed upon between Capt. Thos. Pitman and Mrs. Mary Gualtney, before marriage. Thos. Pitman gives bond that the widdowe Gualtney after marriage with him, shall have the whole disposal of a horse and mare which she now has to dispose of at her own pleasure, as also two pewter dishes and cattle, now called and known to be for the two youngest children, also her youngest son, Wm. Gwaltney, may have two years' schooling.
Signed: Thos. Pitman.
Wit.: Roger Potter, Luke Mizelle.

Page 282. 2 March 1666. Chris. Vaughan sells to ye Hon. Thos. Swann, Esq., two red steers, 780 lbs. tob. debt.
Wit.: Geo. Watkin, Ed. Bushell.

Page 282. 5 March 1666. John Rawlings to Rob. Burgess a bill of sale.
Geo. Watkin.

Page 282. 7 May 1667. Jos. Bridger makes over to Mary Pitt, heir of James Stephens, deceased, stating that she was the heir because she was the daughter of Elizabeth Pitt, sister of Mr. George Stephens, deceased, father of the aforesaid, James Stephens. Property consisted of Land, Tenements, goods, Chattells, personal and real, rents, etc.

BOOK I, 1652-1672                                   59

Page 282. 6 May 1667. James Mills appoints his brother, Arthur Jordan, to appear for him at Surry Court.
Geo. Jordan, James Parsons.

Page 283. 7 May 1667. Deposition of Isaac Tatem, aged 31 years or thereabouts, being at the house of Henry Francis, went into the room where James Stephens, Lyte sonne of Geo. Stephens, doe lay sick upon ye point of death yett sensible & Deponent asking him wherefore he should stay and make his will Jas. Stephens replying he would faire seek ye Doctor first, Ye mother of sd Stephens replyed my it is soone done for he has given yt one half of his Hogs unto his Unkle John Legrand and ye other half to his Brother & ye rest of his Whole estate to me Ye sd James Stephens replying soe I have mentioning ye words over again and further sayeth not.
Margaret Wincester, aged 24 years, or thereabouts, testified to same.

Page 283. 7 6ber 1667. Marmaduke Beckwith sells to Mr. Arthur Allen of Surry County, live stock, household goods, and all the rest of his estate in a debt to Arthur Allen 2400 lbs. tob., Beckwith living at Upper Chippoakes. If suit, then this bill of sale is made void but otherwise in full force.
Wit.: Robt. Spenser, Ed. Bushell.

Page 283. Samuel Cornwall makes sale of one caske of tob. to Thomas Perkings for 10 shillings and to stand unto ye adventure homeward bound what is now delivered unto ye said Rawlings. Thomas Perkings obligates himself and heirs.
Wit.: Capt. John Gregorye.

Page 284. 7 April 1667. Wm. Berkeley appoints Math. Stanton to Com. of Sheriffe of Surry County for the ensuing year, for the performance of the office.

Page 284. 2 May 1667. Thos. Underwood assigns ye Patent unto Thos. Barrlowe with the said land expressed that sd Barlow shall quietly possess ye sd land.
Nath. Stanton, John Legrand.

Page 284. 6 May 1667. Wm. Caufield appoints his sonne Robt. Caufield, his lawful attorney to sue etc. and release ye body of Mr. James Mills for a debt due ye sd Mills to Wm. Caufield.

Page 285. 1 May 1667. Abell James, of Surry County, binds himself and heirs to make over unto Robert Spenser and his assignes certain household goods due unto Abell James from Walter Chiles for ye present year, also all debts which he has, or shall have yett from Geo. Watkin...binds over to said Spenser for security of debt which Spenser is bound unto Francis Mason, as also ye sd Abell James (or Jones) and engages himself not to sell or dispose of ye goods or debts aforementioned till sd Spenser is cleared of ye debt.
Wit.: Wm. White, Henry Applewhite.

Page 285. 17 June 1667. Thirty days after sight...cause to be paid to Coll. Miles Cary, or his order, the sum of ten pounds, nine shillings sterling, money of England and for tobacco laden aboard the ship, Rainbow of Bristoll. Mr. Samuel Wharton Johnson, Raling Street/ Ye subscribers assign all right and title to John Baldwin.
Signed: Miles Cary.

Page 286. 3 June 1667. Edward Bushell bound unto Mr. Arthur Allen for debt.
Stephen Ireland, Robt. Williamson.

Page 286. 24 July 1667. Francis Sowerby complained of unlawful behaviour of Daniell Regan and his wife Eliza. towards himself and his wife, with scandalous words, vile and wicked and several blows and stripes...turbulance to greatly dethrone god, and high treason to his Majestie. Desires that Regan and his wife be bound over to peace. Gives bond until investigated.

Page 287. 24 May 1667. Nicholas Spenser of Lawnes Creek, sells to Capt. Wm. Cockerham a parcell of land formerly his uncle's: Mr. Wm. Spenser,

deceased, and lately bequeathed to Nicholas Spenser by will or right of descent.
Wit.: Nich. Spenser, Daniell Williams.

Page 288. Mr. Nathaniel Stanton sells to Mr. Henry Briggs a filly.

Page 288. 22 May 1667. Nathaniel Stanton is bound for a debt to Henry Briggs for goods received of him.
Wit.: Geo. Jordan, Daniel Roome.

Page 288. 29 Aug. 1667. Thos. Bilbro acknowledges a debt of 2300 lbs. of tob. to John Thompson.

Page 288. 31 Aug. 1667. Thomas Ballard consents to the sale of a heifer by his sister, Hilliard, from her cattle to Francis Gray, and a sow or pigs, for her own and her children's use; but not to be disposed of as by ye deed of gift made by William Thomas to my said sister.

Page 289. 7 May 1667. Thomas Tabb, of the County of Elizabeth Citty, authorizes his friend, Mr. John Barber, his lawful atty. against John Petro? to sue, arrest, etc. for several good causes.

Page 289. 25 May 1667. Indenture between Anthony Spilltimber and Francis Atkinson for land in Surry County, bordering north upon Mr. Meriwether... to a swamp...to the Main Swamp...a patent to said Spilltimber 3 7ber 1667.
Wit.: Geo. Watkin, Barth. Owen.

Page 291. 13 Nov. 1667. John King sells to John Legrande 280 acres of Burson Swamp, adjoining Simmons land; Wm. Lea, and Wm. Gavin. Sale made 13 Nov. 1663.
Wit.: John Rawlings, Walter Thompson.

Page 291. 3 Nov. 1667. Indenture between Thomas Gray of one part and Richard Case and Isabella Case his wife, of Surry County,...where Richard Case is now seated, 100 acres on the west side of Gray's Creek, called Hollowing Point and ye middle neck adjoining to it at the head of Spring Swamp to the end of Sandy Valley.
Rec.: 5 9ber 1667.
Wit.: John Salway, Wm. Dowling.

Page 292. 5 Nov. 1667. Thos. Gray to Thos. Cruse and wife Joane, sells a parcell of land where Thos. Cruse is now seated, about 80 acres on the west side of Gray's Creek, east of Richard Case, by the edge of the old field white oak, south west to Cross Creek to old bridge and old bridge swamp.

Page 293. 1 July 1667. Anthony Young of the Parish of Debford in Kent, marriner, makes Capt. Wm. Browne his atty. for all money and debts due him.
Wit.: Anthony Roope.

Page 293. 6 Jan. 1667. Be it known etc. that Mary Clarke, wife of Thos. Clarke of Surry County appoints her loving friend Ralph Richards to confirm a sale of 150 acres of land to John King, S. E. side of Birchen Swamp, up Chippoakes Creek late sold to John King by my husband, Thos. Clarke.
Wit.: John Smith, Ed. Oliver.

Page 293. Gov. Wm. Berkeley grants to Wm. Gapin 250 acres of land on the south side of Burcyon Swamp, south by Chippoakes Creek in James City County, Simmons, his land. 6 8ber 1651. Thos. Clark and wife acknowledge to John King.

Page 296. 2 Jan. 1667. Indenture between Wm. Butler, sonne and heir of Maj. Wm. Butler, deceased, and Joyce his wife, and Richard Jarret, Surry Co., Lawnes Creek Par., adj. Peter Greene...where Richard Kindred formerly lived ...including old field where Maj. Butler formerly lived, about 200 acres.
Rec.: 7 Jan. 1667. Wm. Butler, Joyce Butler.
Wit.: Wm. Cockerham, Charles Barham.

BOOK I, 1652-1672      61

Page 297. 2 Jan. 1667. Ann Muggett, aged 43 years, made a Deposition.

Page 297. 31 June 1667. Chris. Lewis makes bond with Chris. Lawson for a debt that Thos. Andrews shall have Anthony Rossey.

Page 298. John Rawlings makes a petition to the County concerning his repair of Sunken March Mill, said Mill was all destroyed with the only value the stones, said he disbursed his own small estate to rebuild a mill out of the ruins and built a new mill house according to George Blow's order to keep it till ye orphants came of age. Petitioner has wife and three small children, and to relieve him of ye estate of orphants, and make Capt. Cockerham as overseer of Harris, his estate, for five years rent.

Page 298. 5 Jan. 1665. John Pinken, Planter, makes John Salway his atty.
Wit.: John Hobourne, John Bidford.

Page 299. 7 Nov. 1667. I, James Atkinson, Son of Thos. Atkinson, discharge Thos. Pitman as he marrying the relict of Thomas Atkinson, deceased, and Thos. Gwaltmey, deceased, from all manner of debts or guifts given me by my father's will and also for Thomas Gualtney, my father-in-law, give me by will or any other manner.
James Atkinson.
Wit.: Martin Lacye, Thos. Atkinson.

Page 299. 27 Feb. 1667, Thomas Atkinson, son of Thos. Atkinson, deceased, releases Thos. Pitman of all debts or obligations to him, Thos. Pitman having married the relict of Thos. Atkinson and also the relict of Thos. Gualtney.
Wit.: Martin Layce, James Atkinson.

Page 299. 4 July 1667. Francis Sorsby and wife Katherine acknowledge debts to Daniell Regan and Richard Welbeck.

Page 299. March 1667. Hezekiah Bunnell makes Miles Cary his atty.

Page 300. Wm. Porter and wife Elizabeth sells to Robert Kay of ye County of Isle of Wight, 300 acres of land, being one-half of 600 acres in Surry Co., adjoining Hunifurd land...to Robert Flacke's cart path, a patent to Wm. Porter 23 of April last.
Wit.: Wm. Marriott, Jno. Grove.

Page 300. 4 July 1667. Daniell Regan owes the Court 5000 lbs. tob. They to behave themselves to Fra. Sorsby and his wife.
Wit.: Richard Welbeck.

Page 300. 6 March 1667. Thos. Cruse and Rich. Case declared that the body of Baton Brown found at Coll. Swann's landing, came to his death by drowning.
Samuel Goose, Samuel Magott, Wm. Rose.

Page 301. 2 Jan. 1667. Indenture between Rich. Drew and wife Mabell of the one part, and Richard Harris, Lawnes Creek Parish, 400 acres of land patent to Richard Drew 24 April 1667.
Wit.: Edward Bushell, Anthony Spilltimber.

Page 301. 19 Feb. 1667. Richard Lawrence to the Worshipful Court that urgent occasion takes him to Rapahannock and Potomack Rivers, fears that he cannot attend Court "to answer the suit of Mr. Williamson." Writes from James Citty.

Page 302. 24 Feb. 1667. Mr. Thos. Binns is summoned to appear at the next court to answer charges of John Bird, bricklayer.

Page 302. 4 May 1668. Mary Hux, widdow, makes John Harlow her atty.

Page 302. 20 May 1668. Edward Petway assigns to Mrs. Alyse Carter and George Carter his right in the land where Mrs. Carter lives, during the life of Elizabeth, wife of Edward Petway, except for the fruit.

SURRY COUNTY RECORDS

Recorded 20 May 1668 at the request of Edward Warren.
Signed: Edward Petway, Alyse Carter, Geo. Carter.
Wit.: Samuel Harris, Thos. Flowers.

Page 302. 12 March 1667. Indenture between Mrs. Alyse Carter & Edward Warren for 2500 lbs. of tob., land from the cart path from the Great Swamp to Chippoakes, formerly left to Peter Adams, adj. Wm. Nusam's to Wm. Harris, belonging to Wm. Carter, late husband to Mrs. Carter, 200 acres, houses, etc. for 21 years.
Wit.: Geo. Watkin, Gertrude Watkin.

Page 303. May 1688. Robert Doxwell, Commander of the ship Rainbow of Bristoll, received of Mr. Wm. Cockerham one ship with rudder, oares, tiller, mast, sayles, left in the hands of Cockerham by Mr. Joseph Tucker.
Wit.: John Sugg, Robert Spenser.

Page 303. 7 July 1668. Wm. Thompson, of Surry County, sells to Daniell Regan for 100 acres of land adjoining Francis Sorsby.
Wit.: James Watson, John Phillips.
Wm. Thompson, Katherine Thompson.

Page 304. 6 Nov. 1668. Daniel Regan (Regant) and Eliza. Regant assign to Wm. Thompson, Minister, his patent for 900 lbs. of tob. Thomas Candlis his right to one-half as formerly sold him on 14 Oct. 1667.
Jas. Watkin, John Phillips.

Page 304. Nicholas Meriweather age about 37 years swore that in the year 1666 the Deponent was requested by Mr. John Brady and Thos. Vantore to draw up an Atty. debt. Wm. Thorne, age 25 years, swore to same.

Page 304. 7 March 1667. Thos. Barlow assigns his patent to Samuel Judkins. Eliza Barlow acknowledges the sale.
Wit.: Ar. Long, Thos. -(?)-.

Page 304. 30 June 1668. Chris. Holeman directs that Thos. Pitman receive his pat. of land from John Browne.

Page 305. 16 July 1668. Nich. Spenser, moving, binds and obligates his son John Spenser as servant to Capt. Wm. Cockerham till New Year's Day next seven Years.
Rec.: 16 July 1668.
Wit.: Richard Brock?

Page 306. Roger Williams to pay to Chris. Lewis 1730 lbs. tob.
Wit.: Will Brown, Rich. Wilbecke.

Page 306. 7 July 1668. Thomas Hoge (or Haye), age 23, deposes about a horse.
Francis Mason, age 21 years, deposes about same.
Wm. Dowling, about 50 years, makes a Deposition concerning a conversation between Mr. Richard Lawrence and Mr. Robert Williamson at the Court.
Richard Case, 48 years, testified.
Arthur Allen, age 60 years, testified that he and his brother went to James City to see a horse - two horses for sale; one died. The question of discussion being which horse died.
Daniel Tucker, aged 55 years, testified that while at his brother Allen's house, saw the horse in Mr. Bland's and Mr. Carter's field; but presently saw it in his brother's field.
Wm. Hare, aged 30 years, Testified.
Francis Mason, aged 21 years, said it was his father's horse, James Mason's.
Mr. Wm. Scott, age 25 years, testified.
Mr. Henry Applewhaite, aged 25 years, testified.
John Senior, aged 17 years, testified.

Page 309. 22 Aug. 1668. Whereas Aylse Warren sold one Lease of land for fifteen years to Ed. Colby, if Elizabeth Petway die before fifteen years

be served, to pay her back in tobacco.
Rec.: 14 September 1668.
Wit.: Geo. Johnson, John Hay.
Ed. Colby (or Colly) assigns it to Richard Rogers.
Wit.: Wm. Shorte, John Rawlings.

Page 309. 1 September 1668. James Murray appoints his friend Randall Holt Atty. for debt due Thomas Binns, 450 lbs. Tob.

Page 309. Entry omitted. See last entry before Book II.

Page 309. 15 March 1668. Wm. Porter had a grant of land at Phillip Huniford's to Blackwater for transportation of nine persons 11 Aug. 1667. Wm. Porter assigns this 216 acres of land to John George.
Wit.: Geo. Hancocke, Thos. Flood.

Page 310. 20 Aug. 1668. Edward Petway & Elizabeth his wife to Thos. Ware of Isle of Wight, 200 acres of land in Surry County part of a patent of 700 acres of land secured in 1666 being near the mill path, leading to Geo. Foster's.

Page 312. 6 May 1668. Indenture between Geo. Watkin and wife Gertrude and Joseph Rogers for 500 acres of land on Lawnes Creek and Richard Drew...to Mr. Carter's land, east to Watkins'.
Rec.: 15 March 1668.
Will Browne, Wm. Corker.

Page 311. 3 July 1668. Indenture between Joseph Rogers of Lawnes Creek Parish and Geo. Watkin, 500 acres in Surry County adjoining Richard Drew, Carter's land and Watkins'.
Wit.: Will Brown, Wm. Corker.

Page 312. 25 September 1668. John Senior, aged 17 years, testified. Wm. Bride, aged 30 years testified.

Page 317. 15 Oct. 1668. Widdow Creed makes sale of property.

Page 318. Phillip Simbry? appoints his brother, Benj. Harrison, his Atty.
Wit.: Wm. Scarbrow, Geo. Proctor, Wm. Nance.

Page 319. 7 Oct. 1668. John Preassure, of Nansemond County, and John Rawlings, of Surry County, Sell a water mill and land to John...? on Burchen Swamp, late in possession of Henry Francis.
Rec.: 21 Dec. 1668.
Wit.: Thos. Ballard, John Sallway.

Page 320. 6 Jan. 1668. Ellis Ventor, miller, sells to Roby. Babb, clerke, a mill house and land at Ware Neck...was granted by deed of John Corker and Dorthory, to Capt. Webster.
Wit.: Thos. Warren, Wm. Hill.

Page 321. 12 Dec. 1668. Edward Collier of Buckland, Charles Citty County, Planter, sells to Richard Rogers 300 acres on Chippoaks Creek, called Cabin Poynt, adj. John and Richard Taylor, granted to John & Richard Taylor.
Wit.: Elias Osborne, John Banks, John Rawlings.

Page 321. 25 8ber 1668. Edward Collier, of Buckland, Charles Citty County, planter, assigns to his loving cousin, John Collier, in Surry County, planter, atty. in account, a bill of sale to Richard Rogers.

Page 321. Salem: ye 25th 8ber 1668. Mrs. Thompson, my respects extended being glad to heare of ye welfare as you may remember severall yeares past you had some goods by me and to pay twentye shillings...to pay my sosson (sic) Mr. John Cary, March 1668.
  Yours to serve,    Walter Price

SURRY COUNTY RECORDS

Page 322. March 1668. Wm. Porter and wife Elizabeth to Geo. Mansfield 300 acres of land adj. Philip Huniford.
Wit.: Jno. Grove, Nich. Hill.

Page 322. 23 April 1667. Wm. Porter had a patent from Wm. Berkeley for 600 acres of land adj. Huniford for the transportation of twelve persons.

Page 323. 2 May 1668. Phillip Hunniford and wife, Jane, sell 600 acres to Geo. Manfield.
Wit.: Jno. Grove, Nich. Hill.

Page 323. 20 Feb. 1668. Thos. Flood, Corroner, for the time being, two men drowned watering a horse. Jury members were:

Wm. Rose          Fra. Hogwood
Robt. Warren      John Bird
Fra. Gray         John Meare
Rob. Lee

Page 324. 4 Feb. 1668. Indenture between Samuel Plow and his wife Mary and Wm. Marriott, being a grant to Mr. Wm. Edwards he sold to Blow, adjoining Mr. Binns at Reedy Branch and Crouches Creek.
Rec.: 9 March 1668.
Wit.: Wm. Browne, Thos. Flood.

Page 325. 2 Feb. 1668. Indenture between Katherine Green and John Salway. Katherine Greene, relict of Peter Greene, there being a debt of Peter Greene to John Salway - where Katherine Greene now lives, 200 acres of land on the south side of James River, west side at head of Pawnes Creek adjoining Hill and Richard Drew land at Baker's mill.
Wit.: Rob. Babb, Clerke; Ellis Ventor.

Page 326. 7 Dec. 1668. Jane Tucker, Relict of Samuel Tucker. Her husband sold land to Maj. Nicholas Hill, of Isle of Wight County.
Rec.: 20 Dec. 1668.
Wm. Harris, Thos. Lockett, Henry Randolph, Notary, statement that she was his wife, and probated his will.

Page 327. 4 Oct. 1667. Wm. Webb, of Tewkesbury in Gloucester, shoemaker, appoints his friend Lott Rocketts of ye City of Bristoll, due from Plantation in Virginia.
Wit.: Rich. Hill, Conway Whitehorn, Thos. Newsum, Henry Peyton, Justice of the Peace.

Page 327. Jan. 1668. Est. of Andrew Robinson, by Thos. Binns.

Page 327. 20 Jan. 1668. Mr. Welbeck to implead Marshall Macanna, desires for Mr. Somers to satisfy him.
Wit.: Robert Wilde.

Page 328. George Hopewell, merchant, of Exon, Maj. Nich. Hill Atty.
Wit.: Thos. Lillicrop, Rich. Jarrett, John -(?)-.

Page 328. 22 Aug. 1668. Wm. Shorte to his brother Thomas Shorte land adjoining Thos. Busby's land etc.
Wit.: Thos. Greene, Jno. King.

Page 328. 4 May 1668. John Warren, sonne of Robert Warren of Surry County, to James Riddick, formerly was exor. of "my father's estate." I have received full satisfaction.
Signed: John Warringe.
Wit.: Ed Bushell, John Mabery.

Page 329. Elizabeth Shorte and Wm. Shorte of Surry County, sell to Geo. Midleton of Charles Citty County, a parcell of land one divident at Swamp.
Wit.: Wm. Marriott, Wm. Simmons.

Page 329. 22 Aug. 1668. Wm. Shorte, he moving, sells to Thos. Greene 100 acres of land on the S. E. side of Western Branch of Upper Chippoakes Creek, Patent 7 Jan. 1649 to Wm. Shorte.
Rec.: 4 May 1668.

Page 330. 27 Feb. 1668. Wm. Shorte sells to Wm. Heath 50 acres of land at the head of Western Branch of Upper Chippoakes Creek, where Heath now lives.
Wit.: Wm. Marriott.

Page 331. 17 Feb. 1659. Indenture between Geo. Carter and Mrs. Aylse Parke both of Lower Chippoakes, Surry County, and Peter Adams land called Fig Tree, now in possession of Chambers and Wm. Newsum.
Rec.: 17 Oct. 1668.
Wit.: G. Watkin, Ann Churchman.

Page 332. 1 May 1669. Henry Francis of Surry County appoints John King his atty. in a judgment for 500 lbs. tob. debt to Rich. Welbeck.
Wit.: James Elson.

Page 332. 25 April 1669. Mary Skinner, wife of Richard Skinner, deceased, acknowledges receipt from her husband's estate what John Burgess, deceased, did give to her daughter, Susannah Burgess, etc.

Page 332. 20 April 1669. Patrick Bartley formerly had 100 acres, which did escheat to his Majestie from Henry Meddows and Bartley dying intestate ye heirs and Dorothy Bartley, Relict, Petition for the grant of land to her heirs.

Page 333. 31 May 1669. Patrick Bartley had 100 acres of land at the time of his death on Blackwater River, Patent 20 May 1666.
Signed: Thos. Warren, Wm. Marriott, Ed. Petway, Mathias Merriott, Rich. Drew, Rich. Harris, Wm. Newsome.

Page 334. Wee, Charles Amry and Robt. Spenser and Wm. Oldis of Lawnes Creek Parish, trustees of the Est. of Capt. Wm. Cockerham, deceased, to the Court of Surry County, 60 lbs. of tob., all the estate and tuition of his two sons, William and Thomas Cockerham, and pay William and Thomas their full shares of their deceased father's estate, cattle, etc., when of age. No date.
Signed: Charles Amry, Robert Spenser, Wm. Oldis.
Wit.: Will Sherwood, Geo. Watkin.

Page 335. Know all these presents that wee Charles Amry of Lawnes Creek Parish, Surry County, merchant, Wm. Oldis of same Parish and County and Edward Travis of James Citty Island are bound and obliged to Robt. Spenser of Surry County for 10,000 lbs. of tob. to be paid Robt. Spenser or to his atty. admr. 13 May 1669.
The conditions of this are that Robt. Spenser, special trustee request and desires sd Charles Amry bound on penalty of 60,000 lbs. tob. to the Court of Surry County for the estate of Wm. Cockerham, deceased, and Amry is to indemnify to Spenser also Trustee of the goods and chattels lands from all troubles by reason of delivery of the estate of Wm. Cockerham, and tuition of William and Thomas Cockerham, his sons.
Wm. Sherwood, Geo. Watkin.

Page 336. 4 May 1669. Thos. Binns, sick with distemper, is unable to appear at Court in case against Wm. Marriott and Coll. Jordan's business against himself.

Page 337. 5 July 1669. Thos. Pitman, lame and unable to attend court, makes his wife, Mary Pitman, his atty. to confess judgment to Wm. Marriott and Ed. Bushell for 640 lbs. tob.

Page 330. 22 Dec. 1668. Sir Wm. Berkeley, Gov. of Va., officially appoints the following as Commissioners of Surry County...to be always in full power to hear and determine all suits, controversies...to take depositions, etc.:

  Lt. Col. Geo. Cockerham  Capt. Law. Baker
  Mr. Arthur Allen  Mr. Thos. Warren

Giving unto ye or any four:

  Lt. Coll. Geo. Jordan  Capt. Law. Baker
  Mr. Arthur Allen  Mr. Thos. Warren
  Capt. John Graye  Maj. Wm. Marriott

Page 339. Inquisition 6 June 1669 before Capt. John Grove, Sheriff of Surry County, Va., and Corner and Capt. Law. Baker, one of the Justices upon ye oath of...Jurors Impannelled to find ye cause and manner of ye death of Mary Pope, spinster, aged about eighteen years, servant to one Wm. Cockin of ye county. Mary Pope did some time last May run away from her sd Master's service that day did eat her dinner well and heartily and went away, supposed to be in good health bones being now found by a swamp side near ye house of sd Cockin, and that said Mary was accessory to her own death. Jurors present were:

  Geo. Walker  James Reddick
  Rich. Drew  Rich. Jarrett
  Ar. Long  Rich. Harris
  James Lovejoy?  John Warren
  James Griffin  John Grove
  Thomas Jones  Wm. Chambers
  Henry Baker

Page 339. No date. Sworne before Mr. Holte that a man found in the River fell overboard from a sloop, brought ashore at Mr. Holt's landing.

  Wm. Seward  John Sappington
  Wm. Oldis  James Kilpatrick
  Ed. Tamer  John Casse
  Henry Hagood  John Thomas
  Thos. Clarke  Wm. Kille
  Philip Oberry  Nich. Craford

Page 340. 20 June 1669. Robert Burgess by virtue of a letter of Atty., by Geo. Watkin and Gertrude his wife, did deliver possession of land called Swann Bay, mentioned to ye within named Geo. Seely?

Thos. Blayton, Robt. Cartwright, Wm. Bricknel

Page 340. Ind. 2 Feb. 1666 that Dorothy Thorne is to serve Charles Barham and his wife untill next Christmas six yeares hence to find her lodging and victuals, not to put her into ground and mortar but tach her to sew, to read and give her a cotton suit, etc.

Rec.: 7 Feb. 1669.
Dorothy Thorne, Charles Barham, Elizabeth Barham.
Wit.: Margrit Cornish, Chris. Smiley, Joane Geer

Page 342. 14 July 1669. An appraisement of goods at the house of John Cary, left by Mrs. Fortune Mills, deceased, according to an order of Court. Certain things given by Mrs. Fortune Mills to her son, Walter Flood, not enough to pay her debts, other things are needed; a court cupboard, etc.
Wit.: Ben. Harrison, Nath. Knight.

Page 343. 27 July 1669. Know ye that Wm. Rookings sells to James Elson all his right and title in 100 acres of land known as Novasley extending south to the land my father and Biltrough tooke up, and east to the land I live on...to James Elson.
Rec.: 13 7ber 1669.
Wit.: Jno. King, Daniell Williams, Ralph Rachell
Wm. Rookings makes Ralph Rochell his atty.
Wit.: Henry Randolph, James Coghland.

Page 343. 23 Feb. 1669. Names of the members of the Jury sworn to view the body of a man found dead beside the river near the mouth of Hog Island Creeke.

  Mr. John Gregorye  Mr. Robert Caufield
  Mr. Cornelius Cordenpaine  Mr. Wm. Seward
  Mr. John Skinner  Mr. Wm. Parry

BOOK I, 1652-1672                               67

              Mr. John Barnes          Mr. Wm. Hancocke
              Mr. John Thomas         Mr. James Kilpatrick
              Mr. John Baylie           (or Killybreck)
              Mr. John Peekweeke?    Gulleham Cockerham
              Coralul Barham
The Jury found that he came to his death by some accident and drowned in ye
River, was drowned at Christmas crossing the river with Harris, his horse.

Page 344. 7 7ber 1669. Thos. Bilbrough, planter of Virginia, he moving,
sells to James Elson of Surry County an inheritance of 100 acres on the
S. E. side of Chippoakes Creek, Surry County, west to the Creek, east to
Rookings, his land, so to the woods.
  Wit.: Thos. Stoner, Andrew Frizell

Page 344. 4 7ber 1669. Wm. Harwyes to Mr. Wilbeck a note, makes wife atty.
to confess judgment.

Page 345. 8 July 1669. This Jury impannelled by Capt. Thos. Flood to view
the corpse of a man cast up at the landing of Mr. Ben Harrison, had a blue
shirt with canvas wristbands and canvas baskitt. Jury said he was drowned, had
had no blows on him.
              John Cary               Thos. Thomas
              Ar. Jordan              Jno. Taylor
              Ben. Harrison           Robt. Cartwright
              Thos. Taylor            John Emerson
              Wm. Carpenter           John Smiley
              John Orchard

Page 345. 12 April 1669. Edward Clements appoints his friend Mr. David An-
drews his atty. for all debts due in Virginia.
  Rec.: 3 9ber 1669.
  Wit.: Thos. Benninge, Fra. Lord.

Page 346, 347, and 348. Contains list of tithable. On an unnumbered sheet,
here inserted, which appears to be from the last will book, are the frag-
ments of two wills. The first is the Will of Thos. Smith. Only the con-
clusion is on the page, reading "and Testament, cutting off the annuling of
all other Wills by me assigned in witness whereof I have here unto fixed
my hand and seale this 29th of March 1669."
  Wit.: Rebecca Caufield, Fra. Taylor.
On the same page is the will of John Bruton. Signed by Himself as John
Broughton. "I, John Bruton of the Parish of Lawnes Creek...buried by my
wife in Christian manner...I give and bequeath...my loving wife rest of my
estate. 9 9ber 1669.
  John Broughton.
  Wit.: Jon. Charles, Alse Gregorye, Thos. Clary, Ezra Clary.

Page 345. Inv. Est. of Edward Bushell, sworn to by Relict Mary Bushell.
  James Reddick, Rich. Skinner, Rich. Drew, Rich. Jarrett.

Page 349. 9 9ber 1669. Edward Middleton, of London, makes John Wimberley
of Virginia, planter, his Atty.
  Rec.: 11 Aug. 1669.
  Wit.: John Goring, Edward Amry, Thos. Amry.

Page 349. John Daube and Izabell his wife are negro servants to Mr. Arthur
Jordan.

Page 350. 19 April 1669. Whereas Col. John Flood, deceased, in his last
Will & Testament ordained that that dwelling house, orchard land, etc. to
be sold and certain livestock and two mares to his son Wakter Flood at the
age of 16 years, now Fortune Mills, Relict of Coll. John Flood as also Capt.
Flood & Lt. Col. Geo. Jordan have sold houses and orchards to John Cary, who
married Jane ye daughter of Coll. John Flood, now John Cary pays Walter
Flood, at sixteen years, two good heavy mares, and at 21 years a parcell of
land on the west side of Ware Swamp between the swamp and the land of John

Kindred...when John Cary returns from England.
Rec.: 10 day 9ber 1669.
Wit.: Rowland Place, Rich. Welbecke.

Page 351. 5 9ber 1669. Thos. Busby makes Mr. Richard Welbecke his Atty. in a suit with Jeremiah Ellis.
Wit.: Wm. Browne.

Page 351. 29 9ber 1669. We, the subscribers, have witnessed the corpse of Katherine Patmore, servant to Wm. Seward, dead in the woods near the house of John Case, died a natural death from the cold.

    Chas. Barham    Robert Caufield
    John Sappington    Hen. Goard
    John Antibas    Will Judson
    Christopher Smith    Ed Amry
    Sam Hoyden    Rob. Shaw
    Thos. Jarrell    Rich. Morris

Page 351. 6 8ber 1669. Wm. White married ye Relict and administratrix of Wm. Barbribb, deceased, assigns to Wm. May and Nich. Meriweather, exec. of Thos. Woodhouse, deceased, appoints Elizabeth Bruster, widdow, atty., etc.

Page 351. Sept. 1669. Arthur Allen stands bound for orphants estate, was entrusted by Charles Gregorye, who was entrusted as guardian to ye orphants 1500 lbs. tob. in his possession, ye Allen bound to ye Court of Charles Citty County for ye said Gregorye, his performance as sd Guardian and whereas sd Gregorye was a fugitive lately and privately departed his house and left his wife and children and gone out of ye country, Allen by bond, is bound and asks the Court to give so much of Gregorye's estate to settle the bond.

Page 352. 6 Jan. 1669. John Goode, of London, makes John Wallis and Francis Washington atty. at the Court of Charles Citty for debts due him.
Wit.: Rice Hooe, Otho? Soulcott?

Page 352. 4 Jan. 1669. John Clay, being ill at the home of Nich. Meriweather, cannot appear at Court, appoints against Mr. Watkins, makes Mr. Robert Caufield his atty.

Page 353. 3 Jan. 1669. Thos. Morrison and Thos. Midyett appoint their friend Mr. Wm. Rookings Atty. against Cornelius Owles and his estate.

Page 353. 2 Jan. 1669. Rich. Bullock owes tob. due from Mr. Thos. Busby, Makes Geo. Lee his Atty.
Wit.: Anthony Winn, Mary Tilner.

Page 353. 26 Dec. 1667. Indenture between Peter Greene and Capt. Lawrence Baker, Lawnes Creek Par. for a parcell of land, 40 acres, near a great poplar on James Reddock, along a swamp near a bridge that leads to Baker's. Acct. in Court by John Salway who married ye Relict and axtx. of Peter Greene.
Acknowledged: 4 Jan. 1669.
Wit.: Geo. Watkin, Richard Drew.

Page 354. 17 Dec. 1669. Indenture between Dorothy Evans, late wife of Patrick Bartley, deceased, now wife of Anthonye Evans of Surry, of the one part, and Geo. Watkin for 100 acres of land part of the land formerly granted to Robert Sheppard, and by him given to Dorothy Evans' former husband, Henry Meddows, and after his decease, escheated then to her late husband Patrick Bartley, and since his decease for want of heirs, again to escheat to his Majestie, granted to said Dorothy in her late widdowhood, land on Blackwater to Geo. Watkins.
Rec.: 4 Jan. 1669.
Wit.: Martin Luther, Wm. Sherwood.

Page 355. 4 Jan. 1669. Wm. Newsum and wife Ann sell to Roger Rawlings and and his wife Alse Rawlings a parcell of land 50 acres whereas sd Rawlings

BOOK I, 1652-1672 69

now lives being as follows: between ye College Place to Phillip Clarke's, being ye same divident that Clarke formerly held by lease, if Rawlings have no heir it to return to Newsum.
Wit.: Geo. Lee, Ed. Rumsey.

Page 355. Jan. 1669. John Cary, of Surry County, intending to sail for England and has debts and affairs in Virginia, makes Mr. Benjamin Harrison his Atty.
Wit.: Wm. Hewitt, Jno. Despard.

Page 356. 4 Jan. 1669. Joseph Rogers, Lawnes Creek Parish, Surry County, tanner, gives bond of 10,000 lbs. tob. for his good behavior to John Grove.
Wit.: Maj. Wm. Marriott, Ed. Warren.

Page 357. 4 Jan. 1669. Gives bond for good behavior to King. (Name of the bond giver omitted by E. T. D.).
Wit.: Maj. Wm. Marriott, Ed. Warren.

Page 357. 7 Feb. 1669. Henry Hollingsworth desires to confess judgment to Ed. Napkin before the Court.
Wit.: Randall Holt, Jno. Goring.

Page 357. 16 Feb. 1669. Indenture between Geo. Watkin and Anthony Evans for 100 acres of land on Blackwater, formerly grant to Capt. Robert Sheppard, he to Henry Meddows to Patrick Brady to Dorothy Brady, now Anthony Evans.
Wit.: Wm. Marriott, Wm. Seward.

Page 357. 1 Aug. 1669. Wm. Webb of Tewkesbury, Gloucester, England, swowmaker (sic), acknowledges that Lott Richards of the City of Bristoll, merchant, has paid a debt for selling Webb's land in Virginia to Richard Briggs, 500 acres, at Lower Chippoakes, Sunken Marsh, a patent 29 March 1660.
Rec.: 4 March 1669.
Wit.: Arthur Allen, James Sherbourne, Robt. Turpin, Rich. Peel?, Capt. Nich. Tony.

Page 360. 1 March 1669. Daniel Roome of Surry County and Mary his wife, ye daughter of Geo. Hill, and Arthur Allen, 50 acres of land, adj. William Thomas.
Rec.: 4 March 1669.
Wit.: John Cary, Henry Briggs.

Page 361. 26 Feb. 1668/9. John Beasley, Surry County, appoints his friend Richard Briggs his atty.
Wit.: Geo. Powell(?), Edward Bushell, Francis Master, aged about 18 years.
Rec.: 30 April 1670.

Page 362. Francis Maryson, Esq., a patent granted to John Rawlings, son of Gregorye Rawlings, deceased, 26 acres of land on Chippoakes Creek...formerly granted to John Osborne by patent 26 April 1639, and by John Osbourne, son and heir of John Osbourne, assigned to Gregorye Rawlings, deceased, and now same to John Rawlings being heir to his father's estate this 26 acres for transportation to the colony, sd land granted to Gregory Rawlings, brother to sd John Rawlings by pat. 6 Feb. 1654, by mistake, Should have been John Rawlings as by his father's will appears. 4 July 1662.
This patent assigned by John Rawlings 31 July 1662 to Wm. Dowinge to John Tatem 20 Jan. 1662. On the back of the patent, John Tatem assigns to Robert Burgess, being called Boyer's Point. 21 Nov. 1669.
Wit.: John Rawlings, Rich. Hide.

Page 363. 3 May 1670. John Tatem, of Martin's Brandon, appoints his friend, Wm. Marriott, his atty. to sell 100 acres of land to Robert Burgess and John Kinge.
John Tatem, Eliza Tatem.
Wit.: James Major, Thos. Sharpe.

Page 363. 30 May 1670. John Tatem of Martin's Brandon in Charles Citty County, sells to John King of Surry County land on Upper Chippoakes Creek, extending north by the Great Swamp and Deep Swamp between Tatem and King, was Henry Okeham's, to John Rawlings and by him sold to Dowling, and from Dowling to John Tatem.
3 Nov. 1663.
Wit.: Thos. Winter, Jno. Shipham.

Page 364. 10 May 1670. James Watkin acquits Thos. Steevens of all debt.
Wit.: Thos. Busby, Ellis Watkin.

Page 364. 3 May 1670. Albert Albertson, Daniell Williams, guardian of Wm. Harris, an orphant, 2300 lbs. tobacco due at my plantation Sunken Marsh.
Wit.: John Grove, Wm. Seward.

Page 365. 3 May 1670. Geo. Watkin sells to Robert Burgess 12 acres of land part of 300 acres known as Swann Bay, grant to Watkins, being at Burgess Tobacco House along the Creek.

Page 366. John Harloe, of Surry County, boatwright, and Mary, ye Relict of John Hux, a marriage about to be consummated between sd Mary and John on teh 25th of June. While a widdow had had certain estate, house and land, etc., in her own right, and her youngest son, John Hux, now John Harloe has no children, nor any considerable property to equal Mary's. Harloe will allow John Hux, at twenty-one years, 1700 lbs. of good tobacco above what comes from his own father's estate, etc. 18 June 1668.
Signed: John Harloe.
Wit.: Geo. Jordan, Wm. Marriott.

Page 367. 25 April 1670. Edward Barrett acknowledges a debt to Robert House.

Page 367. 15 May 1669. Indenture between Capt. John Grove and Mr. Robert Caufield, Churchwardens of Lawnes Creek Parish, with the consent of Capt. Law. Baker, and Mr. Arthur Allen, two of his Majestie's Justices, with the consent of the Vestry, bind Thos. Holt, son of Elizabeth Holt, to Geo. Watkin until he is twenty-one years old. 23 Aug. 1667.

Page 368. 15 April 1670. The General Court at James Citty: Present were:
    Maj. Geo. Smith        Henry Corbyn
    Theo. Bland           Coll. Willis

By order of the Court 29 March 1666 desire to learn the extent of damage, grant to Mr. Anthony Stanford agt. ye land of Fra. Newton called ye College and Mr. John Mohun to find ye value of the land by the year and what damage by gust in August what buildings erected by Stanford and Jury of the neighborhood impanneled by the Sheriff find ye value of plantation.
Teste: Rich. Osborne.

Surry County - Inquiry taken of College on 17 May 1670, before Maj. Wm. Marriott, High Sheriff of the County by Virtue of an order of Court held at James Citty 15 April 1670.

Members of the Jury to find the true value of the whole plantation called College in 1666:
    Geo. Watkin          Aug. Hunnicutt
    Rich. Drew           Rich. Jarratt
    Matthias Marriott    Ruch. Brigs
    Daniel Williams      John Salway
    John Kindred         Wm. Chambers
    Wm. Butler           Wm. Newman

The value of the plantation: three sixty-foot wall plate tobacco house, one 50 ft. raftered house, one 40 ft. longe, standing upon ye sd 20 ft. house, one house called a Quarter, of 15 ft. longe standing upon ye sd Plantation to be worth 1200 lbs. of tobacco, or six pounds sterling, and in ye year 1667 ye Gust did Destroy not only all ye houses standing upon ye sd Plantation, excepting two Dwelling houses now standing ye one thirty foote and ye other twenty foote & ye house called Quarter of fifteene foote, but did also blow downe and destroy most of ye Timber trees standing upon ye Plantation and these yet are standing desolate...and winshaken. Therefore we value sd Plantation as it now is att eight hundred pds. of tobacco, or four pounds sterling and ye forty foote tob. house now built by ye atty. of Mr. Stanford up ye sd Plantation. In witness thereof ye Sheriff and Jury have made Inquisition etc. 20 May 1670.

Page 369. 6 July 1670. Christopher Holleman of Isle of Wight County for a valuable consideration paid by Wm. Morris, 300 acres of land on Blackwater Swamp being one-half of ye divident of land of 600 acres adj. Thos. More.
Wit.: John Bramston, Mildred Bramston.

Page 370. 5 July 1670. Jas. Rogers, Lawnes Creek Parish, tanner, by bond dated to Robert Spenser for 30 pairs of shoes 24th July next gave...bond for same.
Wit.: Elizabeth Grove, Sam. Swann, Wm. Sherwood.

Page 371. 15 April 1670. These are to Certify that ye Agreement between ye South Side of James River and this Parish is that sd South Side shall pay unto ye Parish of James Citty for ye yeare 1650 tenn pounds of tobacco, and one bushel of corn per head and forever thereafter to remain in Parish by yourselves with no further payment at all to the Parish.
Rec. by Wm. Marriott.      Wm. Berkeley.

Page 371. 6 7ber 1670. Wm. Warrilow, of Surry County, has sold cleared woodland, 50 acres formerly purchased of sd John Corker by Christopher Vahan and Henry -(?)-. 4 Feb. 1659, assigned to Wm. Warrilow by Vahan, was sold to James Allsop 15 Aug. 1670. Susanna, ye wife of Warrilow gives her consent.
William Warrilow, Susanna Warrilow.
Wit.: Arnoll Cosignat, Hen. Dawson.

Page 375. 27 Oct. 1670. Edward Oliver acknowledges to have received of Thos. Clarke 250 acres of land and one cow to take up his bond with Benj. Harrison.
Richard Joanes.        Edward Oliver.

Page 375. 29 Oct. 1670. Deposition of Thos. More aged about 27 years or thereabouts, said Wm. Myles came to Deponent's house and inquired about a horse he had bought of Thos. Clay. Thos. Clay said at church he had sold to Wm. Holton.

Page 376. 29 Oct. 1670. Coll. Geo. Jordan, trustee of Will of Coll. John Flood, deceased...tobacco paid by John Kindred, planter, unto Mrs. Fortune Mills, ye late wife of Coll. John, she acquits to John Kindred land given in will of Coll. John Flood unto his daughter Jane and Walter Flood's divident, 300 acres. 25 July 1670.
Wit.: Robert Lee, Jno. Harloe, Wm. Sherwood.

Page 377. 24 Sept. 1670. Ind. Mrs. Jane Warren, Relict of Mr. Thos. Warren, late of Surry County, Virginia, deceased, of the one part, and Mathais Marriott, who hath married Aylse Warren, ye only sister by ye whole blood unto Wm. Warren, deceased, and sonne to ye aforesaid Thos. Warren. Witness that sd Jane Warren and Mathais Marriott are and have been at controversie and variance about ye division of of ye aforesaid Thos. & Wm. Warren estate. Now division shall be had and made between...Thos. & William's estates. Covenanted and agreed...First, Mrs. Jane Warren shall have her parte out of ye whole estate of above sd Mr. Thos. Warren his estate and sd Thos. Warren, sonne of above sd Thos. Warren and Jane his wife should happen to die before his sonne comes to age of 21 yeares, ye land which is given to him by his father's will, to fall to Wm. Warren, ye youngest son of sd Thomas Warren and Jane his wife during his natural life and upon and when he dies, land to fall to Mathais Marriott and his heirs for the sum of 1667 lbs. of legal tobacco and caskes out of his share of the estate and likewise further agreed betwixt ye sd Mathais Marriott shall have a white mare, her foale, bed, gold ring, one castor hatt of ye estate of Wm. Warren, and ye sd Mathias Marriott shall have a full share of ye children only if ye abovesaid Thos. Warren, deceased, his estate at ye mannor house where ye said Thos. Warren did live and ye whole dividnt of land thereon itt is situated with all houses, orchards, and appurtenances thereunto belonging and shall remain in fee simple unto Mathias Marriott and his heirs forever.

Itt is further agreed...that ye Mrs. Jane Warren shall peaceably and quietly enjoy ye one-third of the aforesaid mannor house, orchards, and dividents of land hereunto belonging, free egress and regress in and up ye land during her life ye sd Mr. Marriott to have allowed him for his share of ye crop of wheat, etc.

Jane Warren, Mathias Marriott.
Geo. Watkin, Gertrude Watkin.

Page 378. 2 Jan. 1670. Capt. Wm. Woodward makes Geo. Proctor his atty.
Wit.: Martin Quelse?. James Buford.

Page 378. 30 Dec. 1670. Barth. Owen to Richard Welbeck. 3 Jan. 1670.
Geo. Proctor, Henry Brigs, Johannah Owen.

Page 378. 30 Dec. 1670. Robert Shaw pays bill to Mrs. Berber.
Wit.: Edward Bridgman, John Goringe.

Page 379. 3 Jan. 1670. John Brady, Planter, for valuable consideration, sells to John Moring of Surry County, planter, a parcell of land on the west side of Besse's Swamp, adj. Maj. Marriott, 100 acres of land.
Wit.: Robert Babb, Fra. Simmons.

Page 379. 3 Jan. 1670. Geo. Lee of Charles Citty County, Va., for 7000 lbs. of tob. sells to Geo. Watkin a gray mare.
Wit.: Thos. Blayton, Wm. Scarbrow.

Page 380. 24 Feb. 1670. John Hunnicutt and Elizabeth Warren, spinster, both of the County, have contracted to enter marriage...John Hunnicutt to make over to Elizabeth Warren all household goods that she is possessed with. 7 March 1670.
Wit.: John Corker, Jane Warren.

Page 380. 3 Jan. 1670. Depositions of:
        Martin Johnson, aged 30 years.
        Thos. Laine, aged 36 years.
        John Price, aged 21 years.
        John Kindred, aged 35 years.
        Edward Morley.

Page 381. 4 March 1671. Margaret Winchester appoints Jeremiah Ellis her atty.
Wit.: Richard Hide.

Page 382. James Stradling is indebted to Wm. Marriott for 755 lbs. of tob.
Wit.: Robert Babb, Jr., Phill. Howard.

Page 382. Samuel Hayden, aged 26 years, made deposition that two years since he took a Plantation of Mr. Randall Holt in a place called Thimble Point where Wm. Clarke lately lived and looked after hoggs of sd Holt.
Wit.: Robert Spenser.

Page 383. Benj. Amry aged 19 years testified about Hog Island and hogs.

Page 383. 20 April 1671. John George makes Mr. Wm. Sherwood atty. for the estate of John Grove, deceased.

Page 383. 22 April 1671. A dead man found in the river at Thompson's landing, having been dead a long time.

BOOK I, 1652-1672

            Ed. Petway              Wm. Edwards
            Wm. Smith               Wm. Foreman
            John Shiner             Wm. Arnoll
            John Freestone          John Greenwood
            James Fowler

Page 385. 1 April 1671. A dead man found at the landing of Coll. Thos.
Swann, the Coroner out of the County, an able young man drowned in the
river.      Geo. Jordan            Samuel Swann
            Thos. Lillicrop        James Samson
            Thos. Crowes           Thos. Clarke
            Wm. Spring             Harry Rouse
            Wm. Gray               Wm. Hill
    Rec.: 4 May 1671.

Page 385. 26 April 1670. Wm. Sherwood, Sub. Sheriff of the County to the
Worshipful Justices of Surry County for himself and the Public Good at the
Grand Assembly at James City on 7 Oct. 1665 among divers good laws an act
concerning entertainment of Indians, shall be fined 1000 lbs. of tobacco or
one year imprisonment without baile unless security be given. Joseph Rogers
not obtaining a license, employed Indians, severall in his dwelling house,
contrary to law, and were a danger to the neighborhood etc.
    Wit.: Thos. Crows, Thos. Clarke.
    Rec.: 6 May 1671.

Page 386. 7 July 1671. Joseph Antrobus cannot appear at Court, empowers Mr.
John Salway to act for him.

Page 386. 26 May 1671. Will Mays empowers his friend Mr. Nicholas Morrison
to collect debts from Thos. Busby.

Page 386. 7 July 1671. Peleg Dunstan and Andrew Robertson overseers of a
gift of a mare colt to Susanna Robinson by her grandmother Sicelye Dunstant
in her will...loving brother John Dunstan to take in his care the mare and
increase, etc.
    Wit.: Francis Gower, Henry Lucas.

Page 387. 4 July 1671. Thos. Busby has sold to Mr. Wm. Bird of Martin's
Brandon, a grist mill and appurtenances, beginning at ye head of Chippoakes
Creek in Surry County, also 150 acres adjoining, now in possession of one
Heyward, also dwelling house now in possession of Daniell Williams, out of
a patent to Michell...and John Rawlings.
    Wit.: Elias Osborne and William Shorte.

Page 388. 27 July 1671. At Ye house of Capt. Geo. Watkin's, Capt. Law.
Baker, Mr. Chas. Barham, and Mr. Robert Spenser did examine Jane, alias
Hannah Davis, servant to ye Watkin. She testified concerning her child.

Page 389. 22 July 1671. Thos. Busby had a bill of 150 lbs. Tob. which he
owed to Capt. Gray, deceased, for natural love to his dear daughter Grace
Busby, one mare filly to be delivered and marked for her at the age of ten
years, if Grace die, or marry, then to nephew, Francis Allen, son of Anthonye Allen. Wm. Sherwood to Act at the next Court.

Page 389. John Hunnicutt, who has married Elizabeth Warren, daughter of Mr.
Thomas Warren, deceased, has received of Mr. Mathias Marriott his due por-
tion of the estate belonging to ye said Elizabeth as it was given by Mrs.
Jane Warren, and to acknowledge unto sd Marriott for the same.
    20 March 1670.
    Teste: Geo. Watkin.

Page 389. 5 June 1671. Mr. Richard Welbecke is asked by Rowland Place to
arrest Thos. Busby for certain debts and bring him to Court.

Page 388. Thos. Busby sells Mr. Wm. Bird, of Martin's Brandon, 300 acres of
land in Surry County at Michaell Michard? to Wm. Shorte's.
    Wit.: Elias Osborne, Wm. Shorte.

Page 390. John Whitson and Robert Spenser. To all Christian people know that John Whitson of Surry County having married Ann Spenser, daughter of Mr. Robert Spenser of the same County, and having had one daughter called Martha Whitson and her mother being dead, Robert Spenser out of a natural love to his Grandchild and her future benefit has delivered to John Whitson, father of sd child, one mare filly, and some livestock, and deliver to her when she is sixteen years old, or married; if she die, to return to donor.
Rec.: 7 April 1671.
Wit.: Edward Petway, Geo. Watkin.

Page 390. John Clarke appoints Mr. John Blayton to appear at James Town Court in a suit with Henry Brigs concerning a debt. 1 Feb. 1671.

Page 391. 17 June 1671. Thos. Busby, Gent., sells to Roger Potter, 100 acres of land at the head of Chippoakes Creek, extending to Mr. Steven's Mill.
Wit.: Wm. Rooking, Elias Osborne Appoints Wm. Sherwood to Ack. it.
31 Aug. 1671. Samuel Williams, Geo. Lee.

Page 392. 3 Jan. 1671. John Kindred, Lawnes Creek Parish, Planter, sells to Nathaniel Knight 300 acres of land for 4000 lbs. tobacco, given unto John Kindred, formerly a patent, by will of Coll. John Flood, late of the county, deceased, unto his daughter, Jane, and after to Walter Flood, which tract of land lately purchased by Lt. Coll. Geo. Jordan, trustee of the will of Coll. Flood.
Wit.: John Stevenson, Wm. Sherwood.

Page 393. 6 9ber 1671. Indenture between Wm. Hare, of Lawnes Creek Par., carpenter, and Mary, his wife, ye late wife of Geo. Carter, deceased, and Wm. Atkinson, being at the Spring Branch extending to Mr. Newsum's.
Wit.: Charles Barham, Stephen Allen.

Page 394. 31 Dec. 1671. Indenture between John Salway, planter, and Mary his wife, & John Dunstan and James Reddick, and wife Mary. To John Salway, where Salway now lives 200 acres on the south side of James River...adj. Maj. Hill, and Richard Drew...called New Mill.
Wit.: Edward Bechino, Rich. Skiner.
Signed: John Dunstan, James Reddick, Mary Reddick.
Mary Reddick appoints her cozen John Dunstan to ack. the bill of sale.
Wit.: Geo. Watkin, Ed. Bechinoe.

Page 395. 7 9ber 1671. John Salway binds over to Capt. Lawrence Baker the tract of land adj. John Dunstan at the head of Lawnes Creek for debt.
Wit.: Henry Baker, John Balie.

Page 396. 4 July 1671. Indenture between Roger Delke and Rebecca his wife and Wm. Butler...to where Humphrey Allen lived, 90 acres.
Wit.: John Salway, James Reddick.

Page 397. 30 Sept. 1671. Indenture between Roger Delke and Rich. Jarratt, planter, for 1500 lbs. tob., 70 acres of land in Lawnes Creek bordering on Swamp between Robt. Renolds and the Plantation formerly Maj. Wm. Butler's ...to edge of Round Meddow...to Reedy Branch.
Wit.: Jos. Antrobus, Wm. Gray

Page 398. 7 9ber 1671. Phillip Hunniford of Blackwater in Isle of Wight County to Joseph Well 200 acres on the Swamp, of Blackwater, the eastward end of 400 acres of land in Surry County pat. to Hunniford 14 May 1660.
Wit.: Martin Luther, Wm. Sherwood.

Page 399. 7 9ber 1671. Roger Delke, planter, he moving, sells to Robert Reynolds, planter, land in Lawne's Creek Neck formerly held by Thomas ap Thomas and John Burges, land that William Cock now lives upon called Round Meddo Meddows part of 100 acres formerly given and granted to his deceased father, Mr. Roger Delke. Acknowledged by Delke and his wife.
Wit.: Rich. Hill. Robt. Kee, or Kae.

BOOK I, 1652-1672 75

Page 400. 22 May 1671. Indenture between John Browne and John King for five years of lawful service. King to provide sufficient clothing, washing, lodging, etc., and teach him the trade of cooper for five years.
Wit.: Edmunde Shepham, Edward Hutchesson.

Page 400. 23 March 1671. Wm. Townsend appoints his friend Wm. Seward his atty. to release John Bynham and give security.
Wit.: John White, Mayson Maynes.

Page 400. 6 9ber 1671. John Salway sells a bay mare to James Reddicke. The above James Reddicke gives the increase, except the first foal, to his son, Robt. Reddick.
Teste: Geo. Watkin.
Wit.: Thos. Lillicrop, Wm. Cockin.

Page 401. 22 Feb. 1670. Henry Applewhite appoints his friend Mr. Robert Spenser his atty.

Page 401. 6 9ber 1671. Geo. Lee asks to be excused from Court; hurt his foot.

Page 401. 9 June 1671. Vincent Inge empowers his friend Isaih Watson atty.
Wit.: Letetia Barker, Hen. Knighton.

Page 401. 1 Jan. 1671. Roger Williams is arrested at ye suit of Coll. Swann. Mr. Benj. Harrison and Wm. Hux to appear at the next Court 3 Jan. next, and to send his wife as he bitten by a dog.

Page 402. 3 Jan. 1671. Wm. Rose makes a pledge of cartain goods of John Salway, live stock, negro woman, etc., for the security of a debt of 2400 lbs. of tobacco owed to John Salway, 12 Oct. 1671.
Wit.: John Carr, Robert Palmer.

Page 402. Thos. Bentley empowers John Rawlings to be his atty. in a suit with Mr. Geo. Lee.
Wit.: John Legrand.

Page 402. A copy of the estate of Walter Flood, orphants, in the hands of Mr. John Cary.
Wit.: Geo. Proctor, John Emerson.

Page 403. 16 Dec. 1671. John Cary of Surry County, Virginia, being by God's mission bound for England and yere to continue with my wife and children for as far as I yet doe know and whereas I am now guardian unto Walter Flood, orphant brother unto my wife, and Walter Flood being intended to go to England with me and because of the great distance now asks that Lt. Coll. Geo. Jordan and Capt. Thos. Flood jointly to take over the estate of Walter Flood att sea, pay his passage and see after him in England, school, food, and take loving care of him, and give him two mares at sixteen years old and 50 pounds sterling when 21 years old, etc., out of the estate in Virginia.
Rec.: 3 Jan. 1671.
Wit.: Geo. Proctor, John Emerson.

Page 404. 6 9ber 1671. John Dunstant sells a horse to Thomas High.
Wm. Sherwood, Wm. Edwards.

Page 404. Robert Bralye makes his friend Geo. Proctor his atty. between Mr. Hubert Harrell, Wm. Bowles, and himself.

Page 404. 4 March 1671. John Rogers, a Welshman, has run away owing a debt, has run away in to the Bay, and Robert Shaw wants judgment for the debt.
Wit.: James Goring.

Page 405. Maj. Griffin claims land formerly belonging to James Taylor, of Surry County and a Jury impanneled said the land was held jointly by Taylor and Lawrence Baker and did belong to Baker by survival. Case was dismissed. Suit in James Citty. 29 April 1667.

Page 405.  9 March 1670.  Mrs. Alice Allen Discharges Nicholas Sessums of all claims of debts.
Wit.: Wm. Newsum, John Thompson.

## End of Book I

In the back of this book, inserted upside down, are the laws governing all the officers of Surry County, and their duties, Dated 30 April 1650, it begins as follows:

After long and serious debate and advice taken from settling and administeringe of Argmt.  It was unanimously settled & Concluded by the Com. appointed, hereby Authorized by Parliament and by all the Burgesses of the Several Counties & Plantations Respectively untill the further pleasure the Statue be knowne That Mr. Richard Bennett, Esq., Gov. for the ensueing yeare or untill the next meeting of the Assembly with all the Just Powers under authority that may belong to the place lawfull & likewise Coll. Wm. Clayborne by Secretarye of the State with all belonging to that office, and is to be next in place to the Governor.

Next that the Councill of State be as follows Viz.:

     Col.. Samuel Matthewes   Coll. Nathaniel Littleton
     Col. Argall Yar(torn off)   Coll. Thos. Pettus
     Coll. Humph. Higginson   Coll. Geo. (torn off) Endlow
     Coll. Wm. Barnard     Capt. Bridges Freeman
     Capt. Thos. Harwood    Maj. Wm. Taylor
     Capt. Fra: Epps      Lieut. Coll. Jno. Cheeseman

and that they shall have right to Execute and due Right and Equall Justice to all the People and Inhabitants of this Collonye accordinge to ye Instruction as they have or shall receive from this Parliament of England and accordinge to the knowne (torn off) of England and the Acts of Assemblye heere Established and the sd Governments, Sec. and Councill of State are and have such powers and Authorities and to act from time to time as by the Grand Assemblye shall be appointed and granted to their several cos. Respectively from the time above at which all the people which Inhabiting be in this country are hereby Required to take and accordinglye Conforme Themselves thereto.

 God Sabe Ye Commonwealth of England and this Countrye of Virginia.
 Vere Copia Teste.    Jno. Corker, Cler: Dom: Com:
          Robert Stanton, Clerke     1652

(The following entries were omitted by the author and inserted here - R. W. B.)

Page 309.  31 Aug. 1668.  John Barber Makes Mr. Richard Lawrence his Atty. in a debt Thomas Pitman.
Wit.: Peleg Dunstan, Thomas Gully, John Pitkin.

Page 225.  11 Jan. 1663.  Thos. Smith of Dorston in the County of Harroford, yeoman, lawful atty. of Rich. James, and Margery his wife; Rich. Watkin and Jane his wife, all in the county aforesaid, and John Merredith and Mary his wife of Witton in the County of Radnor, release etc., unto Capt. Cockerham, admr. of John Modmore's Est. and unto the Justices of Surry Co. bonds etc. which Thos. Smith, or any of the employees ever had.
Wit.: David Williams, Edward Tanner.

SURRY COUNTY RECORDS

BOOK II, MARCH 1671 TO 5 JULY 1684

The preliminary pages are not numbered.

Page 1.  18 9ber 1679. Capt. Law. Baker qual. as admin. of Herman Hill (in Rt. of decedent's orphans). Sec.: Robt. Caufield & Wm. Edwards.
 Wit.: Benja. Harrison & Will. Foreman.
 Bond: 20,000 lbs. legall tob.

Page 2.  26 Feb. 1679. Robert Ruffin Qual. as Admr. Jno. Goring, deced., with Fra: Mason & Wm. Edwards Security.
 Bond: 80,000 lbs. legal tob.
 Wit.: Thos. Binns & Thos. Senior.

Page 3.  1 July 1679. Jno. Moring qual. as Admr. of Mr. Geo. Proctor, dec., with Lt. Coll. Will. Browne & Robert Ruffin security.
 Wit.: Sa. Swann & Wm. Edwards, Cl. Cur.
 Bond: 100,000 lbs. tob.

Page 4: 1 July 1679. Wm. Reade qual. Admr. Mathais Peach, dece'd. Jno. Moring security.
 Bond: 40,000 lbs. legall tob.
 Wit.: Robt. Ruffin & Wm. Edwards, Cl. Cur.

Page 5.  1 July 1679. Jno. Rawlings, bond 40,000 lbs. legall tob. with Roger Potter & Jno. King surety to deliver orphans of Jno. Collier, their child's part when come of age & bring up orphans: Educate, feed, clothe, etc.

Page 6.  5th 9ber 1678. Joyce Butler, widdow, qual. as admr. of Wm. Butler, dec. Bond: 80,000 lbs. legal tob. with Wm. Newsum and Wm. Seward as Security.
 Wit.: Ro. Kae & Jno. White.

Page 7.  2nd 7ber 1679. Mabell Drew Qual. admx. of her dec. husband Richard Drew; Bond, 40,000 lbs. legall tob. with Ro. Caufield & Wm. Seward surety.
 Wit.: Nathanaell Braxun and Tho. Jarrell.

Page 8.  Date not given. 11 Aug. 1680. Jno. Vincent's bond for 50,000 lbs. legall tob., with Jno. Moring & Dan Roans surety to deliver to orphants of Francis Sowerby, dec., their childs parts of goods of their late Father when come of lawful age etc.
 Wit.: Tho. Jordan, Wm. Edwards.

Page 9.  6 Jan. 1679. Hez: Bunell's bond for 40,000 lbs. legall tob. with Walter Flood & Richard Avery security to deliver to Elizabeth, Orphan of Robt. Cartright, dec., her child's part of the goods of her late Father, dec.
 Wit.: Wm. Thompson & Wm. Edwards, Cl. Cur.

Page 10.  2 Sept. 1679. Jno. Warren's bond for 40,000 lbs. legall tob. with James Watkins & Tho. Melton Security to deliver unto William & Frances, orphans of Francis Hogwood their childs part of their late Father's Est.
 Wit.: Will. Foreman & Wm. Edwards

Page 11.  2d 7ber 1679.  Capt. Ni. Wyatt's of Chas. City Co. bond as Exor. Wm. Rookings, &c., 50,000 lbs. legall tob. with Will'm Simons & Wm. Carpenter security.
    Wit.: Robert Ruffin and Wm. Edwards, Cl. Cur.

Page 12.  Index pages have been bound wrong.  E. T. D.

Page 13.  May 1679.  Jno. Watkins qual. as admr. of Henry Watkins, dec.; bond 40,000 lbs. legall tob. with Wm. Newsum security.
    Wit.: Will. Foreman & John Thompson.

Page 14.  26 May 1679.  Bond of Wm. Gray for 80,000 lbs. legall tob. with Robert Ruffin & Wm. Newsum of Lawnes Creek Parish to deliver to Wm. & Mary Chambers, orphans of Wm. Chambers, dec., their portion of Est. of their late Father when they come of age.
    Wit.: Jno. Price, Fra. Mason, Wm. Edwards.

Page 15.  5 May 1675.  Jury to continue until next Court.  Mr. Wm. Rookings, foreman, 1.  Mr. Richard Drew, 2.        Richard Harris, 3.
                       James Murray, 4.            Wm. Butler, 5.
                       Tho. Lane, 6.               Jno. Dunford, 7.
                       Edwd. Warren, 8.            Sam'll Plow, 9.
                       Robt. Cartright, 10.        Thos. Crews, 11.
                       Jno. Brady, 12.

Page 16.  16 June 1679.  Mary Gray qual. Admx. of Fra. Gray, deced., with Roger Potter & Geo. Foster surety; bond, 40,000 lbs. legall tob.
    Wit.: Tho. Jordan & Wm. Edwards, Cl. Court.

Page 16.  16 June 1679.  Sion Hill qual Admr. Mary Davies dece'd; Bond, 40,000 lbs, tob. with Geo. Williams & Geo. Foster surety.
    Wit.: Robert Ruffin & Wm. Edwards Cl. Cur.

Page 17.  1 July 1679.  John Barnes qual. Admr. Edward Bridgeman dec. Bond, 40,000 lbs. tob. with Robert Caufield Surety.
    Wit.: Fra. Mason & Wm. Edwards, Cl. Cur.

Page 18.  1 July 1679.  David Andrews, Jr., qual. Admr. John Flood, dec. Bond, 50,000 lbs. tob., with Tho. Ironmonger & Geo. Foster surety.
    Wit.: John Thompson & Wm. Edwards Cl. Cur.

Page 18.  1 July 1679.  William Hunt qual Admr. Judah Parker dec. Bond, 50,000 lbs. legal tob. with Wm. Carpinter & Will Nance surety.
    Wit.: Tho. Pittman, Sr., Wm. Edwards, Cl. Cur.

Page 19.  1 July.  Joane Adkins qual. Admr. Richard Adkins, dec.  Bond, 40,000 lbs. legall tob. with Jno. Warren and Thomas Catten sureties.
    Wit.: Wm. Nance & Wm. Edwards, Cl. Cur.

Page 19.  1 July 1679.  Sion Hill qual. as admr. Jno. Spilltimber dec'd. Bond, 40,000 lbs. legall tob., with Joseph Rogers and Jno. Phillips surety.
    Wit.: Benja. Harrison & Wm. Edwards, Cl. Crt.

Folios are numbered beginning here.

Fol. 1.  5 March 1671 and recorded the 8th.  Phillip Hunniford of Isle of Wight Co., Va., cooper, for love and affection to Lovinge Neece Charles Williams son to my well beloved brother, Rice Williams, dec'd., gives 100 acres of land at the Blackwater extending from N. side of land Joseph Wall lately purchased of me & part of my patt., dated 14 May 1666.
    Wit.: Christo. Holiman, Antho. Evans, Wm. Sherwood.

Fol. 2.  5 March 1671, and recorded the 8th.  Phillip Hunniford as above for consideration of Henry Goard of Lawnes Creek Parish, Surry Co., Planter, sells 100 acres of land at Blackwater in Surry Co. on N. side of land this day sold to Neede Chas. Williams, son-in-law to said Goard, part of land by

Patt. 14 May 1666.
Wit.: Christopher Holiman, Anthony Evans, Wm. Sherwood.

Fol. 3. 22 Jan. 1671. John Dunstant sells Wm. Smith a mare named Tibe.
Ackn. 5 March 1671. Rec. 8 March 1671.
Wit.: John ffrestone, Wm. Edwards.

Fol. 3. 22 Jan. 1671. Recd. of Patrick Lesley for 569 lbs. tob. in cask in full of all demands of portion of my wife, Anne, to Arthur Jordan.
Wit.: Wm. Walward, Tho. Moore.

Fol. 3. 2 March 1671. Rec. 8 March 1671. Power of atty. from James Reddick of Surry Co., Planter, to John Salway of same Co. to Implead Jno. Dunstan.
Wit.: Tho. Baker, Joh. Baker.

Fol. 3. 17 Dec. 1671. Jno. Salway of Lawnes Creek Parish, sells Wm. Sherwood 200 acres of land on S. side of James River on W. side head of Lawnes Creek adj. May Hill, Richd. Drew by cart path betwixt Capt. Baker's & the new mill - same obtained by a deed 2 Feb. 1668 by Katherine Greene, dec., or by indenture 31 Oct. last from Jno. Dunstan & Mary Redick, co-heirs of Peter Greene, dec. (mentions James Raeddick & Mary his wife & Joh. Dunston.) (Possession delivered in Mansion House of sd Plantation).
Wit.: Joseph Antrabus, Walter Bartlett, Tho. Lillicrop, Wm. Cockin.

Fol. 5. 20 Feb. 1671. Wm. Sherwood: letter fro John Scott. States that Capt. Cokerham sent a bill for 1 H H D. bread, was landed at Major Coffeldor's Landing - came not on board to pay & next year when I came into ye Cuntery he was desired. Pow. atty. to collect. Mr. Robt.Coffelder informed me he heard Capt. Cokerham acknowledge, etc., when he lay sick etc. Will satisfy you at my coming next year. Geo. Watkins, Clerk.

Fol. 6. 7 May 1672. 24 year of Reign of Charles II. Jon. Dunstan of Lower Chippoakes, Surry Co., planter, to Arthur Long, planter of same co., sells all interest in p'cell of land in Lyons Creeke Psh. which Thos. Clarie purchased of Ralph Dunstan & Hester his wife 1 Sept. 1660, left me by my brother Peleg after the decease of my brother Ralph Dunstan without Ishew by will of my father John Dunstan.
Wit.: Cha. Barham, Ran. Holt, Wm. Sherwood.
Geo. Watkins, Clerk.

Fol. 7. 11 March 1671. 23 year of Reign of Charles II. Nico. Perry of Chas. Citty County by late marriage with Elesabeth Hutton, daughter of Daniel Hutton, dec., was tenant in dower of land whereof wife stood seized by Mr. Arthur Jordan her guardian - indemnified & for leasing land - especially from Richard Avery to whom I lett part of same before my said wife died - sells all right therein to Arthur Jordan.
Wit.: Geo. Jordan, John Danby.
Pow. Atty. to Mr. Rich. Welluck to acknowledge in Surry Court.
Same witnesses.

Fol. 9. 15 April 1672. Land Grant Wm. Berkeley to John Davies & Charles Duthace in Rt. of their wives 100 acres formerly granted to Tho. Boswell, Jr. & lagely Escheated. (Endorsed John Davies and William Duthace their pattent for 100 acres of land in Surry Co.)

Fol. 10. 4 May 1672. Assigned by John Davis, Mary Davis, and Diana Duthace to Richard Briggs of Surry Co., planter.
Wit.: Law. Baker, Nich. Hill.
Pow. Atty. Mary Davis, wf of Jno. Davis of Isle of Wight to Capt. Law. Baker, Gent. of Surry Co. to acknowledge it in court.
Wit.: Nic. Hill.

Fol. 10. 7 May 1672. Wm. Hare makes our 8 head cattle in open court to Capt. Charles Barham & Mr. Arthur Longe, security for orphants estate of George Carter, deceased.

Fol. 11. 4 May 1672. Tho. Stevenson, aged 48 years, says that about 6 years since Humphrey Allen, brother of Arthur Allen, being uppon his death bed gave servant boy Edward Welbanke on 2½ years time he had to serve.
Sworn before N. Wyatt.
Same by Robt. Cobcutt, 60 years old.
Same by Margaret Cobcutt.

Fol. 12. 13 Oct. 1671. Mathias Marriatt sold Geo. Watkins a negro man "Kie," witnesses: John Corker, Will Newsom.

Fol. 12. 7 May 1672. Thomas Nuis pow. atty. to loving friend Isaac Tatem.
Wit.: Wm. Rookings.

Fol. 13. 1 March 1671. John Legrande of Surry Co. sells Ann Dennis of same Co. all interest and Inheritance in parcell of land at Burchen Swamp in Surry Co. adj. Wm. Simons.
Wit.: John King, Wm. Lucas.
Acknowledged and recorded 7 May 1672.

Fol. (not given). 5 March 1671. Depositions Michaell Upchurch aged fifty odd says Geo. Knight on Xmas. Eve last killed deare & asked him if there were not any turkeys & he sd. noe but 2 he killed, etc.
Teste: Geo. Watkins.

Page 14. 17 May 1672. Pow. Atty. Thos. Taberer to "Brother Spenser" as admr. Estate of John Munger, dec., to sue Capt. Thos. Pitman for debt due Munger Estate.

Page 14. 13 April 1672. Stephen Allen, intending for England, pow. atty. to Margaret Allen my now wife & Loveinge Cozen, Mr. Robt. Caufield & Mr. Robt. Spenser assistant to my wife - to buy, sell, etc.
Wit.: Joh. Barnes, Thomas Jarrell.

Page 14. John Pender to Welbeck saus Coll. Jordan is indebted to Him for Mr. Tho. Hunt, and begs him to implead for him at next court.
Wit.: John Bird.

Page 15. 10 April 1672. Richard Cae, planter, and Isabell Case his wife of Southwark Psh., sell Samuel Plow of sd. Co. and Psh., planter, 100 acres of land, plantation whereon Richd. & Isabell lately lived on W. side of Gray's Ck. called Hollowenge Poynte & the Middle Neck adj. to it to the Swampe between the middle neck & the Hay stack swamp, purchased of Thos. Gray, planter,
Wit.: Robt. Caufield, Ni. Meriwether, Wm. Sherwood.

Page 15. 2 July 1672. John Mines? deed trust personal property to Richard Watkins (or Atkins).
Wit.: Tho. Steveton, Geo. Jordan.

Page 15. 10 May 1672. Mrs. Mary Davis, 52 years old. Depositions before Law. Baker about Beast.

Page 15. 1672. Rich. Skinner aged 46 says that he married the Relict of Jab. Burgess & during lifetime of sd Burgess gave his daughter some cattle, deponent removed them to his plantation, etc. Sworn before Law. Baker, Robt. Caufield.

Page 15. 1672. Mary Skinner, aged 40 years saith that what her husband hath declared, she deposeth same. Same Justices.

Page 16. 17 May 1672. Martin Johnson, aged abt. 33, saith he heard Wm. Newsom say Aprill last that he saw the heifer Roger Rawlings he had strayed from him in Thos. Taylor's old field May come 2 years. Geo. Corpe?, aged 35 years about same Roger Rawlings' heifer. Thos. Taylor aged 35 years about same. (Lawnes Creek).

Page 16. 17 May 1672. John Clarke, aged 20, says that when he lived with Wm. Newsom he heard John Kindred bid Roger Rawlings fetch a heifer; sd beast did run at Mr. Watkins, etc.

Page 16. 17 May 1672. Jennet Davis, about 22 years old, says she knew about heifer in controversy between Henry Brigs & Roger Rawlings, etc., speaks of her master.

Page 16. 1672. Wm. Newsom, aged about 24, saith about 3 years ago Roger Rawlings desired him to go with him to John Kindred's place to fetch a heifer sd Kindred had given his daughter Betty - did fetch it Rawlings did mark it; heifer did remain a certain time in "My father Watkins," his pasture, etc.

Page 17. 7 May 1672. John Talbot, aged 22, says returning home from Lt. Col. Jordan's land day before New Year last...12 months, did call in at ffrancis Soreby's house ask for cider; his fellow servant Cotton Robinson. Francis Sorsby followed deponent over bridge & told deponent that his brother Thomas did tell him that Richard Tyas informed him at Joh. Rawlings, his mill, that his Master was going to arrest him, etc.

Page 17. 6 May 1672. Cotton Robinson, aged about 19; John Talbot, deponent's fellow servant, understanding he was to go to Coll. Jordan's landing with deponent's Master Nicholas Meriweather, goodman Sorsby or ffrancis Sorsby; no light in the loft.

Page 17. Pettition of Robert Spenser; Grand Assembly took into consideration prejudice that might issue from too great liberty granted Servants travelling abroad Satturdays & Sundays; In consequence petitioner read law to John Whitson of this Co., requiring observance; refused to obey, etc.

Page 17. 26 August 1672. Depositions of Aylse ffydian; between Whitson and Spenser. Sworn before No. Meriwether.

Page 18. Petition of Robt. Spenser to have John Whitson bound to the peace.

Page 18. 26 August 1672. Elizabeth Phillips, aged 22, depositions that John Whitson was at Stephen Allen's house about 6 weeks ago & fell abusing his father-in-law Robert Spenser; has a child; wife evidently dead. John Phillips aged 36 years declares what his wife has said is true.

Page 19. 2 Sept. 1672. Roger Delke & Rebecca Delke his wife of Surry Co. sell Walter Bartlett of sd county a tract of land in Surry Co., Whereon Robert Gyles & Chas. Willes now liveth bounding E. on Lawnes Creek. Sam(?) branch running out of sd creek and Dividing this from land whereon Robt. Lacy liveth W. on Delk's uttermost bounds & N. on land Mr. Robt. Kee.
Wit.: Jno. Selway, Joseph Antrabus.

Page 19. 20 Aug. 1672. Letter from Wm. Duke to Mr. Sherwood asking that he appear in action as Mr. Richd. Welbeck "att. my suite as marrying ye Relict of Mr. Wm. Bird, dec'd."

Page 19. 28 Aug. 1672. Wm. Drumond letter to Mr. Wm. Sherwood begs to prosecute Wm. Ross at my suit as atty. of Wm. ffowles.
Wit.: Jno. Wright.

Page 19. 14 Oct. 1672. Wm. Thompson of Surry Co. & Katherine his wife assign a patent to Thomas Andrews (Pattent not designated).
Wit.: Daniell Regan, Samuel Thomson.

Page 19. 30 Oct. 1672. Wm. Thomson and Catherine Thompson his wife of Surry Co. in Virginia assign patent to Daniel Regam. (Patent not designated).
Wit.: ffrancis Mason, Wm. Edwards.

Page 19. 25 9ber 1671. Tho. Blayton writes loveing friend Mr. Geo. Proctor to pay Wm. Nance & prosecute Hooper.

SURRY COUNTY RECORDS

Page 19. 4th 9ber 1672. Wm. Hooper Pow. atty. to Thos. Busby.
   Wit.: Tho. Bird, Joane Busby, John Thomas.

Page 19. 29 Nov. 1672. Wm. Tooke, aged 46, says heard Joh. Barnes say that
   Wm. Wells exchanged steeres he bought with Wm. Newsom.

Page 19. 29 Nov. 1672. Tho. Hunt, aged 21, says he heard Wm. Newsom tell
   John Barnes he bought them of Wm. Wells, etc.
   Geo. Watkins, Cl. Court.

Page 20. 14 Sept. 1672. Rich. Welbeck assigns title to certain conveyance to
   John Whitson.
   Wit.: Nic. Meriweather, Geo. Proctor, John Salway.

Page 20. 16 7ber 1672. Andrew Robinson pow. atty. to Wm. Seward to secure
   certain horses, etc., some of which have been sold by John Dunstan who had
   no right to them.
   Wit.: David Williams, Matthew Magnes.

Page 20. 2 July 1672. Rich. Case, aged 53, depositions between Thos. Cray
   & Thos. Cruse--bounds of Cruse--beg. at deponent's cold spring--path that
   goes over to cross creeke, so down to the swamp that runs into cross creek.

Page 20. 2 July 1672. Isabell Case, aged about 56, wife of Rich'd. Case
   deposeth same as husband--also heard that Cruse's wife ask gray (sic) if they
   should not have a small poynt of land that lies by the black stump aforesaid
   & sd Gray answered noe, he did not whether it did belong to him or Col.
   Swann. Cruse's land between 40 and 50 acres.

Page 20. 2 July 1672. Tho. Gray, neare 21 years, deposes same as Case on 2
   July 1672. Joh. Gray, above 21 years saith same as above.

Page 20. 29 9ber 1672. Estate Capt. Cockerham presented by Charles Barham
   & Robt. Caufield. "The ball. being divided into three parts there remains
   due to the 2 orphants 13,400."

Page 20. 20 Nov. 1672. Wm. Heath of Surry Co., Va., Planter, sells John
   Litford of Isle of Wight Co., planter, 200 acres in Chas. Citty Co., beginning at an oak in swampe that parts Chas. Cittye Co. and Surry Co. patt.
   by me, 5 March 1663.
   Wit.: Wm. Thomson and Wm. Sherwood.

Page 21. 5 Jan. 1672/3. Tho. Hane pow. atty. to either Mr. Wm. Edwards or
   Mr. Wm. Sherwood to prosecute my action as Wm. Butler and John Pryse hath
   of Surry Co.
   Wit.: Tho. fferringham.

Page 21. 10 Sept. 1672. Tho. Pitman of Surry Co., gent., bind myself not to
   make use of any part of estate of Lidia Judkins, but she may dispose of all
   estate she now enjoys in her widowhood to whom she pleaseth whenever she
   dyeth.
   Ack.: 7 Jan. 1672/3.
   Wit.: Samuell Judkins and Wm. Hayes.

Page 21. 7 Jan. 1672/3. John Moring with consent of my wife Jane Mooringe
   assigns land to John Smith.
   Wit.: Wm. Corker & ffrances Meriwether.

Page 21. 6 Jan. 1672. Invy. of Michael Micane of Surry Co., dec., upon
   oath of Sarah, the Relict. Included were "7 India bowles," and "1 olde
   Sowe at Mr. Simons." Sarah's petition (states that) Michaell was a very
   sickly man in his life time; has a poore child to bring up," etc.

Page 22. 26 Feb. 1672/3. Thomas Wilkinson asks Mr. Arthur Jordan to appear
   for him to prosecute action as Thos. Pitman. "The debt was made to my
   Predecessor Griffin Dickinson. Also confess Jumt. in my behalf to Wm.
   Wabward.      Wit.: Nath. Knight.

Page 22.  3 Sept. 1672.  Stephen Allen of Southwark Parish, Surry Co. in
Va., pow. atty. to loveing Kinsman Mr. Robt. Gaufield of Lions Creeke Psh.
same Co., to receive all sums of tob., money, Jewells, household stufe,
plate, cattle, Horses, hogs & sows--whatsoever is rightly mine in & upon the
land of Va., etc.
    Wit.: John Cox, Wm. Bridges, 8 Feb. 1672/3.  Wm. Bridges deposes this was
Stephen Allen's hand and he did see him write itt, etc.

Page 23.  24 Feb. 1672/3.  Tho. Parker of Martins Brandon: whereas Elizabeth
Shorte & Elizabeth Shorte (sic) by deed 3 May 1669 did sell Geo. Midleton
part their divident land at Harick, beginning 30 pages S. of the Labour in
Vain House & so down swampe that parts Chas. Citty Co. & Surry Co.  Whereas
Geo. Midleton assigned the same to Thos. Parker.  Thos. Parker sells same
to John Lidford of Chas. Citty Co., planter.
    Wit.: Tho. Busby, Wm. Shorte, Wm. Sherwood.
    Ackn. 4 March 1672 by Wm. Sherwood
    Attur.  Special: Possession delivered above date in presence of Maurice
Rose, Wm. Heath, Tho. Busby, Wm. Shorte, Wm. Sherwood.

Page 23.  4 March 1672/3.  Tho. Warwell pow. atty. to John Whitson to answer
suit of Coll. Geo. Jordan.
    Wit.: Wm. Edwards and Samuell Richardson.

Page 23.  4 March 1672.  Wm. Kite aged 20 years being at Mr. Thomson's house
last Xmas.  Tho. Tias and He were talking about Wm. Foreman's hogs.  Tias
replied he had killed but one--wild--the eares being nailed up at his Godfather's & he would live at Mr. Thompson's or his Godfather if it were but
to kill Wm. Foreman's hogs.

Page 23.  29 Aprill 1673.  William Berkeley--"Gent.  There is a dispute between
my Bro. Culpepper & Coll. Swann of damage my Brother Culpepper may sustain by
hose was leit by Capt. Groves to Geo. Domingoe."  (He) asks for jury to
Commissioners.

Page 23.  25 Aug. 1673.  ffrancis Gray vs Thos. Cruse dispute concerning land
sold by Tho. Gray, dec., to Tho. Cruse.  Land now laid out by Mr. Rich. Lawrence & Capt. Geo. Watkins to be binding.
    Wit.: Tho. Swann, Tho. Hone, Richd. Lawrence, Geo. Watkins, Clk.

Page 25.  27 April 1673.  Inquisition taken Saturday before Capt. Chas. Barham, High Shff. on land formerly in possession of Rich. Blunt--verdict--
plantation contains 300 acres worth annually 350 lbs. tob.

Page 25.  6 May 1673.  Ar. Jordan assigns to Coll. Thos. Swann certain land
& Housing (not designated).
    Wit.: George Proctor, Nath. Knight.

Page 25.  3 March 1672/3.  Rich. Harris of L. C. Psh, Surry Co., planter,
in consideration of marriage formerly had between Walter Taylor & Mary,
wife of sd Walter, one of my daughters, etc., grants to Walter Taylor 100
acres of land now in possession of Walter of L. C. P. pt of tract former by
patt. by me Rich. Harris & Rich. Drew, bounding E. on Richd. Drew, N. on
Mr. Arthur Allen W. & Son  Richd. Harris formerly belonging to one Richd.
Blunt, dec.
    Wit.: Geo. Proctor, Wm. Sherwood.
    (Wm. Sherwood, Attur. Spl.)

Page 25, 24 April 1673.  Tho. Clarke now atty. to John Salway to Implead Jno.
Bird & Joh. Stocke?.
    Wit.: Rich. Lupo, Robt. Palmer.

Page 26.  16 Feb. 1671.  George Midleton assignment to Tho. Parker (land not
designated) acknowledged in court 6 May 1673, also by Sarah Middleton his
wife.
    Wit.: Jno. King, Margaret Ellis, John Morse.
    Acknowledgement & consent of Sarah Middleton presented as by reason of

extreme lameness she can in noe wise waite on the court.
Wit.: N. Wyatt, Wm. Rookings.

Page 26. 28 April 1673. 20th year of Lord King Charles II, Wm. Hux of Surry County in Va. sells Mr. David Andrews of same Co. 25 acres land in said Co. adjoining lands of said Andrews, beginning at Buckmaster's landing at the creek, thence up Buckmaster's run, thence to valley that comes to Thomson's levell, etc., to great Hickory in sd Valley marked 4 ways etc.
Wit.: Wm. Thomson, John Moringe.

Page 26. 6 Jan. 1672. 24th year of Lord King Chas. II, Thos. Busby sold Tho. Hyard 100 acres in Surry Co. bounding on Reedy Branch to Mr. Joh. Barker's line, thence down to the Southern Run along by Michell Micane's etc. to mouth of Reedy Branch begun...as by my pattent.
Ackn. in court on 6 May 1673.
Wit.: Tho. Parker, Wm. Shorte, Tho. Bird.

Page 26. 6 May 1673. Wm. Shorte of Southwarke Parish, Surry Co., Planter, & Mary Shorte his wife sell Joh. Lindford of Chas. Citty Co., planter, 100 acres on western run which part is Chas. City & Surry Cos. beginning at head of tract Wm. Shorte formerly sold Geo. Middleton & is now purchased by sd Lidford & so S. to utmost bounds of land of Wm. Shorte.
Wit.: Thos. More, Wm. Seward, Wm. Sherwood.

Page 27. 6 May 1673. Joh. Clarke receipt to Wm. Newsum acknowledging receipt in full of Estate left me by my deceased father, Richard Clarke.

Page 27. 6 June 1673. Warrant issued by Tho. Swann to High Sheriff of Surry Co. for that Wm. Sherwood, sub Sheriff, complains that Joh. Price of this Co., planter, hath several times assaulted him & on 19 May last past pursued him with intent to do him bodily harm etc., sd Pryse is a common Quarreler and fighter & a Maineteyner of quarrells and affrays at Co. F. and other publique meeting in this county to arrest to court to be held on Monday the 16th this Instant June.

Page 27. 23 August 1671. Bond of Timothy Walker to Mr. Antho. Stanford of London, Mercht., for 2 # 16 s. sterling.
Wit.: Math. Wilkinson, Joh. Mohun.

Page 27. 26 May 1673. Inquisition on Plantation now in possession of Mathew Swann Att. Lower Chipaoks in Surry Co. Sworn before Capt. Chas. Barham, High Sheriff of value of plantation less by reason of lease by Capt. John Grove dec. to Geo. Domingo etc. of land 30 acres on which Mat. Swann now lives--not above 15 acres plantable land for corne or tob.--noe timber trees fit for bords, poles or stakes--1000 lbs. tob. verdict.

Page 27. 26 May 1673. Jury of men near Lower Chippoakes...one other of the Jury hath not assented 500 lbs. tob. More.

| | |
|---|---|
| John Kilpatrick | James Murray |
| Wm. Hare | Wm. Hancoke |
| Rob. Spenser | David Williams |
| Wm. Chambers | Asters? Hunnicutt |
| Charles Amry | John Kindred |
| John Barnes | Arthur Long |

Page 28. 16 June 1673. To Mr. Garwin Corbin, March. in London, from William Berkeley--did last year charge bill of exchange on ye for 50 # sterl. payable to Coll. Thos. Swann if not paid pay him for his order--also another bill of this date for 61 # 16 s. 8 d. Bill follows assignment by Tho. Swann of last bill to Mr. John Beale or his order.

Page 28. 4 May 1673. Maryland, for 26 # Sterl. bill signed "ye loveing friend Thomas Howell to Coll. Joh. Owen in Crutched friers over against ye lumpe to pay to Coll. Tho. Swann of James River in Virginia in the county of Surry assigned Virginia, 24 June 1673, by ye friend Tho. Swann to Mr. John Beale.

Page 28. 5 May 1673. "Sr. Ye loveing friend & Servant Thomas Howell," from Baltimore County in Maryland to "My Honerd friend Collonell Thomas Swann in Surry County in Virginia." "Yours by Mr. Wm. Smith I have rec'd" Wm. Smith talked with ye negro bought him at high rate as he ran away etc. as he ye man Willett & if I heare of Hamleton either in Deliware or New Yorke I will lease him etc.

Page 28. 31 March 1673. Bill signed "Ye loveing Brother Abraham Rowse for ₤ 24 sterl.: addressed to Mrs. Judith Adrian widdow ye backside of ye Royall exchainge as Kensington--to be paid to Coll. Tho. Swann, Esqr. "A second bill recorded, dated 14 June 1673, signed exactly as above for ₤ 11.9.0 sterl.: addressed to Mrs. Judith Adrian Liveninge att Kinsington neare Londone." Both of above assigned by Tho. Swann to Mr. John Beale 24 June 1673.

Page 29. 2 Sept. 1673. John LeGrand of Southwark Parish, Surry Co., Va., Planter, sells Wm. Sherwood of Lawnes Creek Parish, Surry Co., Va., Gent., 180 acres on which I lately dwelt att or neare Upper Chippoakes adj. the S. E. line of Mr. Simond's land W.S.W. upon land of Henry Francis S.E. upon S.W. branch of Burchan Swamp, etc.
Wit.: John Parker, George Proctor.

Page 29. 1 Aug. 1673. Wm. Thompson, Clerk, and Katherine Thomson his wife to Joh. Salway hath of Surry Co. for 6000 lbs. tob. sell that parcel of land comonly called Christo. Lewis nigh the Church at the head of Gray's Creek guessed to be about 70 acres bounded E. by line of marked trees running through Andrew's his old field. Southerly by the swamp which parts sd land from Joh. Whitson's land, Wh. is bounded with a valley running betwixt Wm. Foreman's & the said land N. with young Luke Mizell's line of marked trees.
Wit.: William Corker, Wm. Parker, Geo. Watkins, Mathias Marriott, Tho. Andrews.

Page 30. 14 Aug. 1673. Richard Tias sells Joh. Salway (both of Surry Co.) for a valuable sum 100 acres in Surry Co. nigh Gray's Creek same on which Tias now doth live bounding on land Salway lately bought of Mathias Marriott westerly, being 1/2 of land taken up by one Twy?& by sd Twy? sold to Tias, the other 1/2 comonly called Capt. Wm. Corker, bounds according to patent. Witness to possession gives Stephen Sheafe, Tho. Tias--Rich. Tias also assigns all his interest in the other 100 acres of above devidend specified to be called Capt. Corker's for above amount to sd Joh. Salway same date, same witnesses.

Page 30. 23 July 1673. Mat. Marriott & Alice Marriott his wife sell Joh. Salway for "a Certain piece of land & 10,000 lbs. tob. & caske & more" all that tract of land on which he now lives which was "formerly in possession of Mr. Tho. Warren, comonly called Smith's Forte & Saynes" being 400 acres or above bounded on Gray's Creek, son widdow Gilbert's land & Wm. Marriott's land E. with Rich. Tias his land bounding on the Swamp beyond Stephen Allen's N. Mr. Barrett's land, the whole devident being on S. side of James River in Surry Co., Va.; the land which Mathias Marriott hath in pte. payment for aforesd land lyeth in Surry Co. & formerly belonged to Kett Lewis & sold sd Salway by Mr. Wm. Thomson.
Wit.: George Proctor, Wm. Thomson.
Possession given 30 July 1673.
Wit.: Samuell Plowe, Roy Williams.

Page 31. 23 July 1673. Jno. Selway & Eliza Selaway his wife sell Mathias Marriott, same described on p. 20.
Same witnesses at last above.

Page 31. 2 Sept. 1673. Lease; 25 year of King Chas. II. Wm. Hare of Lawnes Creek Psh., Surry Co., Va., carpenter, & Mary Hare his wife late Admx. of her late husband Ger. Carter, dec., & Wm. Oldis of sd psh. and co., planter: whereas Geo. Carter was in his lifetime possessed in fee of a tract of land in lower Chippoaks in L. C. P., Surry Co., comonly called Carter's land, containing over 100 acres, and by his last will gave sd Mary his wife 1/2

of same for 40 yrs. After his decease & Mary hath made choice of & accepted the here under mentioned for a part of land given her--for 3000 lbs. tob. paid by Wm. Oldis as a fine as incomb as also of the rent & covenants hereinafter mentioned--do demise, let, grat, & to farme lott parcell bounding N. by S. by Chippoakes land & W. to white oak formerly marked for Mr. Wm. Sherwood from thence N. to a marked poplar & by straight line of marked trees to the cart path opposite to Peter Adams' land.
    Wit.: Wm. Thompson, Charles Barham, Wm. Harwood.

Page 32. 2 Sept. 1673. John Barker, Sr., & Ann Barker his wife of Southwark PSh., Surry Co. (she being late wife of & extx. under will of Geo. Marshall late of Martins Brandon in Charles Citty Co., dec'd.), whereas Geo. Marshall was in his lifetime possessed in his dimeine as of fee of certain Plantation at Martins Brandon containing 75 acres which he purchased of widow & orphants of one Joh. Hacker & by his last will dated 9 March 1672, Proved in Chas. Citty Court, bequeathed all his lands to Ann his wife, who since married John Barker, Senr., now in consideration to us paid by John Barker the younger of Psh. and Co. aforesaid, give, grant, alien & confirm to John Barker, younger, aforesaid plantation with all houses etc. as also all other land of which Geo. Marshall dyed seized.
    Wit.: Wm. Sherwood, Robert Lee.
    Ackn. in open Court, Surry Co.

Page 33 (a). 8 March 1672. Invy. of Rich'd Jarrett, dec'd., appr. by James Reddick, Mr. Walter Barttet, Mr. Richd. Briggs & Mr. Wm. Butler
                  1 shag rug & flockbed
                  1 high bedstead
                  trundle bedstead
                  1 suite curt. & vallans
                  1 large table and forme
                  Tho. Davis 3 years to serve, 1600
                  other things
Value: 15,860 lbs. tob. & caske. "This is a true Inventory of my dec'd. husband's estate to the last of my knowledge. Margery Chambers.
    Pd.: Doctor Benton? pounds 1252; Doctor Lidener pr bill 1600; Doctor Taylor pr. andr.; Richd. Drew by debt & legacy 0310; Hen. Baker pr. Legacy 0250; Wm. Gray pr. Legacy, 4 cows, chest, gun, etc.; an a/c of Chas. Jarrots pt of his dec. father, Richard Jarrott, his estate, 2 December 1673; to 1/2 of the appraismt., livestock; per legacy given in will. This a/c. passed & pr. noted pr Robert Caufield, Richd. Drew.

Page 33. 20 Nov. 1673. Wm. Foreman Enters Caveat for west Land lying upon head line Mr. Owens land upon Jno. Shohocings Swamp.

Page 34 (1). 21 9ber 1673. Deps. Charles Beckett. He saw Mr. Jo. Lewis deliver a still to Mrs. Morreing also dishes etc. & said whether he lived or dyed she should have it, etc.

Page 34 (1). 1 9ber 1673. Tho. Warrell of Surry Co., Bricklayer, pow. atty. to Wm. Edwards to Implead Tho. Reeding for a debt.
    Wit.: Jno. Bishop, Jno. Harris.

Page 34. 24 June 1673. Agreement between Joseph Antrobes who agrees to deliver to Jno. Salway before the last of Sept. next so much goods Such as ye sd Salway shall like of as by a true Invoyce shall amount to £ 22.0.10 sterl. at ye first penny in England, ye sd Salway to have ye first choice of wt goods ye sd Antrobus shall bring, send & cont. of England within ten days after arrival of sd goods in Virginia. Bond for £ 30 sterl. on demand. If no goods brought etc. payable on demand after 10th of 8ber next in Lanes Creek Pash. of 4,500 lbs. of sound tob. & caske & to bind, make over unto one servt. maid having 3½ years & upwards to serve called Christian Grimmett, 1 gray mare bought on Richd. Drew, 3 cows, etc.
    Wit.: Charles Amory, Stephen Allen.

Page 34. 20 9ber 1673. Will Corker of Co. of York to Eliza White and Mary White, sisters, in Surry Co., parcel of land on Cypress Swamp on N. side of

Reedy Branch called Tias his branch to ye outward line beginning at ye mouth & extending to ye head of aforesaid branch, Eliza to have 1st part at ye mouth & Mary to have upper part toward ye head equally.
    Wit.: Fra. Meriwether, Rich. Welbecke.

Pages 37 and 38. Estate of Maj. Wm. Marriott, dec.; indebted to Geo. Proctor who married relict and extx., for certain debts and legacyes, etc., "to pd. Wm. Atkinson by will 0140; to his wives legacy 2000.
                  pd Mr. Salway who md. Eliza Peck due by will 1000
                  pd Dr. Allin fol 1,   0060
                  by debts in Henrico Co., 0860
                  by debts in Isle of Wt. Co., 1121
                  by debts in Cha. Citty Co., 2160
                  by debts in Jas. Citty Co., 2461
                  by Dr. Taylor, 1217
                  by 6 pr shooes due from Jno. Rogers
                  by James Bendall, 0132
                  by Dr. Knight by bill, 0188
                  4 silver dram cups
                  3 wine cups
                  1 boule and small tankard, wt. 25 oz.
                  Haverdysaiz
    Rec.: 11 7ber 1673 not final yet. Exam. by Wm. Browne. Capt. Robt. Spencer could not come yet.

Page 39. Coroner's inquest over Mr. Tho. Wilham, cast ashore at Coll. Geo. Jordan's landing, disquieted in drink, got out of Great cabin Port, aboard ye Thomas & Edward, etc., 9 June 1673.

                Benja. Harrison         Edwd. Warren
                Dan Roome              ffra. Hogwood
                Tho. Sowerby            Chris. Foster
                Tho. Bently             Jno. Emmerson
                Tho. Wall               Ralph Rochell
                Abraham Sapcoate       Tho. Jordan
                Jno. Dawkes

Page 39. 21 9ber 1673. Acct. est. Luke Mizell presented by Jno. Smith who md. Deborah relict and extx. of Luke Mizell "allowed mare by court for Spilltimbur's child, & all other demands 0400. Total estate: 12643. Debts 1428; balance of 11215 divided equally between Jno. Smith and Luke Mizell orphant.

Page 39. 6 Jan. 1673/4. Deed of gift from Edward Pettway to George Corpe for 100 acres bounding on Geo. Foster & Tho. Wade, 1 mi. into wood for length & for bredth toward land that Mr. Jno. Salway bot. of Richd. Tias Reserves pine trees fit to saw for plank.
    Wit.: Jno. Salway, & Wm. Edwards.
For want of heirs of Corpse, to return to heirs of Donor.
    Rec.: by Wm. Edwards, 1673, Cl. Cur. (1st found 20 Nov. 1673 as Clerk).

Page 40. 6 Jan. 1673/4. Receipt from Wm. Avary to Wm. Carpinter for whole Estate of cattle, tob., & all other dues owing to my wife Ann one of the orphants of Wm. Knott, dec'd.

Page 40. 30 Jan. 1672/3. Deed of gift from Wm. Avery of Chas. Citty Co. & Ann Avery his wife to our sister Sarah Knot, orphant of Wm. Knot, for heifer, deed to be acknowledged in Surry within 6 months & heifer to be delivered Wm. Carpinder within 10 days who is to have maile increase for looking after them.
    Wit.: Benj. Harrison, Thomas Clarke.

Page 40. 3 Jan. 1673/4. Decision of Law. Baker & Robt. Spenser, two of the Justices of this Co. about the Giddy headed multitude informed abt. 12 of br. (sic) last past a company of seditious & Ride people to the number of ffourteene did unlawfully assemble at ye psh. church of Lawnes Creek with intent to declare they would not pay their publiq taxes, & yet they expected

diverse others to meet them, who failing they did not put their wicked
designe in Execution & by statute of ye 13th of Henry IV, Chap. 7, we sent
out warrant for: the following, to appear.

    Matt Swann             Jno. Barnes
    Wm. Hancock           Wm. Tooke
    Robt. Lacy             Jno. Gregory
    Tho. Clay              Michael Upchurch
    Jno. Sheppard         Geo. Peeters
    Wm. Little             Jno. Greene
    James Chissell

They not being satisfied with their former unlawfull meeting did the greatest part of them, this day meete together in ye old field called ye Dwell's field & did confederate to not discover who were first Instigators of them & have agreed to persistin ye same as appears by open declaring of Roger Delk that if one suffers they would burn all, so have committed the aforesd persons to custody of Sheriff until they find Security for their appearance at next County Court, etc.

Page 41. 3 Jan. 1673/4. James Ghissett & thirteen others this day at house of Capt. Law. Baker summoned to give acct of their riotous assembling at ye church of Lawn's Creek on 12th of br (sic) last; says he came of his own simple head & invited Geo. Peeter to the meeting.

Roger Delke appeared on complaint of Wm. Sherwood sub Sheriff of this county: this day said we will (spoken in a terrifieing manner) burn all before one shall suffer. Said they met at the Church by reason their taxes were so unjust would not tell who invited him & Cyder which they never had.

Others agreed except Michael Upchurch. Robt Lacy said Wm. Hancock carried him to meeting at Dwell's field said he was at meeting at church & Jno. Sheppard told him of it. Jno. Gregory acknowledged he was at church; that heard at Samuell Cornell's by Samuell Haydon that the levies were unreasonable & there would be a meeting to redress them. Tho. Clay said Wm. Hancock told him there was a warrant out for him & was also the first that told him that the levies were unreasonable & about meeting. He was at the Church. Wm. Hancock was at meeting at the church, but was very obstinate about who told him, etc.

George Peeters was at Church meeting, that James Chissett that morning asked him to go to the church to the meeting. Michll Upchurch was at meeting at Church, but tells no more. Mathew Swann was at the Church 12th br (sic) last; meeting was to agree about redress from their taxes, when asked how he knew their taxes were unreasonably laid said Mr. Mason told him & also Mr. Goring. Said Mr. Goring said he would be at meeting if he did not go from Home, Obstinate about lawfulness of meeting & that all or most of ye County were of his minde.

3 Jan. 1673/4. Jno. Greene was at meeting at church, denys to declaire who first told him of it. Wm. Little went with Jno. Barnes to Meeting at the Church. Jno. Sheppard was with others who agreed to meet at ye church to be redressed from their levies; said he heard the levies were unjust by Samll. Corneill who was told so by Mr. Holte so Mr. Corneill said).

John Barnes was at the Church; sayd he heard the levies were unreasonable by Every Body. Wm. Tooke was at meeting at Church, denys by whom he first heard levies were unreasonable, etc. Warrant to take them into custody until they give security for their appearance at Ware Neck on Tuesday the 6th inst. at the Court there to keep peace, etc.

Signed: Law. Baker, Robt. Spenser.
Separate Warrant for Roger Delke.

Page 43. 2 Jan. 1673/4. Deps. of Fra. Taylor called before Capt. Law. Baker, Mr. Robt. Caufield, & Capt. Robert Spenser concerning meeting on Fryday, 12th br, 1673, at Lawnes Creek Psh. Church; being at home looked out & espyed Jno. Grigory going thru field; called him & asked him to make me a wastcoate, said he would make me to go to church; great part of parish met this morning concerning the levies; was not concerned being no housekeeper, was going to Mr. Caufield's to make measure of one of his men for his freedom clothes & would hollow for me as he came back. We went together, found about half a score of men setting there, etc. Coll. Swann was to have 5000 lbs. tob. for his trouble; others did not come; resolved to speak about it next Sabbath being Sermon day said levy only on this parish; in Interim on Saturday, I being at Mr. Sherwood's, asked to see the list of Levy, was on all the County, which I spake of at the Church.

Page 43. 3 Feb. 1673/4. Assignment Coll. Thos. Swann of all interest in Estate as Admr. of Tho. Stevinton to "ye sd Proctor."
Wit.: Jno. Salway, Fra. Summer.

Page 43. 23 Feb. 1673/4. Discharge from Lt/ Coll. Geo. Jordan, Exor. of Tho. Hunt, to Jno. Barnes.

Page 44. 3 March 1673/4. Jno. Barker, Sr., to Jno. Barker, Jr. Whereas my son, Jno. Barker, Jr., did convey to me on 1 8ber 1673 75 acres of land at Mertins Brandon Psh., Chas. Citty Co. (we hath then being of Surry Co.), which land formerly passed unto him by Ann, my wife; now reconveyed to Jno. Barker, Jr., noe pte of the consideration was ever by me performed.

Page 44. Whereas Mrs. Ann Barker, Mother-in-Law to me, Jno. Barker, Jr., conveyed to me 75 acres of land by deed 2 7ber 1673, noe part performed by me of consideration surrender said land to sd Ann; sd land in Martins Brandon. Acknowledged in open court at Southwarke.

Page 44. 10 Jan. 1673/4. Deed from Wm. Sherwood to Coll. Thos. Swann, Esq., for "within mentioned land," written on backside of a deed from Jno. Salway to Wm. Sherwood. Recorded in this court office 8 March 1671.
Wit.: Law. Baker, Chas. Barham, Richd. Welbecke, Fra. Taylor.

Page 45. 3 Feb. 1673/4. Pow. Atty. from Geo. Lee to Mr. Proctor Respects to wife and rest of yr family have reced nootes from Mr. Besse to Mr. Place for his tot, & for Mr. Wenters, & most of rest I shall gett except Crooketts (not this year). Send you bill of Samll. Magetts for £ 1200 tob. and caske; get me an order for it next court, have demanded it several times; promise to pay it to Coll. Jordan but has never done it, etc.

Page 45. 27 7ber 1673. Tho. Ludwell to Justices of Surry Co. yr Clerk Mr. Watkins being dead I could no less than present ye bearer Mr. Hill to be clerke in his stead because he hath bin so particularly recomended to ye Governors & my care by ye Lord Ffitzharding who hath laid too many obligations on me to denye him any Service & is so ready to advance ye good of this Collony. I suppose he is a Sober man, & I hope will prove able.
14 8ber 1673. When clerke sworne no order to deliver records to him; therefore meet at Mrs. Watkins on Thursday next to see all records & papers delivered to him. Tho. Swann to Capt. Law. Baker, Capt. Robt. Spenser, & Capt. Chas. Barham.
Rect. from Wm. Hill, Clk. of Surry County Court to above gentlemen dated 16th 8ber 1673 for:
    1 new book in folio with a leather cover
    2 new books in folio covered with parchment
    2 old books in folio covered with blue linnen
    3 old books in folio without covers being part
      torne & lost
    13 bundles of papers of several concernments
      as alsoe ye printed & written acts of Assembly.
Wit.: Wm. Edwards, Fra. Meriwether.

Page 46. 3 March 1673/4. Deps. of Wm. Thomson, Jr., aged 16, came to Tho. Worwell's w or 3 days after mischiefe done in my father's tob., saw 1 door down and ye house was hole without any further damage, abt. 800 lbs. of good tob. of ye dep's father in bulke and it was all spoyled.
Teste: Gulielmi Edwards, Cl. Cur., 1673.
Deps. of Wm. Aylett, aged 17. Came to Tho. Worwell's house; heard him say he would turn his cattle in ye tob. house where was Mr. Wm. Thomson's tob., saw door down, etc. Cattle were in, etc.; abt. 800 lbs. of tob. of ye Dep's Masters in ye house.

Page 46. 3 March 1673/4. Deps. of Jno. Skinner and Mary Skinner his wife. Tho. Holmes, Tho. Worwell, and Joshua ffittchett came to deps. house a little before Xmas, last was 12 mos. & requested to sett them over the River, could not having other use for his boate, heard Tho. Holmes say come we will take Mr. Thomson's boate for I have order to carry her to James Alsope to be <u>trimed</u>. Tho. Worwell sd noe we will borrow something of Jno. Skinner & you shall free her, & Joshua & I will Rough.

Page 46. 12 Feb. 1673. 7 Jan. 1673/4. Invy. of Capt. Geo. Watkins presented by Mrs. Eliz. Watkins late wife and co-extx. appr. Wm. Thomson, Rand. Holt, Robt. Spenser, Ffra. Mason, sworn before Lt. Coll. Geo. Jordan, 38,658 lbs. tob.

  trundle bed, stead, cord, and mattress  0060
  1 new sealeskin righening trunk & 1 old one
  1 low brass vadlestock, 1 pr. brass snuffers
   & brass mortar & pestle, 1 brass sausepan
    0080
  21 old books of small volumes  0250
  Kearsye, Lockerham fine Dawlace, 3/4 hummells,
   canvis, 3/4 penistone (Ells of goods),
   sheeting, English soape 15 lb.
  Large andirons, 3 Dernix table carpets, Irish
   stockings, 1 gro. brest gimp buttons, Broad-
   cloth bed, etc., and 1 ham co. 1 pr. pistolls
   and holsters, 83 lb. pewter, 2 old flagons,
   2 pewter candlesticks, 1 pewter cup, Tankard,
   and 1 stone jug  1000
  1 pr. Iron Doggs, xl copper kettle, xl old brass
   kettle, 1 brass skillet, 1 brass skimer, 1
   doz. milk trays, 27 trenchers, 1 old couple
    2000
  1 Silver tankard, 6 silver spoones, 1 silver dram
   cup, 1 small box surveying Instruments, 1
   chaine, 1 pockett compass, and 1 Jacob staft
    0400
  1 diseased negro man called Kiah  04000
  1 woman servant bamed Jennet  01600
  also 1 old small broken silver hatband and
   other articles.

Presented by Mr. Robert Ruffen who married ye relict, 7 7ber 1675. Items marked with an x taken by Elizabeth under will.
(This only includes part of Estate what I wanted to note - V. E. S.)

Page 49. 12 Feb. 1673. Sale of Capt. Geo. Watkins' Estate as given by will to his Cousin Mr. Xo. Watkins, appraised at 19355 lbs. tob., sold for 21049, publique notices given at ye Psh. Churches of this Co. at house of Mrs. Elizabeth Watkin, Wm. Edwards bought 2 oxen for 1210 lbs., a brown steere, 1 blk., 1 red, 1 pied steere for 1310 lbs., 11 pr. shooes, 00440. Other buyers were:

  Mrs. Watkin    Capt. Barham
  Mrs Wm. Thomson   Jno. Price
  Mr. Caufield    Wm. Newsum
  Coll. Jordan    Wm. Sherwood (who bought
  Capt. Spenser      surveyor's instruments)

Page 50. Probate Mary Gilburt's will by Elinor and Mary Gilburt, 7 April 1674. Given at James City by Sr. Wm. Berkeley, Knt., etc.

Page 50. 7 April 1674. Probate Xo. Lewis' will by James Jones. Given at James City by Sr. Wm. Berkeley, Knt., Governor, etc.

Page 51. 7 April 1674. Probate Tho. Well's will by Fra. Hogwood. Given at James City by Sr. Wm. Berkeley, Knt., etc.

Page 51. 7 April 1674. Probate Capt. Geo. Watkin's will by Mrs. Eliza Watkin, relict, and Capt. Chas. Barham.

Page 51. Capt. Robt. Spenser's bond to exors. of Capt. Geo. Watkin for use
of Mr. Xo. Watkin of London for 175 lbs. tob. convenient in Surry Co. Same
for Jno. Price and Robt. Caufield for 771 lbs. tob. Same for Wm. Edwards
and Wm. Sherwood for 9960 of tob. convenient in Surry Co. to the River. Same
for Wm. Sherwood and Wm. Edwards for 1380 lbs. tob. convenient in Surry Co.
 Also for:   Geo. Jordan          Wm. Thomson
             Wm. Newsum           Mathew Swan
             Robert Caufield      Elizabeth Watkin
             Robert Spenser       Chas. Barham
 Wit.: Wm. Sherwood, Wm. Edwards, Geo. Proctor, Ran. Holt, Robert
Spenser, etc.

Page 53. 4 April 1674. Elizabeth Watkin's bond to Robert Spenser as counter
security for 6354 lbs. tob. due in settlement with Est. Due Mr. Xo. Watkin
of London, etc.
 Wit.: Jno. Thomas, Wm. Edwards.

Page 53. 22 March 1674. Deed lease to lett farm from Geo. Corpe and Gartrid
Corpe his wife of Surry Co., planter, to Thos. Lane of same, planter, for
100 acres of land adj. Geo. Foster and Thos. Ware toward the land Mr. Salway
bought of Richd. Tias, being land conveyed from Edw. Pettway to us, Geo.
and Gartrid my wife, leases house and everything for 99 years from date for
a valuable sum paid, and empower Mr. Wm. Sherwood to ackn. in open court.
 Wit.: Tho. Senior, Wm. Edwards.

Page 54. May 1674. Den. Roomis pow. atty. to Wm. Sherwood in difference with
Warsh Mr. Benj. Harrison as atty. for Mr. John Cary.

Page 54. 5 May 1674. Wm. Heath (Adam Heath Security) bond as guardian of
Roger Gilbert, orphant of Elinor Gilbert, for his estate 4 cattle, 1 sow,
14 shoots, noe pigs in hands of Wm. Heath, but when he finds them to give
bond, etc.

Page 54. 10 June 1654. Deed Thomas Rolfe to Wm. Corker 150 acres of land
between Smith's Fort old field & the Divell's Woodyard Swampe & all houses,
etc., being due unto the sd Rolfe by guift from the Indyan King.
 Wit.: Ja. Mason, Edmund Howell.
On backside assigned by Wm. Corker to Wm. Barber, 22 Aug. 1654.
 Wit.: Richd. Webster, Sam Suklemoe.
Assigned by Wm. Barber to Roger Gilbert and Xo. Mitchell on 1 Dec. 1654.
 Wit.: Wm. Marriott, Jno. Brady.
Interest assigned by Chr. Mitchell to Roger Gilbert.
 Wit.: Jno. Corker.

Page 55. 2 June 1673. Joseph Antrobus has delivered to Robt. Caufield 3 cows,
Sweetin, Old Cherry, and Young Cherry to secure £.6.8 sterl. to be paid
Caufield at the next returne of ye shipe from London to Va. in such goods
as Caufield shall give a note for at first cost out of the Shoppe in London.
 Wit.: Owen Macke, Wm. Proser.

Page 56. 5 May 1674. Lt. Tho. Busby's mark for cattle, etc., is a crop on
the Rt. Ear, 2 slitts in the crop, & a halfmoone on the left ear. His daughter, Janis, mark is acrop on the Left Ear, 2 slitts in the crop, and a half
moone on the right ear.

Page 56. 6 July 1674. Richd. Smith's sale to Richd. Drew of 2 steers 6 yrs.
old apeace named Swann and Sweetinge. To be taken as bond for 9 hundred
weight of tob. and caske.
 Wit.: Ffran. Sumner and Henry Baker.

Page 56. 7 July 1674. Deps. of Ffra. Taylor aged 43, bin several times at
(Peter?) Bartletts and by my desire have obtained sometimes a pottle of
ale, sometimes a gallon, and have bought both rum & sugar of him. Sometimes
requesting a bottle to be drunk in his house, sometime to be made in flipp
with Rum, sugar, and beer, and have passed a bill for rum and sugar to Mr.

Bartlett on behalf of Mr. Richd. West. Ale was sold at 15 lb. tob. a gallon. Same deps. of Roger Delke, aged 40.

Page 56. 6 June 1674. Com'n. of Capt. Samll. Swann as one of the Commissioners of Surry Co. to be of Sworun (Quorum?) by William Berkeley, dated at Greene Spring.

Page 57. 23 March 1673/4. Edward Pettway releases all right to the Pines mentioned in within deed (deed gift for 100 acres of land to Geo. Corpe) & he to take all his land on the N. side of path comonly called B...nd's Path.
Wit.: Jno. Phillips.
Bond to acknowledge above in open court.
Wit.: Wm. Blunt, ackn. 7 July 1674.

Page 57. 7 July 1674. Rect. of William Forman for a head of cattle belonging to Luke Mizell, rec'd of Jno. Smith.

Page 57. 14 June 1674. Report of Will. Browne & Robt. Caufield on Exam of debts due Jno. Bishop by Mr. Geo. Proctor as marrying the extx. of Maj. Wm. Marriott; with consent and good liking of sd Bishop and Proctor, awarded amt. due Bishop out of Maj. Marriott's Est.

Page 58. 28 May 1674. On back of Pattent dated 28 Jan. 1662 for 480 acres granted to Jno. King; assigned all right being just 200 acres from Jno. King to Jeremiah Ellis.
Wit.: Edward Greenwood, Jno. Warren.
Confirmed by Jane Plow who disowns any claim she has to sd Patent.
Wit.: Jno. Bishop, Geo. Foster.
7 Sept. 1674. Reacknowledged by Jno. King with notation "his heirs, Exors. & Admrs."
Wit.: Geo. Proctor, Mrs. Marriott.

Page 59. 1 7ber 1674. Deed from Roger Delk of L. C. P., Surry Co., planter & Rebecka Delk his wife to Robt. Lacy of same psh. planter for parcel of land in fork of branch issuing out of Lawns Creek to Delk's head line, to S. line of land sold by Delk to Walter Bartlett, to 1st station.
Wit.: Jno. Goring, Wm. Hancock.

Page 60. 22 April 1674. Bond of Tho. Hux to deliver certain personal property to Mary Rawlings, dau. of Jno. Rawlings, dec., when of age or married & to Jno., son of Jno. Rawlings, dec'd., when of age. If Mary die before of age or married her share goes to Jno. If Jno. died before of age his share returns to Tho. Hux.
Wit.: Roger Potter, Jno. King.

Page 60. 7 Aug. 1674. Roland Place to Doctor Geo. Lee to implead actions in court.

Page 60. 1 7ber 1674. Deps. of Tho. Lane, aged 39, summoned with Jno. Price to appraise est. of Thos. Taylor, sworn before Capt. Chas. Barham; to meet at Mr. Arthur Long's house; when got their sheriff (Jno. Salway, sub. Sheriff) gone to Austin Honicutt's Long said he would go with them to Sheriff when came against Taylor's house Long said some things there you must appraise; appraised them; went to Austin Honicutt's; met Shff. all went together to Jno. Kindreds; appraised a heifer Sheriff & Mr. Long made up their accts. We signed them by generall consent went to the Tenn House; appraised a patt. Mr. Long would have taken all and pay all. Mr. Salway refused etc.
Jno. Price, aged 24, same deps.

Page 61. 3 May 1674. Wm. Hare is indebted to Mr. Fra. Mason & hath departed etc. Exon. issued by Chas. Barham to Sheriff. By virtue of which attached 1 heifer at Mathew Swan's by Jno. Salway, Subvice Com'r.

Page 61. 1 7ber 1674. Rebecka Delke wife of Roger Delke relinq. dower in land sold by husband to Robt. Reynolds on 2 Xber 1671.

Page 61. 1 Aug. 1674. Deed exchange signed by George Foster & Elizabeth Foster his wife of Southwark Psh., planter to Samll. Plow of same psh., planter for land, whereby sells Plow 200 acres land by Patt. whereon Geo. and Elizabeth lately dwelt bounding on S. side of W. branch of Crouches Creek (anciently so called) by Swamp dividing this land from land that was formerly Tho. Woodhouse S. by E. parallel with Woodhouse land by marked trees from thence N. by W. parallel with Jno. Troy's land to marked tree standing in reedy swamp which is above sd western branch & down sd swamp to beginning which formerly belonged to Geo. his father, dec'd.
    Wit.: Tho. Crues, Jno. King.

Page 62. Estate of Tho. Harte dec'd is Dr. 7ber 1673.
| | |
|---|---|
| funeral charges | 0600 |
| pd a steere to Jno. Sheppard | 0300 |
| pd Wm. Edwards for drawing this account | 0500 |
| Whole estate | 14250 |
| Debts paid | 8443 |
| Rest | 5807 |
| My wife's third part is | 1935 |

Rest due to three orphants of Tho. Harte, dec., viz.: by Tho. & Robt. Harte Subscribed 3 9ber 1674 by William Newsum.

Page 62. Titheables 10 June 1674 Glory be to God.
   By Benjamin Harrison 59 psh.   3  53  Col. Jordan's list
      James Jordan's with Arthur Jordan
      Tom Jordan's with Geo. Jordan
      Owen Morick & Tom Lewis are shoemakers.

Page 63.
| | | |
|---|---|---|
| By Ni. Meriwether | 25 | |
| By Robt. Spenser | 83 | Maj. Browne is chg. with Berkeley |
| Psh. | 1 | |
| Coll. Swann to psh. | 07 | |
| Mr. Thomson to psh. | 7 | |
| | 238 | Southwark |
| Lawnes Creek Parish | | |
| Rand. Holt's list Hog Island | 17 | |
| Chas. Barham's list | 47 | |
| Robt. Caufield's list | 53 | |
| Law. Baker's list | 65 | |
| Capt. Law. Baker chgd with Geo. Prime (or Prince) | 182 | |

Page 64. 11 May 1674. Appr. Estate of Jno. Warren, dec'd presented by Mary Warren, relict and admx., apprs. James Reddick, Richd. Bridges, Richd. Harris, Jno. Price. Sworn before Capt. Law. Baker & presented for recording 3rd 9ber 1674 by Jno. Denfield who married sd relict.
| | |
|---|---|
| 1 Cattaile bed and bolster | |
| 1 old rug | |
| 2 old blankets | 0300 |
| Total | 18,111 lbs. tob. and caske |

Page 65. 28 8ber 1674. Deed exchange signed Samuell Plowe & Jane Plowe his wife to Geo. Foster, planters, sells that plantation bought of Richd. Case containing 100 acres on W. side of Gray's Creek called Hollowing Poynte and the middle neck adj. it bounded with head of the Spring Swamp to end of the Sandy valley on N. side, runs E. by marked trees from Sandy Valley to Swamp betwixt middle neck & Haystack Swamp.
    Wit.: Wm. Rookeings, Edmund Howell.

Page 65. 3 9ber 1674. Letter Atty. from Capt. Law. Baker to friend Jno. Browne of Carolina to collect debt from Francis Thom.

Page 66. 23 8ber 1674. Deed sale from Thomas Senior of Southwark Psh. to Jno. Price of L. C. P., for 50 acres part of a dividert on which Senior now lives on the Great Swamp between the land of Jno. Bishop & Myne,

beginning at a deep valley about 100 yds N. from the foot path from my house to Jno. Bishop's, up the head of the Swamp, S. into the woods E. from place begun at up the deep valley to a hollow run, thence S. into woods parallel thehead of the 1st Southern line on the E. side.
Wit.: Wm. Edwards, Wm. Hill.

Page 66. 8 May 1674. On attachment Ro. Caufield vs Joseph Antrobus, Jno. Salway Subvice <u>comes</u> attached parcel land & housing 12 May.

Page 66. 10 June 1674. On attachment Thos. Crow vs Est. Cornelius Cordipaine attached 11 hogs, shoats, and pigs. 11 June 1674.

Page. No date. Recorded about 9ber 1674. Petition of Robert Lee to the Commissioners of Surry Co. to be released out of Prison; says he was in error.

Page 66. 16 8ber 1674. On backside conveyance land Thos. Busby to Roger Potter recorded 7ber 1671, assigned by Roger Potter to Geo. Midleton "within bill of sale for land."
Wit.: Wm. Rookings and Jno. Mosse.

Page 67. 4 9ber 1674. On backside lease of parcell of land from Geo. Corpe & Gartrid his wife to Tho. Lane recorded 9 May 1674, assigned by Thos. Cane (<u>sic</u>) to Thos. Gibbons.
Wit.: Wm. Sherwood, Wm. Hill.

Page 67. 4th 9ber 1674. Deps. of Wm. Swett aged 37 years says was in company of Jno. Dunstan last May two years, in Wm. Smith's house in Towne & Jno. Dunstan said he had given foale of mare that always came to Mr. Mason's house, to the child of Wm. Smith & asked me to mark it & deliver it to the child for her use & I branded it with Wm. Smith's mark.

Page 67. 3 9ber 1674. Rect. from Jno. Clarke and Wm. Clarke to Edward Warren for full of our whole estates.
Wit.: Wm. Thomson.

Page 67. Continuation indebtedness estate Maj. Wm. Marriott to Mr. Geo. Proctor as marrying the Relict, from p. 37 this book.

Page 68. Blank.

Page 69. 23 Sept. 1674. By Wm. Berkeley, Gov. and Capt. General of Va.; remits fines of Mathew Swan and the other poor men fined in Surry County Court, provided they acknowledge their faults in the county Court.

Page 69. 16 June 1671. On backside Pattent of Mr. Thos. Hunt for 836 acres of land in Surry Co. dated 14 March 1666 was written: the 836 acres taken up and surveyed by Capt. Thos. Flood, decd., and Mr. Arthur Jordan, who at the request of Mr. Tho. Hunt were willing to take out pattent in their own names he paying for survey and patent they reserved to themselves 100 acres to each of them at E. end and the other 636 to Thos. Hunt's, which 200 acres they settled during lifetime, or Mr. Tho. Hunt as his Exor. Geo. Jordan inserts this acknowledgement being his order upon his death bed.
Wit.: Geo. Proctor, Nath. Knight.

Page 69. 5 Jan. 1674/5. Pow. atty. from Thos. Pittman, Sr., to loving friend Wm. Sherwood, to answer or implead in court, etc.

Page 70. 5 Jan. 1674/5. Deed sale from Francis Grey and Mary Grey his wife, planter, to Tho. Crews, planter, for pcell of land called Haystack Neck, near mouth of Grey's Creek, quantity not known, bounded E. by Thos. Grey, S. by Geo. Foster & the sd Thos. Crews & N. by W. by lands of Coll. Thos. Swann, Esq., said land being marked by agreement by both parties.
Wit.: Wm. Thompson, Fran. Sumner.

Page 70. 26 Jan. 1674/5. Acct. of tob. Jno. Dunford has paid for Estate of Jno. Warren more than allowed; to appraisers for a/c James Minsey has us a bill in appraisement & to Dr. Francis Taylor. Total 30 lbs. Bond of Jno. Dunford to Lt. Richd. Skinner and James Griffin for 30,000 lb. tob. convenient to the River for counter security for a bond of even date for estate of Robt. Warren, son of Jno. Warren, dec., of L. C. P.
Wit.: Roger Delk, Wm. Edwards.

Page 70. 4 March 1672/3. Reced. 29 Jan. Jan. 1674/5. Pow. atty. from James James of Chas. Citty Co. to Wm. Sherwood to appear in all suits for him personally or as Exor., Xo. Lewis.

Page 71. 25 Jan. 1674/5. Jeremiah Ellis to Maj. Browne saying he cannot come to Court as his wife is newly brought to bed and now lieth in with none but myself to look to her.

Page 71. 25 Jan. 1674/5. Pow. Atty. Wm. Rookeings to Elias Osborne to confess jmt. to Ri. Hill for 1 Bbl. salt porke etc.
Wit.: Tho. Busby, Tho. Mudgett.

Page 71. 14 Nov. 1674. Pow. Atty. from Thos. Marston to Wm. Sherwood to Collect balance on Wm. Roland's bond.

Page 71. 25 Jan. 1674/5. Pow. Atty. Wm. Nance to Mr. Sherwood to answer suit of Jno. Causey.
Wit.: Edwd. Oliver, Donell Williams.

Page 71. 16 March 1674/5. Report of Will Browne, Rich. Welbecke & Fra. Meriwether in difference between Mr. Jno. Barker and Mr. Richard West; stated a/c Ric. West is Dr. 1674 for several items including tob. sold to Mr. Sam'l. Shrimpton in New England, Hides sold in New England to 4 hamakcoes etc. totaling 58,12,06. He is Cr. with items including "french heeled shoes delivered to Jno. Barker," making of pickle, Joshua Barker's passage to New England and clothing and necessities and for his dyet, washing and lodging from 22 May 1673 until last 8ber 1674 (allowing 11,00,00 for this but could not agree on it) totaling 58,12,06.

Page 71. 15 March 1674/5. Pow. Atty. Will. Rollinson to Elias Osborne in business in Surry Court in this Instant March 16th.
Wit.: N. Wyatt.

Page 72. 28 Jan. 1674/5. Pow. Tho. Hudgett to Elias Osborne to confess jmt. to Coll. Thos. Swann and to Fra. Sowerby.
Wit.: Wm. Rookinge, Jno. Legrande.

Page 72. 16 March 1674/5. Order past us Est. Capt. Geo. Watkin for fees due Wm. Sherwood Sub Sheriff itemized 900 lb. tob. and 20 s.

Page 73. 12 Feb. 1674. Henry Randolph states that Wm. Rookings has in his possession a negro woman, jointly purchased by Jane, the mother of said William, and me, Henry Randolph, the subscriber (now God being pleased to take, William my son to himself), I doe hereby confirm to William and his heirs all my right and title etc. to said negro woman...provided if said Wm. Rookings and his children should dye without heirs, then the whole stock, descending from said negro, return to ye heirs of me ye said Henry ...anything to the contrary notwithstanding.
Signed: Geo. Lee, Wm. Randolph.

Page 73. 16 March 1674/ On back of a sale of land in Surry County, made by Wm. Marrilowe and wife to James Alsope, bearing date 16 Aug. 1670, the original being recorded in this county office. James Alsope and Judith his x wife, for valuable considerations, assigned same to Edmund Howell of Surry County.
Signed: Wm. Edwards, Jno. Salway.

Page 74. 14 Nov. 1674. Wm. Berkeley appointed Robert Spenser High Sheriff of Surry County.

Page 74. 4 May 1675. Benjamin Thompson, aged 34, testified.

Page 74. Ebenezer Kirtland, aged 19, testified concerning happenings at Geo. Proctor's.

Page 74. 4 May 1675. Eleanor Kyrtland, aged 19 years, testified about happenings at Geo. Proctor's Sworn before Coll. Thos. Swann, Esq., Lieut. Col. Geo. Jordan, and Maj. Wm. Browne.

Page 75. 4 May 1675. Capt. Robert Spenser testified concerning same.

Page 76. 5 May 1675. Isabella Forbus, aged 50, testifies concerning same.

Page 76. 4 May 1675. Thomas Pittman, Sr., aged 60, examined sayeth What he knew about the happenings at Geo. Proctor's.

Page 77. 4 May 1675. On the back of an Order (26 Jan. 1674), 26 July 1674, On obedience to this Order Wee have viewed the within named David Williamson and Albert Albertson and doe find as Justly due upon balance of Rent...to Christmas last the sum of 5197 pounds of tobacco and seaven barrels, two bushels and one-half of Indian corn, and nine bushels of wheat when it is acknowledged due by said defendant.
Law. Baker. Rob. Spenser.

Page 77. 4 May 1675. Know all men that I, Thomas Hunt, doe binde over to Robert Cartwright sec. of Debt which Cartwright is bounde to Maj. Browne. Signed: Geo. Foster, Thos. Gibbons.

Page 78. 4 May 1675. Deposition of Thos. High, aged 78, concerning Geo. Proctor.

Page 80. A Petition to the Rt. Hon. William Berkeley, Capt. General of Virginia, by Henry Francis, most humbly sheweth: the Deponent, about ten years ago, purchased of John Legrand a parcel of land in Surry County containing about one hundred and fifty acres, and have possessed it peaceably and quietly...being informed that his land is escheat land, and desires that he be satisfied in regard to this.
A jury was ordered impanneled of the neighborhood to inquire whether the said land doth escheat to his Majestie, or not, and return said inquisition to the Sec....this sufficient warrant. 16 Nov. 1674.
Signed: Wm. Berkeley.
To: Thos. Ludwell, Esq., Escheate Genll. of Va., or his Deputy.
Deputes Wm. Edwards to execute this writ, provided he act according to the laws and customes of the Collony. 17 Nov. 1674. Rec. 29 Apr. 1675.

Page 81. 1 Jan. 1674. David Owen, of the Citty of London, appoints his friend, Thomas Barlow of ye Upper Parish of Isle of Wight County, planter, in Virginia to be his lawful attorney for all bills, bonds, etc., in his Majestie's Collony in Va. Rec.: 5 May 1675.
Wit.: Geo. Proctor, Thos. Cocke.

Page 82. 26 June 1675. Christopher Brasse, aged 25 years or thereabouts, sayeth that on that Monday the 21st instant in the morning, the Deponent met with Nicholas Paine, his fellow servant, in the mount, and asked him how he durst throw bricks at his master, the said Nicholas replied: a plague take the d...gate, if it had not been for that I would have hit him. This Deponent answered him that he did believe it would be the dearest brick that ever he threw in his life, etc., etc.
Signed: Xpher Basse.

Page 82. 26 June 1675. The Deposition of Phoebe Jeweller, aged 21 years, saith Sweeping off the porch, saw Nicholas, servant with this deponent to Coll. Thos. Swann, Esq., throw five or six bricks, or brick bats at his master.

Page 82. 26 June 1675. Deposition of Mary, an Indian servant of Coll. Thos. Swann, Milking, she saw two bricks thrown at her master.

Page 83. 5 May 1675. Wm. Spring against the Est. of Warburton for 700 lbs. of tobacco. By virtue of a writ, May 1675, what tobacco was due to sd. Warburton is in the hands of Thos. Crews and Thos. Ironmonger.

Page not given. Wee, subscribed by the Grand Jury, present, doe present as Followeth: Persons not frequenting the Church: I, Thomas Clarke, presenting myself, and:

| | |
|---|---|
| Nathaniel Knight | Henry Briggs |
| Wm. Rookinge | Barth. Owen |
| Wm. Nance | Rich. Parker |
| Geo. Midleton | Jno. Moss |
| Rich. Tias | Thos. Senior |
| Edmund Howell | Jno. Orchard |
| Old Mrs. Symonds | John Barker, Jr. |
| Wm. Short | Wm. Harvey |
| Wm. Draper | Edward Greene |
| Long John Phillips | Jno. Hunnicutt |
| James Watkins | Addam Heath |
| Jno. Miniard | Thos. Busby |
| Rich. Royes | Thos. Buirde |
| Daniell Williams | Jno. Sminner |

On back of attachment by Wm. Spring agst. Est. of Warburton for 700 lbs. of tobacco, 6 May 1675, signed by Maj. Wm. Browne that tobacco was in the hands of Thos. Crewes and Thos. Ironmonger. Rec.: 9 July 1675.

The names of the following presented for wrong doing:

| | |
|---|---|
| Rich. Welbecke | Thos. Clarke |
| Robt. Burgess | Thos. Sowerby |
| Jno. King | Fra. Hogwood |

Court order, fated 26 Jan. 1674, requesting Capt. Law. Baker, Capt. Robert Spenser in regard to exors. of Capt. George Watkins, deceased and find balance due to Wm. Aloorson, 3 July 1675.

Judith Randolph writes to Mr. Benjamin Harrison about business and thanks him for assistance, 7 April 1675.

Page 84. Deposition of Jno. Bardy, aged 74, concerning Jno. Watkins, Geo. Proctor and himself. 6 July 1675. Dep. of Henry Watkins, 21 years.

Page 85. William Gray sold to Jno. Salway a mare 12 Oct. 1675. Testified by by William Buttler and Sion Hill. John Salway assigned to Mathias Marriott, he assigned to Jno. Stocke, who assigned it to Geo. Proctor.
Testified by W. Arnoll.

Page not given. 5 July 1675. Thomas Baker requests a letter of reference from Mr. Salway.

Page not given. A letter from Jno. Jennings, Clerk of the Court of Isle of Wight County, 1 May 1675, and signed by the Court's Order to the Hon. Coll. Thomas Swann, Esq., and the Worshipful Justices of Surry County. "This day at a Court held for Isle of Wight County, the Hon. Coll. Joseph Bridger, Esq., and the rest of the Worshipful Justices Ordered and Commanded me to signify to you Honor & ye rest of the Worshipful Justices of your County, that they are both willing and ready to treat and concludewith you about the laying out and bounding of Isle of Wight and Surry County, and that ye Honor and ye Rest of the Gentlemen may find by then that they have no thoughts of porogation in this necessary work, but to finish and end it in a friendly & Honourable way without charge and further trouble to the peace and comfort of the Inhabitants on both sides and they have appoynted certaine Gentlemen appoynted for that purpose to treat and conclude about it and have thought fitt that on Whitsun Tuesday next their may be a meeting but if ye Honorables think it may not be then convient, they request your Hon. to appoynt the day and place for meeting & that your speedy answer may be returned here in

& this day they thought good to move you with in the behalfe of themselves and the Inhabitants, Etc." 9 May 1675.

Page 86. At a Court held at Southwarke for this county on this day, 4 May 1675. This day was produced and read at Court by the Hon. Col. Tho. Swann and a Letter from Capt. John Jennings and Importing an offer of the Honorable Coll. Joseph Bridger and the Justices of the County of Isle of Wight to ascertain the dividing line between that County & this which Letter was by the said Coll. Swann and the whole Court received with kind and hearty acceptance and the amicable tenour thereof deserving noe less the termes being Honorable and convenient for the peace and satisfaction of the Inhabitants and sufficient evidence of the worth and prudence of the proposal, Coll. Swann and the Coms. of this County hath Therefore unanimously commanded me to return this answer that they doe most willingly Imbrace the Motion and will by the Grace of God, Health and Weather permitting, attend the Gentlemen of that County upon Whitsun Tuesday at Harding's Mill, that is to say Coll. Thos. Swann and two or three of the Coms., not doubting but then and there to finde soe equall and concordant a proceeding as may bring a satisfactory end to th s affaire this by order of the Court is signed at Southwarke the day and yeare above written. Ye Honorable and most Humble & Obedient servant, William Edwards, Clerk. 9 May 1675.

At Southwarke, in Surry Co., 16 Aug. 1675, Wm. Thompson, minister, to the Governor in regard to unorthodox preaching by Robert Parke, a young man lately arrived, and residing at the house of Mr. Randolph Holt, in Hog Island, without permission or consent of Wm. Thompson, who is Minister in the Parish. On July last at Lawnes Creek Church, Parke, at present sick in Isle of Wight County, This preaching brought about by Mr. Holt and encouraged by him and invited Inhabitants in next Parish below to hear him.

Page 87. John Brasseur, of ye County of Nansemond, makes John Rugherhood of Surry County, his power of Attorney.
Teste: Henry Bailey, and John Brasseur, Jr. 10 7ber 1675.

Deed of gift from David Andrews and wife Elizabeth to their only son, David Andrews, 8 7ber 1675.
Teste; Charles Barham, Wm. Sherwood.

Page 89. Elizabeth, wife of Francis Hogwood, and her second husband a gift to Elizabeth Beckwith, orphan, she being godmother to said orphan; also to Edward Oliver. If orphan die or Marry, to go to Grace Beckwith, her sister. 7 7ber 1675.

Grace Warren, wife of Ed. Warren, a gift to her grandchild and god-daughter Grace Beckwith, orphan, also to Edward Oliver. If Grace die to her sister Elizabeth. 7 7ber 1675.

Rober Potter, bound for debt which Minyard owed Swann. 7 7ber 1675.

Fra. Mason and Arthur Allen appointed Com. of Surry County by Wm. Berkeley. 2 Aug. 1675.

Page 91. 25 Aug. 1675. Wm. Duke requests Thos. Busby to appear at Court for him against Roger Potter and Henry Briggs, Notice for High Sheriff sent by sonne of Mr. Thompson from house of Wm. Rookings and at his wife's funeral. 25 Aug. 1675.

Deposition of Thomas Barlow, aged 40, concerning a horse race between George Proctor and Jno. Price.

Deposition of Thomas Adams, aged 42, concerning horse race between Seward's horse and Proctor's. 7 Oct. 1675.

Page 92. 13 7ber 1675. Richard Walabancke, being lame, did not appear in Court on time.

BOOK II, 1671-1684        99

Page not given.  Thomas Bird being sick, his family could not attend court.
Date same.

Page not given.  30 Aug. 1675.  Those whose names are signed below were appointed to view the dead body of James Goodridge, and found no wound, or mark, believe he was sick from natural causes and lay down in the Swamp and died.  Signed: John Rutherford    Rob. Burgess
                Francis Hogwood     Will Simons
                Roger Potter        Henry Francis
                Thomas Bentley      Wm. Carpinter
                Jno. LeGrand        Jno. Collyere
                Sam. Mathews        Thos. Tine

Page 96.  6 Jan. 1675.  Ind. between Giles Bland, Esq., Charles Citty County & Walter Bartlett, of Surry Co., for 16,000 lbs. tob., two parcels of land, parts of the division of Edward Bland, dec., in Lawnes Creek Neck Parish in Surry County adj. Roger Delk...near Deboll's field...Sold by Giles Bland...against him the said Giles Bland, his heirs, etc., against Edward Bland, Theodosia Bland, both uncles of said Giles Bland...and against Edward Bland, the sonne and heir of Edward Bland, deceased & his heirs, etc.  Giles Bland, attorney of Jno. Bland, Esq., his Father.

Page 97.  5 Jan. 1675.  Ind. between Giles Bland, Esq., Charles Citty Co., and Edward Tanner for 14000 lbs. tob., 150 acres in Lawnes Creek Parish, Surry Co., now in tenure of John Barnes and Widow Tooker or some of them... being a divident of land of Mr. Edward Bland, deceased, & defends Edward Tanner against all claims of Edward Bland as heir of Edward Bland, his father, deceased, or any son or sons.

Page 98.  5 Jan. 1675.  Giles Bland makes Robert Kae his attorney...deeds to Tanner and Bartlett.

Page 99.  25 Jan. 1675.  Martha Marriott, Surry County, makes over her man servant, Thos. Bagg(?) to Mr. Ni. Meriweather for security in debt to him.

Page not given.  25 Jan. 1675.  Jno. Gray...planter, grants or letts to Jno. Moring land at head of Grey's Creek, quantity not known.
  Wit.: Jno. Watkins, Fra. Sumner.

Page not given.  25 July 1675.  Robert Ruffin to Thos. Giles of Nansemond County, my plantation that my late deceased father, Wm. Ruffin, of Isle of Wight County, lived on at the Cypress and another patent not out of land Office to Giles, exempting 200 acres formerly deceased father's, to Katherine Thornton, 25 July 1675.
  Wit.: Edm. Prime, Eliza Ruffin, Robert Ruffin, Wm. Ploie?

Page 100.  1 Jan. 1675.  Ind. between Wm. Hux, Surry Co., and George Proctor of sd county...parcell of land at Croos Creek to Grey's Creek.
  Wit.: Tho. Ironmonger, Richard Greene.

Page not given.  20 Jan. 1675.  Jno. Bird constitutes his wife, Ann Bird, his attorney.
  Wit.: Thos. Dunn, Ni. Witherington.

Page not given.  20 Jan. 1675.  Roger Rawlings appoints his father-in-law, Richard Skinner, his attorney.

Page 101.  25 Jan. 1675.  Wm. Hux...sells to Edmund Howell land in Southwarke Parish in Ware Neck, part of a divident there where Wm. Hux now lived, adjoining Thos. Jenning's old field...50 acres.
  On back of bill of sale...made by Wm. Warrilow wife to James Alsoope 15 Aug. 1670, the original recorded Oct. 1670, rec. 20 March 1674.  Edmund Howell to Wm. Heath all right and title to the land, 18 ber 1675.
  Signed: Edmund Howell, Rebecca Howell.
  Wit.: Henry Baker, Rich. Wilbeck, Wm. Edwards, John Edwards.

Page not given. 18 Dec. 1675. Richard Hill appoints his friend Jno. King his attorney against William Rookings in a debt to obtain judgment.

Page 102. 26 Jan. 1675. Ann Kersey for love etc. to her son Jno. Kersey binds her son to Richard Brassier as an apprentice until he is 21 years old. Certain provisions are made in this agreement.
Signed: Ann Kersey, Rich. Barker, Geo. Lee, Wm. Edwards.

Page 103. 16 Jan. 1675. Thos. Adams, aged 41, made a deposition concerning Coll. Swann and a sloop, and William Spring. Edward Warren is also mentioned.

Page 105. 24 Jan. 1675. Alexander Davison, planter, makes Adam Tapley his atty. to recover from John Bird all debts, etc.
Signed: Rich. Carlisle, Ann Sizer.
Adam Tapley signed over to Wm. Rookings.

Page 106. 28 March 1676. Jno. Flood acknowledged receipt from Eskiah Bunnell what he had of Jno. Flood that came from Flood's father.
Signed: Jno. King, Ralph Ratchelle.

Page 106. 28 March 1676. Depositions of Margarett Allen, aged 28, concerning Mr. Richard Hill, and Mr. Lee.

Page 106. 10 April 1676. Deposition of Mary Fletcher, aged 28, concerning Mrs. Jane Hill, wife of Richard Hill.

Page 110. 14 Apr. 1676. Jno. Price of Surry Co. sells to Robert Ruffin 300 acres bequeathed to Jno. Price by will and test. of Geo. Watkins, deceased.
Signed: Jno. Price, Mary Price.
Wit.: Edmond Prime, Timothy Walker.

Page 111. 1 Jan. 1672. Thos. Busby, of Surry, moving, sells to Edward Green land on Blackwater Swamp.
Acknowledged in Court 1676.
Wit.: Jno. King, Wm. Nance.

Page 111. 17 April 1676. Thos. King to appear in Court for Thos. Blayton.

Page 111. 23 Feb. 1676. Susanna Jones, being lame, appoints Nicholas Jonson to appear in Court for her against Wm. Newsum.

Page 111. 17 Apr. 1676. Tho. Hone appoints Wm. Edwards his atty.
Wit.: Fra. Mason, Edward Ramsey.

Page 112. 17 April 1676. Martha Williams, widow, testifies to Justices of Surry concerning Capt. Charles Barham & Robt. Caufield on her husband's estate.

Page 112. 5 April 1675. Richard West, of Boston in New England, appoints his friend, Mr. Charles Barham, of Surry County, in James River, Virginia, his attorney to see after bonds and interests.
Wit.: Samuel Swann, Fra. Taylor.

Page 112. 29 April 1676. Ind. between Lawrence Baker and Henry Gray, planter, Capt. Lawrence Baker and wife Elizabeth sell Henry Gray 200 acres on second Blackwater Swamp.
Wit.: Hen. Baker, Jno. Baker.

Page 112. 24 April 1675. Richard Leech owes a debt to Thos. Newhouse.
Wit.: Jno. King, Margaret Ellis.

Page 116. 29 Jan. 1675. Walter Vahan indebted to Wm. Edwards.
Wit.: Law. Mizell, Jno. Bishop.

Page 119. 23 June 1676. Thos. Barlow having to be absent from Court, desires certain transactions done for him, relative to Capt. Pittman, Thos. Gibson, Mr. Mason, and Mr. Salway.

Page 119. 8 Oct. 1675. George Marable of James Citty, gives power of attorney to Wm. Edwards to collect debts.
Geo. Mason, Fra. Mason.

Page 119. 10 Aug. 1676. Mr. Edward, Clerk, is to record a gift from Christopher Lewis, deceased, to Katherine Owen, daughter of Bartholomew Owen.
Signed: Bartholomew Owen.

Page 120. 26 March 1677. The following acknowledged debt to the King, Jno. Clemts, Edward Pettway, Wm. Pettway, Wm. Blunt, Thos. Gibons, Jno. Skelton, Mathew Magnis, Stephen Aston, on penalty of 10,000 pounds sterling to keep the peace.

Page 120. 31 March 1677. Surry County Magistrates (Justices of the Peace), Capt. Law. Baker, Lt. Coll. George Jordan, Capt. Barham, and Mrs. Robert Caufield, Capt. Robert Spenser, Mr. Ben Harrison, Capt. Arthur Allen, and Mr. Fra. Mason.

Page 121. 8 March 1676/7. Richard Lawrence is proclaimed a "Rebell & Traytor," to be fined 2130 lbs. tobacco (estate seized to pay it) by Robert Caufield.

Page 121. 1 May 1677. Deposition of Judith Case, aged 36, Concerning the purchase of a servant girl by Mr. Seward. Servant's name is Margaret, and was formerly owned by Henry Brooks.
John Cary, aged 17, testified to same.

Page 121. Deposition of Obedience Dunn, aged 23, wife of Jno. Dunn, concerning ill treatment by Mr. Geo. Lee, of his maid, Mary Fletcher.

Page 124. 18 May 1676. Will. Thomson of Nansemond County, appoints George Proctor his attorney to collect for Robert House of Surry.

Page 126. Year 1677. Margery Chambers delivers to Charles Jarrett, son of Richard Jarrett, his inheritance.
Margery Chambers, Charles Barham, and Wm. Gray.

Page 124. 20 March 1676. Thomas Senior sells to Wm. Edwards "where I live," 150 acres.
Wit.: Wm. Vicers, Isabell Smith.

Page 124. 2 Sept. 1671. On back of a sale made to Joseph Wall by Phillip Huniford for 200 acres, recorded 2 September 1671, was written in effect this: that Joseph and Susan Wall of Surry sold Richard Jordan, Jr., in Surry, land on Blackwater, 1676.
Wit.: Chris. Holleman, Thomas Pittman, Jr.

Page 127. 15 June 1677. Deposition of Jno. Price, aged 27, in regard to Wm. Chambers' gift to his son William Chambers.
William Kelle, aged 31, testified to same.

Page 127. 15 June 1677. Wm. Carpinder, aged 44, testified that Thos. Hux, Jr., had made a certain gift.

Page 127. 15 June 1677. James Sowerby, aged 66, made deposition concerning John Orchard. Thomas Sidway, aged 22, testified about a conversation with Mary Orchard, now wife of Thomas Hux, Jr.

Page 127. 23 June 1677. Various depositions:
Sarah Austin, aged 21, about conversation between Robert Cuddiford and Mrs. Thompson, a threat.
Robert Austin, aged 35, testified that he and his wife, servants to Mrs. Thompson, testified that he and his wife, were persuaded by Robt. Cuddiford and his presant wife to run away to the Southward.

Thomas Mason, aged 35, made deposition.
Ann Kersey, aged 30, made a deposition.

Page 130. 4 July 1677. Wm. Blackburne, aged 26, testified about Jno. Orchard.
Abraham Wallis, aged 28, testified.

Page 130. 3 July 1677. John Clarke, aged 25, testified that three men from Nansemond County, pressed him to show them the way to Roger Rawlings... they had Capt. Long's warrant & paper for Mr. Collins.

Page 130. No date given. Wm. Kitte, aged 37, saith he was ordered by Mr. Long to prepare boats. Kitte went to Long, at Chippoakes & told him boats were small, carrying about eight people. When at Towne, Mr. Alsope said they had all the Governor's goods, etc.

Page 130. Jno. Price, aged 27, made a deposition that at the home of Mr. Long's where Roger Rawlings came that Rawlings was to carry Long "over to Towne," that the Governor was landing with several Judges to "destroy us all." 4 July 1677.

Page 131. 3 July 1677. John King, aged 32, testified about the happening at Geo. Lee's home, when Nathan Reynolds appeared.

Page 131. 4 July 1677. Jeremiah Ellis, aged 34, testified about being at home of Henry Francis and a conversation about Rookings and Robert Lee, also about a horse of Capt. Barham's & Thos. Bentley.

Page 131. 3 July 1677. Wm. Challoner, aged 34, testified concerning Goody Hux, Mrs. Thompson, Jno. Orchard, and Thos. Hux, Jr.

Page 132. 3 July 1677. On deed from Thos. Senior to Jno. Price, 1674, was found assignment by Jno. Price and wife Mary, to Stephen Lewis, his heirs, etc.

Page 132. 14 June 1677. John Grascome appoints his friend, George Lee, of Surry Co., chrurgion, his attorney.
   Geo. Proctor, Arthur Long.

Page 132. 2 July 1677. Thos. Hunt appoints his friend, Jeremiah Ellis, to collect from John Salway.
   Teste: Mary Ellis.

Page 133. 3 July 1677. Thos. Hux, Sr., makes Elias Osborne his attorney.
   Signed: Sarah Tayler, Robert Cuodifer.

Page 133. 4 July 1677. At a Court held for Surry County, Arthur Long appeared in Court with a rope about his neck and on his bond made a statement that he repented of his Rebellion, and on his knees implored pardon of his God and King, etc.

Page 134. 3 July 1677. Jno. Price, aged 22 years, testified that about the twenty-third of last September, the Deponent prisoner at the house of Arthur Allen, heard Capt. Arthur Long command Thos. Gibbons to take his gun and shoot into Allen's cattle; Later, deponent was given leave to go home by Capt. Pittman and Long and to bring dogs in the morning to catch Allen's cattle...some were killed, and Allen's wheat ground in a hand mill, then the deponent was sent back to prison.

Thomas Gibbond, aged 30 years, testified to about the same thing.

Page 134. 3 July 1677. Elizabeth Blesley, about 29 years old, testified that she was Arthur Allen's house when it was taken or seized by Rebells; Joseph Rogers and one man more came armed. About three-quarters of an hour afterward, it was entered by the Rebell Crew, with whom deponent had no discourse that night, but afterwards answered queries about Mr. Allen's plate, where it was hid, etc. Joseph Rogers and a man brought a large

Dutch case to Mr. Allen's house, with about six or seven three pint bottles, etc.

Page 134. 9 July 1677. Mary Hodge, wife of John Cooper, aged 22, testified that shortly after Mr. Arthur Allen was forced from his house by wicked Rebells, her husband found a saddle with bolster, and put them into a chest, but Joseph Rogers came to Deponent's house and demanded three saddles, locked in the chest, pushed deponent away and took them with other things.

Page 135. 16 July 1677. Elizabeth Elisley, aged 29, testified that Capt. Robert Burgess (who afterwards was heard to be called Lieut.) with about seventy other men in Arms, entered the house of Mr. Arthur Allen and seized all his estate that they could find, making havoc etc....inquiring for a man of Mr. Allen's called John Fenley, said he had taken him prisoner; the house was robbed of valuables.

Page 135. 16 July 1677. Jno. Fenley, aged 24 years, testified that being sent by his Master, Mr. Arthur Allen, from James City to Coll. Swann's, from thence to go home to his sd. Master's house, was by Robert Burgess on the road near Southwarke Church, commanded to stand...took his horse, carbine, etc. The deponent was carried a prisoner to the house of Robert Jones in Flower-de-Hundred, thence to Nevitte Wheeler's in Martins Brandon and remained eleven weeks, though he solicited his liberty.

Page 135. 16 July 1677. Walter Tayler, aged 33 years, testified that he saw Rebells at the house of Mr. Arthur Allen commanded by Wm. Rookings, amongst whom were Robert Burgess...Mr. William Simons, who carried the colours, had title of ensign. Those men carried away books and other Possessions of Mr. Allen.

Page 136. 13 August 1677. Charles II allows a Governor for the time being to reside in Virginia except when commanded to England, then appoints Deputy until a new Governor arrives. All lands now possessed by Planters shall be confirmed to owners and heirs etc. Escheat land to be enjoyed by Inhabitants, who pay two pounds of tobacco for every acre, which is the rate set by the Governor. Gov. to try crimes, murders, etc.
  Copia est.: Robert Beverly.

Page 137. Sam Firth, merchant, bound on Voyage, constitutes his beloved friend, Wm. Archer, merchant, and Alex. Sheppard, planter, or either of them Attorney to Collect debts, etc.
  Wit.: Hugh Owen, Lance Fletcher.

Page 138. 2 Oct. 1674. Lott? Richards, of Bristoll, England, merchant, appoints Mr. Robert Caufield, of Surry County, his Attorney to collect debts, wtc.
  Wit.: John Needy, William Morgan.

Page 141. 6 July 1677. Thomas Busby sells to Richard Race (or Pace) one Indian woman called Ann, aged about twenty-five years.
  Wit.: Geo. Lee, John Moring.

Page 143. 3 Sept. 1677. Bartholomew Owen sells to Richard Tias, the elder, 100 acres of land on the North side of Johnseahagen Swamp.
  Wit.: Ni.: Meriweather, Eliza Meriweather.

Page 143. 8 7ber 1677. Bartholomew Owen makes Ni.: Meriweather his Attorney, etc.
  Wit.: Margaret Thomas, Joan Meriweather.

Page 143. 15 7ber 1677. Martin Thorne appoints Wm. Seward his attorney in a suit with Christopher Smith.
  Wit.: Sion Hill, Walter Taylor.

Page 144. 8 7ber 1677. A petition of Ayles Stock, a poor widow and relict of Jno. Stock.

SURRY COUNTY RECORDS

Page 144. 7 4br. 1677. Deposition of Rowland Davies concerning Robert Kae touching his Tithables. Kae had four men servants called James Johnson, Jno. Collins, Evan Humphrey, and John Esquire, also one negro woman called Judy, and Kae himself and myself (being Davies) and Kae a son called Robert Kae.
Roger Delke, about 48 years, testified to the same.

Page 144. 4 8ber 1677. Thos. Watson, aged 30, testified about Owen Myrick, at the house of Fra. Mason. Thomas Gibbons, aged 30, testified also.

Page 145. 15 Nov. 1677. Wm. Gray and John Gray of Surry County, Joint heirs of Thomas Gray, their Brother, deceased, for 4000 lbs. tobacco sell to Thomas Swann, Esq., 100 acres of land at Smith's Fort Creek, or Gray's Creek.
Wit.: Thos. Busby, Robert Penny.

Page 149. Deposition of Alice Marriott, aged 32 years, about a conversation with Wm. Freeman, Lawrence Meazle, Katherine Witherington, and Thos. High, in which Coll. Swann was called "Old Rebell, or Traytor" etc. Katherine Witherington, aged 31, swore to same, as did also Lawrence Meazle, aged 26 years.

Page 149. 6 Feb. 1676. List of pardoned Rebells in the "Late Disloyal Rebellious Collony," etc.

Walter Vahan
Ni. Johnson
Ja. Forbes
Stephen Lewis
Jno. Skinner
Wm. Newitt
Thos. Senior
Samuel Plowe
Geo. Williams
Wm. Blunt
Mayow? Magnus
Alex. Spenser
Wm. Bugby
Geo. Proctor
Fra. Evans
John Phillips, Sr.
Edmund Howell
Edward Davis
Jonas Bennett
Stephen Allen

William Jones
Jno. Hunnicutt
Richard Green?
Jno. Clements
Thos. King
Wm. Heath
Jno. Garvett
Jno. Pulystone
Rob. Evans
Edward Pettway
Tho. Gibbons
Cor. Cordonpaine
Hen. Baker
John Shelton
Robt. Judkins
Samuel Judkins
Wm. Pettway
Thos. High
Geo. Harris
Thos. Pittman, Sr.

Page 150. 16 9ber 1677. John Cary, of London, moving, appoints Benjamin Harrison of Surry County of James River in Virginia his true and Lawful Attorney to collect debts.
Signed: Tim Briggs, Notary Publique.
Wit.: Henry Briggs, John Warner, Timothy Walker.

Page 150. 15 Sept. 1679. Christopher Foster, aged 27, makes deposition that he was at Coll. Swann's house the same day ye late Gov. Sr. Wm. Berkeley sallied out of towne; Coll. Swann, thinking ye county in some danger, sent Deponent to Mr. Busby's to see if any Guards were kept there and wanted to speak to Busby, but found only Mrs. Busby at home, a woman, two men, and Wm. Pickerell, a lame man, etc.

Page 151. 20 June 1677. Robert Welbeck of great Marlowe, Buckinghamshire, apothecary, makes Wm. Browne, of James River, in Va., Gentlemen, his Attorney to collect money, etc., in Virginia.
Wit.: Samuel Looke, Robert Mitford, Thos. Grewe.

Page 154. 14 day of 9ber 1677. John Bird appoints his wife, Ann Bird, his Attorney.
Wit.: Samuel Mathews.

Page 154. 15 9ber 1677. Richard Hill constitutes Elias Osborne his lawful Attorney.
Wit.: Kerper? Miller, Hannah Pickerell.

Page 154. 15 9ber 1677. Wm. Kitto, aged 38, swore that Susannah Jones, widow of said Jones, before her death was at the home of the Deponent and said that if she did not go to liver with Henry Baker, she must perish for her son, Ni. Johnson, " grutched ye victuals she ate," etc. Therefore she would give what she had to Henry Baker and leave her child, Alice, to sd Baker.
Dorothy Killo, aged 34, swore to same.

Page 155. 18 March 1676/7. The following testified that the dead body of Mary Gasgoville, servant to Jno. Salway, found in the Marsh at Gray's Creek, drowned herself. Signed by:

| | |
|---|---|
| Wm. Blunt | Jno. Smith |
| Jno. Clements | Alex. Spenser |
| Thos. Kinge | Jno. Vinson |
| Henry Watkins | Henry Baker |
| Stephen Aston | Edward Pettway |
| Edmond Howell | Jno. Smith |
| Thos. Pittman, Sr. | James Forbes |

Page 155. 16 9ber 1677. Deposition of Thomas Shrewsby, aged 44, in regard to being forced from his habitation; went to John Rutherford's. John Rogers, and Mr. Wm. Rookings, who were then Chief Commander. Mr. John Salway's house was locked, but opened by John Rutherford, Jno. Rogers, and others, entered and drank wine, etc. Nic. Witherington, aged 30, testified to same.

Page 156. 13 April 1676. Capt. Robert Spenser ordered the body of Ann Amy, wife of John Amy, found dead by the Swamp side near her home to be viewed.
Signed:

| | |
|---|---|
| Robert Ruffin | Hen. Hunnicutt |
| Wm. Powsum | Timothy (Walker?) |
| Joseph Rogers | Wm. Chamble |
| Peleg Dunstone | Richard Prime |
| Jno. Kindred | Thos. Lane |
| Ralph Houlston | Wm. Baiden |
| Jno. Hodge | |

Page 156. 4 Aug. 1677. John Senior sells to Wm. Edwards land adjoining Fra. Mason.
Wit.: Francis Everist, Wm. Thompson

Page 157. 3 9ber 1677. Stephen Lewis sells to Wm. Edwards a Molatto boy, Kiketan, seven years old, for 1000 lbs. of tobacco.
Wit.: Jno. Phillips, Nicholas Johnson, Lewis Williams.

Page 157. 14 9ber 1677. Septhen (sic) Lewis sells to Wm. Edwards 50 acres bought of John Price, Price bought of Thos. Senior, 1674. Sold by John Price and wife Mary to sd. Lewis.
Wit.: Robert Spenser, Robert Ruffin.

Page 158. 10 9ber 1670. Julian Allam and Herbert Ferrell sell to Stephen Lewis a horse; Stephen Lewis sells to John Edwards.
Wit.: Wm. Edwards, Tho. Hone?

Page 158. 5 Nov. 1677. Gov. Herbert Jeffries for the better Administration of Justice in the county, etc., to appoint Inferior Courts of Justice and Commissioners for the same. On the 28 June 1642, Commissioners were appointed for every county for keeping monthly courts, and since continued.

On the 2 March 1661, it was said eight men, the most honest and Judicious in the County, eight, or four of them a Quorum, etc. Some to be empowered out of Court to act and do all such things as by ye Laws of England and to be done by Justices of the Peace thereof. These take the oath of allegiance. Now two more persons to be added.

Lt. Col. Geo. Jordan          Capt. Lawrence Baker

SURRY COUNTY RECORDS

        Maj. Wm. Browne                Mr. Robert Caufield
        Mr. Arthur Allen                Capt. Samuell Swann
        Capt. Charles Barham        Capt. Robert Spenser
        Mr. Benj. Harrison            Mr. Nicholas Meriweather
        Mr. Francis Mason be of the Quorum

Page 160. 1 Jan. 1677. Walter Flood acknowledges to have received what was due him from John Cary, Walter Flood, now of age, and from Mr. Arthur Jordan, who was collaterally bound for payment and now discharge John Cary and Benj. Harrison, attorneys and Arthur Jordan.
    Wit.: Geo. Jordan, Chris. Easter.

Page 160. 28 Dec. 1677. John Plough? empowers his friend Wm. Thompson his Atty. in a case pending between him and James Forbesse.
    Wit.: Fra. Berkeley, George Marble.

Page 160. 31 Dec. 1677. Jeremiah Ellis seals to Hezekiah Bunnell 150 acres of land on Chippoakes Creek, adjoining Dr. Lee's land, Richard Hide's land, 100 acres escheat and 50 bought of Richard Hide.
    Wit.: Wm. Thompson, Kath. Thompson.

Page 160. 31 Dec. 1677. Elias Osborne appoints his friend, Geo. Lee, his Atty. in an amount due from Col. Swann.
    Wit.: Francis Shrewsbury, Samuel Parker or Packer.

Page 161. 18 Jan. 1677. John Hodge, who married Margaret the Relict of John Cooper, deceased, claims 2801 lbs. of tobacco and caske due est. on balance of 2724 lbs. on acct. now exhibited. One-third belongs to petitioner (Jno. Hodge) in right of his wife; and the other part to Elizabeth, only child of the deceased, and makes bond for same.

Page 162. 30 Dec. 1677. Probate granted Wm. Cocke on the will of Wm. White.

    18 7ber 1677. Mary Weekes granted probate on the will of Stephen Weekes.

    18 7ber 1677. Tim. Essel, Sen., granted Probate on the Will of Amara Dotson.

    18 7br 1677. Geo. Branch granted probate on the est. of Capt. Corker.

    30 Dec. 1677. Mr. John Goring, on the will of Henry Goard.

    31 Jan. 1677. Jane Owen, on the Est. of Bartholomew Owen.

    31 Jan. 1677. Mary Kindred on the Est. of John Kindred.

Page 162. 8 Dec. 1677. William Rose, Sr., did in his life time Record a mare with increase for the use and benefit of four of his children: Jane, William, Ann and Mary; until the children come of age or married, and then to receive an equal part. Jane, the eldest, married and her husband sold her share to Wm. Rose...now William Rose wants the stock divided, and to be possessed with his half. Wm. Rose is indebted to his sister fifty pounds of tobacco to be wholly theirs. Ann Rose, Mary Rose.
    Signed: William Rose.
    Wit.: Wm. Browne, John Moring.

Page 163. 8 March 1677. James Bish asks Mr. Geo. Lee to present widow Parker into Court for debt owed him. Benj. Harrison.

Page 163. 4 March 1677/8. Henry Clarke, very sick, not able to attend Court, confesses indebtedness to Mr. William Mathews, Murrur Markina, and confesses judgment.
    Wit.: Rand. Holt.

Page 165. 18 Feb. 1677/8. John Rudds, Mariner, appoints Richard James his atty. and implores Mr. Geo. Lee, Atty. for Mr. Grassome for a debt of 400

lbs. of tobacco due him.
Wit.; Robt. Hunnicutt, Robert Grove, Jas. Vinson.

Page 165. 19 March 1677. Sarah Drummond, living in London, England, is a widow of William Drummond, of James City County, Virginia, relict and administrator of her late husband, gave power of Atty. to Capt. Samuel Swann, of Surry Co., Va., to manage the est.
Signed in London, in presence of: Jno. Liddiard, Parton Paul, Jacob Hayes, Joseph Holden.

Page 166. 5 March 1677. Richard Tyas, aged 49 years, sworn said that Mr. Thomas Warren possessed and enjoyed for their own right the Plantation on which John Salway is now seated, commonly called Smith's Fort, about thirty-four years without any suits or troubles, etc., that about twenty-five or twenty-six years since the said Warren did begin to build the same without being forewarned or disturbed by any person and that Mr. Rolfe was then living and lived several years afterward and was commonly at ye said Warren house before and whilst sd house was building, and Mr. Barrott, father to this Barrott, now living and was likewise alive when the house was building...and never did claim any right...noe more the 1200 acres of land ...at mouth of Gray's Creek. Deponent was at Warren's house...with Mr. Warren and Mr. Thos. Rolfe aforesaid and Mr. Mason and others, some time before Warren built brick house, where he saw Mr. Rolfe write a bill of sale with his own hand...did sell from him and his heirs to sd Warren... plantation called Smith's Fort, etc.
Thos. Pittman, Sr., testified to same.

Page 168. 1 March 1677. Ind. between Thomas Blunt, only son of Richard Blunt of Surry Co., deceased, and Thos. Drew, son of Richard Drew, both of said County. Whereas 300 acres of land was granted to Robert Warren, dec., a patent dated 6 August 1649, Robert Warren sold to Richard Blunt, by assignment of patent 2 April 1650, and lived on it. It went to Thomas Blunt at the death of his father, was under age; and Richard Harris held the same and now sells 300 acres to Thos. Drew.
Henry Briggs and Mary, his wife, make over all their right and title in this estate to Thomas Drew, 5 March 1677.

Page 169. 24 April 1678. Com. of Admr. granted to Mary Collier on Est. of Jno. Collier.

24 Apr. 1678. Com. granted to Maj. Wm. Browne & Mr. Benj. Harrison on Est. of Jer: Knight, dec.; also on est. of Nath. Knight.

24 April 1678. Admr. granted to Joseph Barlowe on the Est. of Jno. Carr, dec.

24 April 1678. Admr. granted Mrs. Eliza Cocker on the Est. of William Cocker, dec.

24 April 1678. Admr. granted to Lt. Coll. Geo. Jordan for orphans of Francis Hogwood, dec., on the est. of Richard Hogwood, dec.

Page 170. 15 May 1678. Edward Travis appoints his wife, Elizabeth Travis, his lawful atty.
Wit.: John Champion, Wm. Harrison.

Page 170. 6 Apr. 1678. Inv. of Est. of Jeremiah Knight, deceased. John Moring, Ar. Jordan, Thos. Sowerby, Wm. Norwood.

Page 171. 7 May 1678. Jno. Goring debtor to Henry Goard's estate, by Martin Thomas, Charles Amry.

Page 172. 7 May 1678. Deed of sale confirmed of 100 acres of land sold by Bartholomew Owen, 3 7ber 1677, to Richard Tias.

Page 172. 7 May 1678. Thos. Sowerby gave John Collier son of John Collier, deceased, a yearling, and wants it recorded.

Page 172. 14 Sept. 1677. A contract of marriage between Jno. Rawlings and Mary Collier.

Page 173. 7 May 1678. Indenture between Richard Blow and Robert Caufield for 5000 lbs. tobacco, land on Blackwater called "Blow's Land."
Wit.: Jno. Goring, Jno. White.

Page 175. 7 May 1678. Deposition of Jeremiah Ellis, aged 35 years, sworn said that Henry Francis, the younger, was born in the year 1660 in November.

Page 175. 7 May 1678. Deposition of Robert Howes, aged 64 years, that Henry Francis was born the same year that the king was proclaimed.

Page 176. 7 May 1678. Indenture between Wm. Harris, the only son of Thomas Harris, of Surry County and Thomas Jarroll, for 1500 lbs. of tobacco sells 100 acres of land on...College Run...bounding on the head line of William Newsum, and Robert Ruffin in Wm. Newett's line, etc.
Wit.: Robt. White, Jno. Goring, Jno. White.

Page 178. 8 May 1678. Herbert Jeffries, Gov. of Virginia, a Proclamation, or letter states that Capt. Arthur Allen and Mr. Robert Caufield as Members of a Court, held at Southwarke for the county of Surry, had opposed the order that Capt. Swann should be High Sheriff of the County, and "Filled the eares of the People in a full Court with Amasion't and doubt but drew the rest of the Commissioners to Comply with them," which...was a bad example, etc., and suspends Robert Caufield and Capt. Arthur Allen from sitting in the Commission or any other Majesterial authority, etc. Swann's Point 8 May 1678.

Page 180. 16 Feb. 1677. James Barrett, of James Citty County, son and heir of Capt. William Barrett, sells to Maj. William White, of James Citty County, Land granted by Patent to "My said father," 2000 acres in Surry County on Crouches Creek.
Wit.: Sherwood, Enoch Woodward, Henry Bates.

Page 181. 1 March 1677. Indenture between Thomas Blunt and Richard Washington of the one part, and John Goreing of the other part. Whereas Charles Ford was in his lifetime and at his death, in possession of 250 acres of land, 50 acres held of the King by Patent 19 May 1638, James Citty...at Dancing Point...upon Col. John Flood, lately in possession of Nath. Knight, dec'd., granted to Charles Ford, the first Proprietor, Charles Ford died without a will and land escheated to the King...went to Thos. Blunt and Richard Washington then orphans and sons-in-law unto Charles Ford, and now to Jno. Goring.

Page 182. 20 April 1678. Indenture between Robert Burgess, blacksmith and Mr. John Mooring and Mr. Geo. Proctor of Surry County, Robt. Burgess having been kept in prison in said county...at entreaty of Burgess, Geo. Proctor and John Mooring became bound to Capt. Arthur Allen for payment of same etc., etc., and Robert Burgess was delivered out of prison with consent of Ann, his wife, sells all that land where Burgess now lives on Chipoakes Creek, 112 acres, houses, building, etc., to Jno. Mooring and Geo. Proctor.
Signed: Robt. Burgess, and Ann Burgess.
Wit.: John Weaver, Jno. King. 17 July 1678.

Page 183. 5 March 1677. Depositions of Wm. Simmons, aged 29, that he was at the house of Henry Francis and was requested by him to go to Thomas Bentlie's etc. Deposition of Wm. Lucas, aged 23, to the same. 5 March 1677.

Page 184. 12 7ber 1678. Mary Clutterbuck of the Island of Barbadoes, in America, widdow, appoints...her friend, Thomas Jordan of Virginia, Gent., her attorney to receive from John Whiddon, otherwise John Whitney of Virginia debts. etc. Wit.: Ni. Meriweather. John Parrocke, John Watkins

Page 185. 8ber 1678. James Stringfellow owes debt. Appoints his friend
Jno. Phillips his Atty.
Wit.: Lewis Williams.

Page 186. 10 Aug. 1678. Indenture between John Barker, Sr., of Martin Brandon in Charles City County, planter, of the one part, and Benjamin Harrison of the other part, land in Surry County at the head of Chipoaks Creek, where he formerly lived. Pat. 18 Dec. 1662, 1800 acres for 16,000 lbs. of tob.
Signed: John Barker, Ann Barker.
Wit.: Elias Osborne, Jethro Barker.

Page 187. 12 7ber 1678. Mr. Edward Bland, merchant, Lawnes Creek Parish, in Va., had certain possessions, whereas after the death of Edward Bland, Mr. Theodorick Bland, late of Westover in Charles City County, one of His Majesties Commissioners of State of Virginia, afterwards deceased, and Theodoric Bland, by power from John Bland and Co., calling to account all who were indebted to Edward Bland in America, and England, John Barker, Sr., purchased of Theodorick Bland 1800 acres of land, and was confirmed to Benjamin Harrison by John Barker and Ann, his wife.
Wit.: Wm. Simmons, David Phillips, Henry Francis, Humphrey **Folph?**

Page 190. 5 9ber 1678. George Branch, Jr., of Isle of Wight Co., Va., planter, marrying Mrs. Susannah Corker, daughter of Capt. Corker of the county of Yorke, deceased; Whereas Wm. Corker by a deed of gift, 20 Nov. 1673, confirmed to Mrs. Eliza White and Mrs. Mary White, sisters, land in Surry County, which land was to be equally divided between Elizabeth and Mary White as directed in the deed. Now, since the gift, Eliza is deceased and her father desired the bequest to second daughter. Susannah "my now wife" and Robert Spenser, Gent., married sd Eliza White and now is to have half the estate.
Wit.: John Goring, George Proctor.

Page 191. 5 9ber 1678. George Vahan gives a heifer to his son Stephen Vahan by deed of gift.

Page 193. 5 9ber 1678. Capt. Wm. Corker, dec'd., gave to John Vinsent 50 acres of land in Surry County on Johnsychawkin Swamp. Now George Branch, Jr., and Susannah his wife, one of the daughters and coheirs of sd William Corker, deceased, confirms to John Vinsent the 50 acres aforesaid.
Wit.: Robert Spenser, Ni. Meriweather.

Page 194. 15 9ber 1678. Jno. Flood marrying Mary Creeds received full satisfaction of John Warring for his wife's estate, and acknowledges it, and acquits Warring.
Signed: Jno. Flood.
Wit.: Jno. Rawlings, Ar. Jordan.

Page 194. 30 Dec. 1678. Thos. Sowerby, Jno. Watkins, Sam Judkins and John King, Grand Jury, present to the Court, Thos. Hunt and Robert Lee for not attending church. Also Thomas Senior, Edward Davis, Jno. Hewliston, Nich. Johnson, Robt. Evans, Walter Vawhan, Richard Tyas, Jr., preferred by Tho. Crews. Martin Thorn, Nich. Wilson, Math. Swan, Robert Kae, Grand Jury in the Lower Parish, present not attending church: Jno. Bynam, John Shepheard, Daniel Wade a vagrant and not settled and not attending church.

Page 194. 23 Jan. 1678. Will of Mary Simmons deceased, presented in Court by Maximiliam Mansfell.

Page 195. 6 Jan. 1678. Francis Taylor, lame for 32 days, desires Mr. Osborne to appear for him in court with a suit against Coll. Swann.

Page 196. 14 Feb. 1678. Petition of Daniel Wade, of Abingdon Parish, Gloucester County, free planter, unto Rt. Hon. Sir Wm. Berkeley, Capt. Gen. of Virginia, stating that at a General Muster in said County, 3 Feb. 1672, and in service, his gun exploded and he lost one of his hands and (is) incapable of service; desires release from service and of paying

Parish levies, as he has no way but his own labor and industry to maintain himself, his wife, and a small child. Petition was granted.

Page 197. 31 Dec. 1678. At Middle Plantation: Present were Hon. Chickley, Knt., Deputy Governor, etc., Coll. Nathan Bacon, Lt. Coll. Dabiel Parke, Coll. Joseph Bridger, Coll. Wm. Cole, Ro. Wormeley, Esq., and Richard Lee, Esq.

Ordered that Mr. Robert Caufield, Mr. Arthur Allen, and those other Gentlemen of Surry County that were suspended from ye Commission of the sd Court in the same qualification they were formerly. To the Justices of Surry County.
Signed: Hn. Hartwell.

Page 198. 4 March 1678. Wm. Hancock acknowledges he has received full satisfaction for all rights in purchase of Rowland Hudson, in his life and for himself and wife, and confirms to Jude Hudson, his wife, to her and his child. 27 April 1667.
Signed: Wm. Hancock, and Eliza Hancock.

On reverse deed was written: Deed of sale from Geo. Blow et ux to Rowland Hudson and Wm. Hancock. Rec.: Nov. 1664.

Page 198. 4 March 1678/9. Robert Kae, and Mary, his wife, of the Upper Parish of Isle of Wight County, Virginia, for 30,000 lbs. of tobacco paid by Robert Caufield of Lawnes Creek Par., Surry Co., Va., sell 300 acres of land, part of a Patent of 1,000 acres, granted to Roger Delk, deceased, land sold by Roger Delk (only son and heir of Roger Delk, and Rebecka, his wife) to Capt. Thomas Adams, late of Isle of Wight, deceased, Nov. 1659, and by William Adams, of Kenton in County Devon, in England, brother and heir to Capt. Thomas Adams, both in his own right and his sister, Dorothy Pegraff, of County of Devon, sold and conveyed to sd Kae, 10 March 1664, and residue to Roger Delke, and Rebecca his wife, 10 Nov. 1666, and deeds to said Caufield, Now delivered 4 March 1678/9.
Signed: Robert Kae, Mary Kae.
Wit.: Thos. Pittman, Sr., Jno. Barnes, Robert Kae, and Samuel Swann.

Page 203. 6 May 1679. Ind. Arthur Allen to Capt. Law. Baker 350 acres of land east side of second swamp, Blackwater, Pat. 14 June 1678.

Page 201. 14 March 1678. Charles Judkins, an orphan, is to stay in custody of Thos. Pittman, Sr., until he is 21 years old at the request of Thos. Pittman's deceased wife.

Page 205. 5 May 1679. William Little sells to George Peeters and Mabell Peeters for some consideration.
Wit.: Wm. Seward, James Murray.

Page 206. 6 May 1679. Jno. Miniard to Roger Potter some stock, a debt for which Capt. Roger Potter is bound with me to Mr. Arthur Allen for 652 lbs. of tobacco.
Wit.: Robert Randall, Jno. Rawlings.

Page 206. 26 April 1679. The following men viewed the body of a drowned seaman and swore before Capt. Charles Barham the verdict.

| Wm. Seward | | Wm. Prosser |
| Fra. Rowland | | Jos. Seale or Seele |
| | Christopher Smith | Richard Andrews |
| Wm. Hancocke | | Jno. Greene |
| Thos. Clary | | Edward James |
| Jno. Cary | | Walter Bartlett |

Page 207. 13 Nov. 1678. Sarah Curtis, found dead, is said by Jury to be lame and dropsical and she died of exposure. She was former servant to Mary Skinner, of Isle of Wight County. The Jury members were:

BOOK II, 1671-1684     111

    Ni. Willson    Jno. Gray
    Richard Drew   Joseph Foard
    Walter Taylor   Thos. Smith
    Jno. Dunford   Henry Gray
    Jos. Barlow    James Reddick
    James Largie.

Page 209. 27 Mar. 1679. Administration on estates granted to the following:

Mabell Drew on est. of her husband, Richard Drew.

Mary Gray on est. of her husband, Fra. Gray, deceased.

Jno. Case on est. of Edward Browne in right of orphans.

Roger Potter, admr., on est. of Thomas Foserreft, dec'd., for orphans.

Sion Hill on est. of Mary Davis.

Jane Spenser on will of her husband, Robert Spenser.

Mary White and Mrs. Lucy Corker on will of John White, deceased.

Eliza. Claye on the will of her deceased Husband, Thos. Clay.

Ni. Williams on the will of Joseph Pharlow.

Page 211. 16 June 1679. Robert Ruffin declared that at the house of Lewis Williams, of Lawnes Creek Parish, late deceased, he heard Mrs. Williams say that her husband, before he died, gave his son to Wm. Newsum, and his girls to Sion Hill, and his wife and daughter-in-law, named Mary, to Mr. Thompson and ye others of his daughters-in-law to the disposing of his wife. The wife died, and the child went to Mrs. Edwards.

Page 211. 8 May 1679. Benjamin Harrison made High Sheriff.

Page 211. 6 May 1679. Est. of Jno. Collier, deceased, debtor on Jno. Rawlings, Oct. 1679, being divided between the Relict, (and) Thos., Jno., Joseph, and Mary, orphans of said deceased.
 Signed: Jno. Rawlings.

Page 213. 1 March 1677. Thos. Drew, Lawnes Creek Par., and Faith, his wife, sell to Richard Drew land adj. Long and Capt. Baker, part of a patent to Robert Warren, 6 Aug. 1649, and by Warren assigned to Richard Blunt, and by Thos. Blunt, only son and heir to sd. Richard, sold and conveyed to Thos. Drew and he this 50 acres to Richard Drew.
 Rec.: 1 July 1679.
 Wit.: Charles Barham, Ar. Allen, Robt. Ruffin.

Page 214. 1 July 1679. John King, aged 33 years, sworn and said that he heard Wm. Rookings say he would carry his will to his brother, Wyatt's, and there subscribe it.

Page 223. 2 7ber 1679. Wm. Harris and wife Mary sell to Wm. Gray 494 acres, part of pat. for 850 acres granted 2 June 1661, adj. Rich. Briggs, dec.

Page 215. 1 July 1679. Thos. Binns acknowledges receipt from Mr. Fra. Mason of 85,850 lbs. of tobacco, being his part of his (Binns') father's est.

Page 229. 9 8ber 1679. Jury called to view the dead body of a man:
    Zachariah Jackson  Daniel Wade
    James Ellis    Jno. Phillips
    Edmund Howell   John Porteus
    James Rowles    James Forbus

SURRY COUNTY RECORDS

      Thos. High      Henry Baker
      Thos. Binns     James Warren

Page 229. 17 Feb. 1678/9. Power of Atty. branted to Sarah Bland before Nicholas Hayward, Notary in London; she wife to John Bland, merchant in London, Sarah Bland now bound from London to Virginia and principally Mr. Bernard Sykes and Mr. Dodd and take in...Plantations of Bartlett Kin, Herring Creeke Mill, Jordains, Westover, Upper Chipoaks, Sunken Marsh Plantation, Basses Vhoice, James Towne Lott, Lawnes Creek and all other land and Plantations due, owing, or belonging to sd. John Bland, etc., etc., administrator on Theodorick Bland, late of Bartlett Upon James River in Charles City County, Va., merchant, deceased.
  Wit.: Anthony Fenn, Robert Mittford, Edward Montaigne, Thomas Tanner, Humph. Hegynison?

Page 230. 6 Oct. 1679. Sarah Bland, Atty. and wife of John Bland, confirms to Walter Bartlett all purchases made by him from Giles Bland.
  Wit.: Robert Caufield, John Mover.
Confirms to Edward Tanner, likewise. 4 9ber 1679.
On back of this deed was written warrant of Atty. to Richard Clarke, Sheriff, to acknowledge the indenture.

Page 233. 26 9ber 1679. Charles Moryson writes to his friend, Mr. Robert Caufield, merchant, excusing himself for not writing from Col. Bridger's concerning Mr. Goring's estate. Said he forgot, being just leaving the country, full of troubles and distractions, as he was bound for New Yorke with the Indyans wch came from Barmudus, who I am commanded to carry to the abovesaid place, etc." He stated that he wished Caufield to secure the Rapier, Pistolls, and Holsters he had lent Mr. Goring, etc.
  Signed: Ch. Moryson.

Page 235. 6 May 1679. Acct. of Est. of Jno. Barton, deceased.

Page 236. 9 9ber 1679. On the back of a Patent for 250 acres of land granted to Robert House, dated 14 March 1666, is written that Robt. House, Sr., for 4000 lbs. of tobbacco, paid by John Warren, sells to John Warren, his heirs, etc.
  Wit.: Wm. Edwards, Jeremiah Ellis.

Page 236. 18 Dec. 1679. A Jury was summoned at the house of Henry Clarke, in Hog Island, to inquire into the death of a child, being left alone fell into the fire:
      Timothy Easell, Sr.   Edward Tanner
      Wm. Prosser     George Easell
      Walter Bartlett    Jason Skinner
      Henry Clarke     Jno. Barnes
      Thos. Edwards    Wm. Hancocke
      Charles Amry     Owen Mise?

Page 238. 4 9ber 1679. Thos. Busby explains that on the 20 June 1677 he sold an Indian girl of nine years as a slave to Wm. Duke. Wm. Duke died before the sale was consummated and Wm. Archer married the Relict and administratrix of Wm. Duke. He confirms the sale of the Indian girl, Bess, to Wm. Archer.
  Wit.: John Tirrey, Dorothy Tirrey.

Page 239. 15 Dec. 1679. Fra. Lord, of the Parish of Wallingford, in James Citty County, etc.,...whereas Edward Gunnell owned 1426 acres of land in Surry County, by Beaver Dam Swamp...was Patent from Sir Wm. Berkeley 8 9ber 1670, and sold to Wm. Stento, 731 acres and Wm. Stanton died before acknowledging the deed, although in his Will he gave the land to his wife, Dorothy, and Fra. Lord, having married sd. Dorothy has become the rightful owner of said land as Wm. Stanton had sold the 713 acres to Henry Briggs, and confirms to Henry Briggs the same etc.
  Signed: Fra. Lord.
  Wit.: Jno. Hamelin, Robert Netherland.

Page 241. 31 May 1678. On the back side of a lease of 50 acres of land, leased by Andrew Robinson to Jno. Clay for 99 years, dated 1 March 1661, was written that Roger Archer married the Relict and Executrix of Mr. Jno. Clay, late of Isle of Wight County, exor. of Mr. John Clay, Sr., deceased, sells to Mr. Arthur Allen of Surry Co., all their right and claim to the 50 acres.
Signed: Robert Archer, Mary Archer.
Wit.: Wm. Edwards, Fra. Mason.

Page 243. 15 Dec. 1679. Wm. Edwards, Atty. for Thos. Robley, states that Henry Willis owes him eight barrels of corn, but is privily departed out of the country, attaches Henry Willis' Est. This est. of Henry Willis in the hands of Joseph Malden.
Signed: Wm. Foreman, Baycliffe.

Page 246. 28 9ber 1679. Ind. between John Bynum and Richard Jordan, Land on which John Bynam bought of George Blow, 600 acres.
Signed: John Bynam, Rose Bynam.
Wit.: Richard Jordan, Jr., Richard Lane, Rich. Blow.

Page 248. 6 Jan. 1679. Francis Taylor makes Richard Ruffin his Atty.

Page 248. 1 Jan. 1679. Elizabeth Rochell makes Jno. King her Atty. to get an order against Capt. Nicholas Wyat, exor. of William Rookings, deceased, in Surry County for money due her late husband, deceased.
Wit.: Wm. Phillips, John Willson.

Page 248. 29 Dec. 1678. Jno. Baxter, of Charles Citty County, appts. Jno. King his atty. between himself and Edward Farned in Surry County Court.
Wit.: Margaret Ellis, Luke Meazle.

Page 248. 25 9ber 1679. Thos. Robley makes Mr. Wm. Edwards his Atty. to collect money in Surry County.
Wit.: Robert Penny, James Ellis.

Page 248. 5 Jan. 1679. Owen Myrick appoints his wife, Mary, his Atty.

Page 249. 12 Dec. 1679. Edward Farned appts. Elias Osborne his Atty.
Signed: Wm. Crabb.
Wit.: Benj. Harrison, John Tirrey.

Page 250. 27 Feb. 1679. William Lyle, of Southwarke Par., married Judah, only daughter of Rowland Hudson, of Lawnes Creek Parish, deceased, and now sells to John Smith and to his heirs land purchased by Rowland Hudson and Wm. Hancocke of George Blow and Margaret, his wife; deed dated 7 May 1664, and by sd. Hancocke to the heirs, etc., of Rowland Hudson; deed 27 April 1667, and now sold to John Smith.
Signed: Wm. Lile, Judia Lile.
Wit.: Thos. Pittman, Sr., John Gaiffing?
Rec.: 2 March 1679.

Page 250. 2 March 1679. Ind. between Richard Blow of Blackwater in Surry County, and Nicholas Seesam (Sessoms), 100 acres of land on Green Swamp.
Wit.: Ni. Smith, Sion Hill.

Page 252. 31 Oct. 1677. Ind. between Robt. Parke, Clarke, and Mary, his wife, and Wm. Gray for a grist Water Mill, "Bushell's Mill," and ground on which it stands, etc.
Rec.: 10 May 1680.
Wit.: Fra. Taylor, John Mathyson, Will. Evans.
On the back of this deed was an assignment by Wm. Gray to Robert Kae of Isle of Wight County, and Ni. Willson of Surry, 23 Aug. 1679.

Page 255. 27 May 1680. Jasper Gransome appoints his wife Elizabeth his Atty.... Signed: Jas. Gransume. Wit.: Bartholomew Figgers, Wm. Hunt.

SURRY COUNTY RECORDS

Page 255. 14 May 1680. Elizabeth Gransome appoints Thos. Jordan her Atty.

Page 255. 28 May 1660. Mr. Robert Caufield is appointed High Sheriff of Surry County, by Henry Chickley.

Page 256. 10 May 1680. Gov. Thos. Culpeper makes Proclamation empowering all Civill Magistrates and Militia to execute their respective powers and commands as given them by Rt. Hon. Sr. Henry Chickley, His Majesties Deputy Governor, etc.

Page 257. 30 July 1680. Ind. between Wm. Harris, only son of Thomas Harris, late of Lawnes Creek Parish, Surry County, deceased, and Mary his wife, and Thomas Jarrell...100 acres of land a lease for 98½ years (7 May 1678) now makes void the lease and they sell Thomas Jarrell 120 acres of land part of 850 acres, formerly granted to Thos. Harris, deceased. Pat. 13 Feb. 1657, etc.
   Wit.: Robt. Ruffin, Wm. Newsum.

Page 258. 19 July 1680. Phillip Shelly married Ann Mason, acknowledges to have received of Jno. Sugar as marrying ye Relict and extx. of Thos. Clay, deceased, due to Wm. Shelly by a bond of Thos. Claye in the Clerk's office of Surry County, and is satisfied; acquits Jno. Sugar from same.

Page 259. 6 July 1680. John Smith, Lawnes Creek Parish, and wife, Mary, sell to Thos. Barrow 150 acres of land, conveyed by Wm. Lyle and wife Judah, sd. Fra. Mason's land and Jno. Bynam in Green Swamp.
   Wit.: Ni. Smith, Will Seward.

Page 260. 6 July 1680. Thomas Pittman, Sr., makes a deed of gift to Wm. Pittman, son of Thomas Pittman, Jr.; gift is a heifer.

Page 261. 3 June 1680. Peter Field of Henrico County appoints Elias Osborne his Atty. to prosecute Thos. Pittman at court in Surry Co.
   Wit.: Thos. Jordan, Will. Simmons.

Page 261. 25 May 1680. I, Jno. Epps, exec. of my father, Jno. Epps, deceased appoints Elias Osborne his attorney.
   Signed: John Epes.
   Wit.: N. Wyatt, Wm. Harrison.

Page 264. 8 7ber 1680. Ann Dennis makes over to her son-in-law, Abraham Evans all her right in 60 acres of land sd Evans is now possessed with, part of a parcel of land I bought of John Legran...adj. Jno. Harris, Wm. Simmons, and Jeremiah Ellis.
   Wit.: Jeremiah Ellis, Elizabeth Simmons.
Underneath a conveyance of land sold by John LeGrand to Ann Dennis on 1 March 1671, recorded in Surry County 9 May 1672, was written, Ann Dennis sells to Wm. Lucas one-half of abovesaid land.

Page 265. 4 8ber 1680. Nicholas Hoskins has privately departed the county, owes Robt. Caufield, who attaches the est.

Page 271. 30 Aug. 1670. Ind. between Charles Barham, of the one part & Joseph Rogers of the other part, land granted Capt. Cockerham and to Barham by Joint Patent, 14 May 1666. "Pocatinck."

Page 272. 9 Oct. 1680. Ind. between Thos. Senior and Thos. High for 113 acres of land granted to Thos. Senior by Patent 20 April last past.
   Wit.: Mary White, Fra. Mason.

Page 272. 30 8ber 1680. Ind. between Wm. Sherwood, of James Citty Co., and wife Ratchell and William Carpinter, of Surry County, land where John Le Grand formerly lived and Wm. Sherwood purchased of Le Grand, 180 acres.
   Wit.: Robert Jones, James Bibgley.
On back of this, Ratchell Sherwood empowers her nephew Maj. Samuel Swann to acknowledge the deed as her voluntary act.

Page 273. 25 8ber 1680. On Complaint of Jno. Clarke, the Estate of John Miller, departed out of the county, is attached.

Page 274. 7 April 1680. Ind. between Thos. Busby and wife Susannah, and Daniel Room for land on Chipoakes Creek, adjoining Wm. Short, 100 acres. This sale, later disputed, because the land was claimed to be in a tract belonging to Wm. Bird of Martins Brandon, deceased. Paid Thos. Bird the difference.

Page 275. 12 9ber 1680. Robert House's patent, dated 14 May 1666, was conveyed to Jno. Warren, and John Warren conveyed it to Owen Myrick.
Signed: Jno. Warren, Mawdlin Warren.
Wit.: Wm. Thompson, Elias Osborne.

Page 276. 29 Oct. 1680. Deed of gift of a heifer from Hannah Holton to her godson, Edward Browne.

Page 276. 9ber 1680. Jno. Pittford stated that Jno. Atkinson, godfather to Sarah Pittford, gave her a cow and a calf. Jno. Pittford acknowledges the receipt of it.

Page 278. 4 Jan. 1680. Maj. Samuel Swann, and wife Sarah, sell to Roger Williams, 248 acres of land, a Patent to Swann, 18 ber(?) 1668.

Page 279. 7 Jan. 1678. Wm. Sherwood and Thos. Moore became security for the payment due the orphans for the payment due the orphans of Peter Bagley, and John Litford, who married the Relict of said Bagley, did...bind over all his rest estate, and the land of Lidford, deceased, escheated. Now, the orphan Peter Bagley, Jr., gives power Attorney to Hugh Bagley, his brother, to possess themselves of the est., which John Litford possessed and they will recover 250 acres of land in Surry County.
Wit.: Robert Kae, Ro. Evans, Walter Bartlett.

Page 279. 15 March 1680. Edward Norwood appoints Elias Osborne his Atty. Richard Case, Thos. Howe.

Page 279. 24 Jan. 1680. Thos. Hunt appts. Elias Osborne his Atty.

Page 279. Susannah Busby, wife to Thos. Busby, makes Charles Gardner her Attorney.

Page 280. 1 May 1680. Roger Williams, and wife Mary, sell to Richard Blow 60 acres of land bought of Maj. Samuell Swann and Sarah his wife.

Page 282. 16 April 1681. Arthur Allen and Wm. Newsum sell to Jno. Leer, of Nansemond County, 432 acres of land on Blackwater River. Katherine Allen, and Ann Newsum, wives to the above men, relinquish their dower.
Wit.: Wm. Swett.

Page 283. 3 May 1681. William Shivers acknowledges receipt of all his estate from his Guardian, Mr. Wm. Carpinter.

Page 283. 28 Feb. 1680. Elinor Eliote appoints Elias Osborne her Atty. Thos. Wallis, Thos. Marshall.

Page 283. 19 May 1681. Owen Myrick makes Elias Osborne his Attorney. Lancelot Beck, Thos. Wallis.

Page 286. 15 June 1681. Jno. Vincent makes deed of gift to Francis Sowerby, orphant of Francis Sowerby, deceased, of a cow calfe.

Page 287. 15 June 1681. Thos. Wiggins withdraws his account with Elinor Elliott.

Page 287. 5 July 1681. George Lee, once resident of Surry County, is now in James Citty County. Any business with him will be done at James Towne, in James Citty County.

Page 289. 28 July 1681. Robert Dearemon is indebted to various people.
Signed: Joseph Malden.

Page 294. 6 7ber 1681. Wm. Kitto, Sr., to Wm. Kitto, Jr., a mare given him by Thos. Edwards.

Page 295. 18 8ber 1681. Wm. Briscoe, of James Towne, appoints Roger Rawlings of Surry County his attorney.
Wit.: Geo. Spenser, Will Browne, Wm. Edwards.

Page 296. 5 9ber 1681. Henry Briggs and wife Margery sell to Thos. Blunt, planter, land that was sold to Briggs by Wm. Stinton, late of James Citty County, who died before acknowledging the sale. Francis Lord married the relict of said Stinton, and was confirmed by Francis Lord for 150 acres of land.

Page 297. 22 8ber 1681. John Bynam and wife Rosamund of Surry County, sell to Wm. Webb, of sle of Wight County, land in Surry County on the west side of the branch from the Plantation where Webb now lives.
Wit.: Robt. Ruffin, Samuel Thompson.

Page 297. Wm. Shivers, of Surry County, sells to Thomas Piddenton 200 acres of Woodland "given to me by my father in his Last Will and Testament," the rest given to my sisters and fallen to me by their death. The said land was purchased of Ralph Creed and sold to my father. The said Thomas Piddenton is to have first choice of all my land, except 400 acres.
Signed: William Shivers.
Wit.: Daniel Regand, Jno. Rodwell, Wm. Senod?

Page 298. 5 June 1680. Roger Williams, of Surry County, sells to Jno. Watkins 200 acres of land on Pidgeon Swamp purchased by Williams of Maj. Samuel Swann.

Page 300. Robert Lacey, of Surry County, and Mary, his wife, late Relict and extx. of Wm. Cooke; whereas Wm. Cooke about A. D. 1677 sold Thomas Ward, late of Surry County, deceased, 100 acres of land on the south side of Second Swamp, Blackwater, in the Lower Parish of Surry County, part of a Patent for 800 acres granted to Cooke on 10 9ber 1670, but died before sealing, now confirm the sale.

Page 301. 14 Feb. 1681. Wm. Fordman, Atty. for Susanna Busby, wife to Thomas Busby, relinquishes her dower.

Page 301. 20 Xber 1681. Ind. between Thos. Busby, Sr., and Susannah his wife, and Edward Greene for a tract of land, 200 acres...at James Jones' line at Blackwater Swamp, to Sec. Reedy Branch above Greene's Plantation.
Signed: Robert Wyatt(?), Beng. Harrison.

Page 302. 6 8ber 1681. Wm. Allen and Samuel Swann, Justices. Whereas Capt. Lawrence Baker in his Will nominated and appointed Maj. Arthur Allen and his Relict execs., probate is asked to dispose of grants by Allen and Baker, Wm. Brown and Sarah Swann. Mrs. Eliza Baker and Arthur Allen Probate on Lawrence Baker's will.

Page 302. 6 March 1681. Jno. Rogers, Sr., empowers his friend Elias Osborne his lawful attorney.
Robert Lee, John Vincent.

Page 302. 7 March 1681/2. Maj. Samuel Swann, Lawnes Creek Par., Surry County, eldest son and heir of Thos. Swann, Esq., for 30 pounds sterling paid by Mary Swann, widow and Relict of the above deceased, in consideration of her relinquishing her right of dower to land and housing etc. of deceased, of which she was dowerable...do sell and deliver to Mary Swann...a parcell of land...containing 300 acres by Gray's Creek, N.,....in line between said Swann, and William Gray, the son of Francis Gray, 100 acres patent thereof

BOOK II, 1671-1684                                               117

as by deed dated 15 Nov. 1677, doth appear, part of a patent to deceased
father of 1950 acres on 4 Oct. 1645.
 Wit.: Earth Biggers, Thos. Hagard, Wm. Pollard, Wm. Edwards.
Sarah Swann, wife to Samuel Swann, relinquishes her dower.
 Wit.: Wm. Newsum, Wm. Pollard, Wm. Edwards.

Page 303. Sarah Swann, wife to Samuel Swann, relinquishes her dower, and
appoints Lt. Col. Wm. Browne, and Mr. Benjamin Harrison, either of them,
her lawful attorney to act in this acct.
 Wit.: Wm. Newsum, Wm. Pollard, Wm. Edwards.

Page 303. 25 Feb. 1681/2. Madam Mary Swann...relict of Coll. Thomas Swann;
whereas her son, Samuel Swann, eldest son and heir to Col. Thos. Swann,
deceased, hath enfeoffed me, the said Madam Mary Swann, of 300 acres...upon
Gray;s Creek, now acquits Sam. Swann, eldest son and heir of sd. Coll. Thos.
Swann, her said husband, deceased, and assigns all Dower rights, except
rights in house and land that her husband was possessed with, in James Citty,
late in possession of John Everett, and dower in house at Warenock where an
ordinary was lately kept...
 Wit.: Bart. Biggers, Thos. Hagard, Wm. Pollard, Wm. Edwards.

Page 304. 25 Feb. 1681/2. Mary Swann, widow, Relict of Thos. Swann, appoints
her brother Wm. Edwards, her lawful attorney of that due to Samuel Swann.
 Wit.: Thos. Jordan, Jno. Greene.

Page 304. 7 May 1681. Anthony Evans gets ear mark for cattle.

Page 304. 10 April 1682. Wm. Pollard gets ear mark for cattle.

Page 304. Interrogatory of Jno. Smith, carpenter, with Maj. Swann whether
there was an agreement between them for carpenter's work to be done to the
house rented of him in James Citty.

Page 305. 9 March 1681. Hezekiah Bunnell withdrew suit against Robert Lee.

Page 305. Jeremiah Ellis withdraws a suit against John Rogers, Sr.

Page 305. Richard Bigton gets ear mark for cattle.

Page 305. 22 April 1682. Joseph Malden appointed High Sheriff for the year
1682. Henry Chichley.
 Rec.: 4 May 1682.

Page 305. Arthur Jordan claims that Robert Lee owes him 1600 lbs. tobacco
and 7 bus. of wheat, and has departed from his Habitation and not enough
goods in the estate to pay.

Page 309. 7 Feb. 1679. Inv. of Est. of Mary Long, widow, one small Bible and
one old chest given to her son, George Long. Walter Taylor, Thos. Drew.
Presented by Robert Caufield, 4 July 1682.

Page 310. 5 7ber 1682. Arthur Allen of Lawnes Creek Parish, to Wm. Newsum,
all right and interest in 554 acres, granted to him to Newsum, jointly, by
pattent dated 26 7ber 1678, on a branch of Blackwater River. Samuel Swann,
Daniel Pugh. Katherine, wife of Ar. Allen gave consent.

Page 310. 5 Sept. 1682. William Chivers of Southwarke Parish, indenture for
1500 lbs. merchantable tobacco, to Thos. Hux, 100 acres of land adj. land
sold to Wm. Hunt, divided from the remainder of my land by marked trees,
from Mr. Benj. Harrison's land to Wm. Knott's land...to dividend where I
now live.
 Thos. Piddenton, Wm. Hunt.
7 6ber 1682. Elizabeth Chivers, wife to above, relinquishes her dower.

Page 310. 7 6ber 1682. Wm. Chivers, indenture for 2000 lbs. of merchantable

tobacco paid by Wm. Hunt, two necks of land on the N. E. side of Gravelly Run Branch, 100 acres bounded by Gravelly Run Bottom, to Thomas Piddenton, to Round Island, to land of Wm. Knott, being part of a divident where I now live, with houses, etc.
Thos. Piddenton, Thos. Hux.
Wife relinquishes her dower.

Page 312. 6 7ber 1682. Wm. Chivers indenture and Bill of Sale, planter, for 1750 lbs. of merchantable tobacco paid by Thos. Piddenton, cooper, one neck of land, containing by estimation 100 acres on the south side of Gravelly Runn Bottom Branch, including all the land without the said branch run, extending to Mr. Benj. Harrison's line...to Wm. Knott's line, part of a divident where I now live, 100 acres with houses, orchards, etc.
Wm. Rose, Edward Pettway.
Wife relinquishes dower.

Page 313. 5 day 7ber 1682. On the back side of a conveyance of land from Jno. Smith to Thos. Mathas, 3 Jan. 1680. Rec.: 19 Jan. 1680, was written Conveyed to Alexander More, or his heirs, 5 day 7br 1682.
Test.: Nich. Smith, Peter Michell.
Signed Thomas Mathas (or Mather).

Page 313. On the back side of a conveyance of land from Jno. Smith to Alex. More, Mary, wife of Jno. Smith, Relinquished her dower. Dated 3 Jan. 1680.

Page 313. 7 7ber 1682. This day appeared in Court Mary, wife of Alex. More, and relinquished her dower in a deed of land sold by her husband to Hen. Baker.

Page 313. 5 day 7ber 1682. Alex. Moore to Henry Baker.
Samuel Thompson, Richard Andrews.

Page 314. 10 May 1682. Ind. between Hezekiah Bunnell, of Surry County, and Richard Jones of Martin's Brandon, Charles Citty County, with the consent of Jane, his wife, 150 acres of land bought from Jeremiah Ellis 31 Xber 1677, for 3400 lbs. of good tobacco.
Nich. Smith, Walter Flood. 5 7ber 1682.
Signed: Hezekiah Bunnell, Joane **Bunhill.**

Page 314. 5 7ber 1682. Edward Pettway sells to his daughter Joyce Fiveash, a parcel of land, 50 acres, part of the land I live on at the head of Crouch's Creek and Hogpen Swamp, to Henry Hart's land.
Thomas Edwards, William Edwards.

Page 315. 5 7ber 1682. Edward Pettway to son Wm. Pettway, sells 80 acres part of the land I live on, beginning at the head of Thunderbolt Valley... to the land of Henry Hart, to Great Swamp, to branch of Crouch's Creek.
Thomas Edwards, William Edwards.

Page 315. 5 7ber 1682. Alex. Moore, of Surry County, Virginia, to Thos. Mather of the same county, a parcel of land formerly taken up by Maj. Marriott, lying upon Nicholas Sessums on the Swamp, to the mouth of Bold Robin's Branch, for 99 years, for a valuable consideration.
Nick. Smith, Thos. White.

Page 316. 6 7ber 1682. Robert Caufield, and Eliza. his wife, for 4400 lbs. of tobacco sell to Joseph Wall a tract of land on the Main Blackwater Swamp, 2250 acres, granted by patent to Caufield...to land granted to Thos. Warren, south by Blackwater, west by Deep Branch, 500 acres more or less.
Ro. Caufield, Eliza. Caufield.
Philip Shelley, Edward **Pamoast?**

Page 318. 7 9ber 1682. John Rogers, Sr., appoints his wife, Mary Rogers ye elder, his lawful attorney to collect his debts etc. Josiah **Hacume?**, John Rogers, Younger. Jno. Rogers, Jr., made oath to same.

Page 319. 7 9ber 1682. Roger Gilbert, of Surry County, Colony of Virginia, planter, sells to Alex. More of said County, half of my land at the head of Gray's Creek near the mouth of the Swamp called Warrelow's Swamp and the land of Sam. Thompson.
Wm. Thompson, Saml. Thompson, Katherine Thompson.

Page 319. 7 9ber 1682. Alex. Moore assigned to Jno. Thompson.
Alexander Moore, Mary Moore.
Hen. Baker, John Giles.

Page 319. 12 Xber 1682. Robert Burgess of Upper Chipoakes appoints Elias Osborne his Attorney in a suit between me and Mr. Rumbell. 7 9ber 1682.
Bartholomew Figgers, Jno. Battell.

Page 319. Owen Myrick appoints Elias Osbourne his Lawful atty. in a suit against Ralph Poole. 6 6ber 1682.

Page 320. 7 9ber 1682. Roger Gilbert, planter, sells to Nicholas Witherington for 4000 lbs. of tobacco, 75 acres of land lying between Gray's Creek ...the Upper Parish, one-half of a greater quantity...the other moiety already disposed of to Ellexander More, adjoining certain land known as Smith's Fort, the which land is in possession of Joseph Malden, from Smith's Fort to the adjoining line, the whole tract sold by me to the above mentioned Ellexander More, and the said Nicholas Witherington, the first above mentioned 75 acres to be possessed by Nicholas Witherington with manor dwelling house and orchard, etc.
Wit.: Rich. Clarke, Robert Penny, Thos. Waller, Ri. Lane.

Page 320. 7 9ber 1682. Roger Williams for 4500 lbs. of Tobacco paid by Jno. Collins sells him a parcell of land containing 200 acres, part of the land I bought of Maj. Samuel Swann, 4 March 1680, the other part by me sold formerly to Richard Blow, this being the whole of the before mentioned parcell of land bought, except Blow's, is bounded by a patent for the whole, by me assigned to said Collins (Blow's only excepted) to Jno. ollins.
Will Evans, Wm. Edwards
Mary, wife of Roger Williams, relinquishes her dower.

Page 321. 3 9ber 1682. Indenture between Thos. Weller of Surry County, and Richard Lane of the other, for 210 acres of land in the Lower Par. of said county, 420 acres lately taken up by said Waller on the North side of Deep Branch, West to Robert Caufield's South to Thomas Waller, East to John Binum.
Signed: Thos. Waller, Mary Waller.
Wit.: John Coker, Wm. Pitman, Richard Jordan, Sr.

Page 321. 4 9ber 1682. Lancelott Beck appointed Thomas Jordan his Attorney against Jno. Smith Elias Osbourne and whatever Mr. Thomas Jordan shall act or doe in my behalf shall stand.
Jno. Rawling, Rich. Winder.

Page 322. 7 9ber 1682. Estate of Lt. Coll. Geo. Jordan. (Payments?) Dr. to:

| | |
|---|---|
| Wm. Broadrib | Geo. Hogwood |
| Mr. Arthur Jordan | Wm. Jordan children |
| Mr. Robert Ruffin | Capt. Roger Jordan |
| John Miniard | Mr. Thos. More |
| Richard Hide | Benj. Harrison |
| Maj. Francis Epps | Fra. Gray |
| Alex. Spenser | Mr. Hobson and Broadrib |
| Rob. Coleby | (schoole) |
| Capt. Clemons | Contra by appmt. |
| Mr. Henry Briggs | Wm. Clarke |
| Thos. Cotton | Mr. Jos. Malden |
| Mr. Robert Caufield | Capt. Wyatt |
| Wm. Hall | Mr. Walter Flood |
| Jno. Watkins | Wm. Blackburn |
| Maj. Arthur Allen | Mr. Wm. Thompson |

SURRY COUNTY RECORDS

Robert Gullett
Henry Bunnell by Col. Bacon
  per George Norwell
Robert Archer
Mr. Wm. Sherwood
Mr. Henry Hartwell
David Andrews
Mr. Wm. Edwards
Thos. Sowerby
Wm. Reade
Mr. Thos. Raply
Nat. Roberts
Mr. Jno. Moring
Mr. Wm. Simons
John King
Sam. Maggott
Jas. Sowers
Warren and Hogwood Est.
Jer. Ellis
Capt. Wm. Fisher
Capt. Roger Potter
Mr. Thos. Busby
Owen Mirick
Mr. Wm. Thompson
John Warren
Daniel Rome
Coll. Cole
Robert House
Harry's Ordinary
Mr. Henry Briggs
Christor Foster
Wm. Draper
Mr. Morgan
Tim Izard
Coll. Wm. Browne
To church by will
Benj. Harrison
Geo. Loveday
Capt. Potter
Mary & Sarah Swann
Wm. Browne

Mr. Geo. Lee
John Rogers, Sr.
Ab. Evans
Maj. Samuel Swann
Thos. Bentley
Barth. Brittle
John Flood
Francis ap Thos. Bentley
Richard Pace
Mr. Elias Osborne
An Sorsby
**Mrs. Merriweather**
John Johnson
Jno. Wilkerson
Thos. Andrews, his wife
John Warren
Mr. Edward Baley
Wm. Arnold
Wm. Lyle
Robert House, Sr.
Jno. Dauby
Ja. Mathew
Mr. Geo. Marable
Catrina Sorsby
Geo. Foster
Thos. Sowerby
John Wilkerson
Mr. Jos. Maldon
Edward Baly
Mr. Wm. Edwards
Mr. Wm. Hall
Thos. Blayton
Mr. Robert Ruffin
Coll. Bell
Est. due in money
Henry Prosson
Madam Diggs
Mrs. Mary Browne
Eleanor Hux
Dr. Hainsworth
Benj. Harrison

Page 323. 7 9ber 1682. Wm. Archer, Chas. Citty Co., appoints friend Elias Osborne atty. Hugh Davis, Ralph Poole.

Page 323. 7 9ber 1682. Est. of Wm. Marriott, deceased, Dr. to Jno. Moring, Admr. of Mr. Geo. Proctor, Est.
Amt. due Mr. Samuel Thompson as marrying ye surviving of ye two orphans, out of which 1500 is to be paid and deducted from funeral charges of the dec'd orphan by order of Ct. Rec.: of Mr. Thompson in right of his wife 9ber 1681, ex. and settled Maj. Marriott's estate.
Wm. Browne, Wm. Edwards.

Page 324. 7 9ber 1682. Est. John Price settled. Maj. Price Admr. dec'd.

Page 324. 1 Jan. 1682. William Springer of Chas. Citty County appointed Mr. Elias Osborne atty. in Suit between Wm. Pickerell and Thos. Hayard.
Paul Williams, John Harrison, Geo. Jennings.

Page 324. 5 Jan. 1682. Indenture between Robert House, Jr. (who married Martha Spilltimber) of Southwark Parish, in Surry, carpenter, for and in consideration of 5000 lbs. of tobacco paid by Robert House, Sr., 100 acres of land...bounded by a patent of land granted to...Anthony Spilltimber dated 6 Feb. 1648, doth appear, which said patent is assigned to the above named Robert House, Sr., 16 Jan. 1682.
Martha House relinquishes her dower, 5 Jan. 1682

BOOK II, 1671-1684    121

Page 326. Feb. 1682. Wm. Kitto, Lawnes Creek Parish, binds certain household articles to Roger Rawlings for debt.
Rob. Ruffin.

Page 326. 5 March 1682/3. Wm. Chambers receives from his guardian, Wm. Gray, "my father's estate, and sister Mary her estate."
Rob. Ruffin, Martin Johnson.

Page 326. 6 March 1682. Estate of Geo. Proctor, by Jno. Moring, a list of debts due the estate of Mr. George Proctor, out of date.

| | |
|---|---|
| Richard May | Charles Denison |
| Roger Rawlings | Jno. Rawlings |
| Thos. Senior | Capt. Thos. Pittman |
| Wm. Spring | Thos. Clarke |
| Rob. Gulley | Alex. Spenser |
| Rich. Avery | Wm. Rowland |
| Mt. Marriott | Rich. Harris |
| Thos. Bentley | Thos. Robley |
| Roger Nicholls | John Bishop |
| Walt. Vahan | Math. Swann |
| Wm. Blackborne | Owen Miro |
| David Williams | Dr. Stratton |
| Ni. Johnson | Rich. Miller |
| John Bayneham | Maj. Swann |
| Thos. Sowerby | Cr. Cardinpaine |
| Capt. Potter | Capt. Spenser |
| Rich. Andrews | Hen. Armstrong |
| Ch. Amry | Mr. Mason |
| Jos. Foard | Lt. Coll. Jordan |
| Robt. Kae | Jno. Case |
| Jno. Jones | Edwd. Davis |
| John Clarke, Sr. | Jno. Smith |
| Wm. Peacock | Thos. Hy |
| Wm. Newitt | Ja. Murry |
| Rich. Prince | Thos. Cotton |
| Thos. Waller | Dr. Newsham |
| Martin Thorne | Edmond Howell |
| Jno. Amry | Rich. Morris |
| Ni. Johnson | Wm. Swett |
| Rich. Blow | Martin Golborn |
| Rand. Holt | Jno. Rutherford |
| Jo. Newner | Jos. Wall |
| Fra. Taylor | Capt. Wiggins |
| Jno. Prince | Thos. Barlow |
| Edw. Bridgman | Fra. Sowerby |
| Antho. Cornish | Jno. Atkinson |
| Wm. Harris | Ar. Davis |

Page 327. 6 March 1682. Deposition of Wm. Pollard, aged 20 years, concerning an accident to Thos. Sowerby and Thos. Jordan's mare was killed.

Page 327. Deposition of Wm. Broadrib, aged 18 years, concerning Thos. Jordan's mare.

Page 328. 6 March 1682/ Christopher Foster, aged 33 years, testified in a like deposition. Luch Corker, aged 24, also deposed.

Page 328. 9 Feb. 1682/3. Mary Rogers, wife of Jno. Rogers, makes Edward Baly her atty. in right of dower to sell to Edward Grantham. Jno. Rogers was of Isle of Wight County.
John Due, Rich. Lucas.

Page 329. 17 March 1682/3. Thomas Arnold, belonging to the ship, Culpeper, a carpenter, appoints his friend P. Perry, merchant, his attorney to sue for recovery from James Parrott and Mr. Jno. Nicholls, execs. of the Will of Ann Arnold and that the Plantation was formerly my brother's: Edward

Arnold, of Chickahominy in James Citty County, Va., and in his Will of 14 Aug. 1679, left said plantation to her for life, and at her death to me and my heirs. My attorney to see after this. 3 July 1683.
Wm. Chischester, Robert Ruffin, Will Evans, Thos. Arnold.

Page 330. 27 April 1683. Indenture between Wm. Chivers of the Lower Parish, planter, sells for 3500 lbs. tobacco, 200 acres of land to Thomas Sidway, adjoining the land sold to John Hux...Arthur Allen survey, part of where I live. 3 July 1683.
Elizabeth Shivers relinquished her dower.

Page 330. 27 April 1683. Geo. Dowing appoints Elias Osbourne his attorney.

Page 331. 6 June 1683. Thos. Cole of James City County appoints his friend Thomas Jordan his attorney to bring to judgment Thos. Clarke of Isle of Wight in court, 6 June 1683. Signed: Thos. Cowle.

Page 331. 3 July 1683. Indenture between Sam Thompson who married Mary, only daughter of Maj. William Marriott, deceased, and Thomas Mathas of the other part, land adjoining Nicholas Sessums, 150 acres at Sessums Swamp, etc. Thos. Flood, Wm. Thompson.

Page 334. Geo. Blake, the elder, about 46 years old, deposes in a law altercation between Richard Andrews and Christopher Smith.

Page 334. Geo. Blake, the younger, aged 22 years, deposes to same.

Page 338. 6 9ber 1683. Wm. Harris, of Lawnes Creek Parish, only son and heir of Thomas Harris of the same Parish, deceased, and Mary his wife of the one part, and Robt. Ruffin of the other part, for 400 lbs. of tobacco sells 20 acres, part of 850 acres of land granted to Thomas Harris, deceased, by patent dated 13 Feb. 1657...on Sunken Marsh adjoining Thos. Jarrell...to Carter's land, etc.
Wm. Harris, Mary Harris.
Wit.: Wm. Newsum, Thomas Jarroll.

Page 338. 6 9ber 1683. Henry Hart acknowledges to have received of his father & guardian, Wm. Newsum, his part of father and Uncle Jno. Shepard's estate due by will or otherwise.
Robert Ruffin.

Page 339. 6 9ber 1683. Daniel Roome and Margarett his wife give to Thomas Farmer 50 acres of land.
Walter Flood, Jennit Jordan.

Page 339. 15 8ber 1683. John Clarke indebted to Roger Puleston.

Page 340. 7 Jan. 1683. Philip Randolph sailing in his boat in haste to get to Nansemond tomorrow his ketch laden, should be ready to saile, sends papers and desires Mr. Flood to appear in person for him, if not get Thomas Jordan.

Page 341. 12 Xber 1683. Launcelott Beck makes complaint of John Dun, formerly an inhabitant of this county, is privately departed out of the country and is indebted to Beck.

Page 341. 1 Jan. 1683. Nicholas Mason makes his wife Mary his attorney.
Henry Clarke, Wm. Holt.

Page 342. 1 Jan. 1683. On the back of a patent of land granted to Jno. Rogers, 14 May 1666, was written: John Rogers, Senior, of Surry County, with consent of his wife, Mary Rogers, and 1000 lbs. of tobacco, sells 200 acres to Edward Grantham, 23 9ber 1682.
Thos. Jordan, Chris. Tatum.

BOOK II, 1671-1684   123

Page 342. 15 Dec. 1683. On the back of sale of 150 acres of land sold by Bartholomew Owen and Joane, 6 7ber 1674, was written: Wm. Foreman for 2800 lbs. of tobacco assigns all right, title, and claim, to Richard Jordan. Will Browne. 15 Dec. 1683.
Roger Potter, John Clough.
Wife Hester relinquishes dower.

Page 342. 27 Xber 1683. Wm. Chivers of Va., planter, Surry County, sells to Jno. King all the divident of land adjoining land lately sold to Thomas Piddenton...Benjamin Harrison land down to Dibdall's path.
Wm. Knott, Geo. Nicholson, Rich. Dualos?, Wm. Chivers, Elizabeth Chivers.

Page 343. 1 Jan. 1683. Wm. Chivers for 1100 lbs. of tobacco sells to Hezekiah Bunnell, planter, 50 acres of land Upper Sunken Marsh, Surry County, to Wm. Blackbourn's, etc.
Richard Moonk, Jno. King, Richard Winclos?

Page 343. 8 Dec. 1683. Samuell Swann, for 1550 lbs. tobacco, sells to Thos. Jordan a house at Warenoke formerly belonging to Thos. Swann, now in possession of Thos. Jordan, and land belonging at least one-half acre belonging to said house, extending west to Samuel Thompson to Mill Swamp except dower to Madam Mary Swann.
Sarah Swann's consent. John Ironmonger.

Page 344. 5 7ber 1683. Wm. Baldwin of the Upper Parish and Elizabeth his wife, and Joseph Foard, part of a patent of 275 acres dated 20 April 1682, 80 acres of land in the Lower Parish of Surry County, to Arthur Davis' line to sd. Wm. Balden, adj. Geo. Cripp's land, to Geo. Harding's line.
Elizabeth Balden relinquishes her dower.
Know that I, Elizabeth Baldwin, wife of Wm. Baldwin, of Isle of Wight County, appoints Wm. Evans Attorney to acknowledge deeds of sale for land of her husband sold to Joseph Foard and Thomas Smith of Isle of Wight both dated 5 9ber 1683, to Joseph Foard 80 acres, to Thos. Smith, 70 acres.
Elizabeth Balden, Jno. Gray, Robt. Brocke. 27 Xber 1683.

Page 345. 5 9ber 1683. Ind. between Wm. Baldwin of the Upper Parish of Isle of Wight and Elizabeth his wife to Thos. Smith, 70 acres a patent of 275 acres 20 Aprill 1682 & on Main Blackwater River adj. Arthur Davis & Capt. Lawrance Baker, deceased. Jos. Foard, William Evans.

Page 345. 26 Feb. 1684. Ind. 25 Jan. 1660 between Alice Parke and George Carter, her son, of Lower Chipoaks, Surry County, to Aug. Hunicutt, 400 acres of land, 300 acres bounded as follows, east upon Mr. Dunstone...Mr. Pettway's door, for 99 years. Aylce Parke, Geo. Carter. G. Watkins, Matthew Townes.

Page 346. 4 March 1683. Wm. Howgood of Southwarke Parish, Surry County, acknowledges to have received of Jno. Warren his whole estate of all kinds and quality, etc.
Wm. Howgood, Ben. Harrison, Thos. Hux.

Page 347. 4 March 1683/4. George Branch, ye Younger, and Susannah his wife, sell to Mr. Henry Baker, merchant, 120 acres of land on Blackwater in Surry County, on the south side of Cypress Swamp.
Thomas Thropp, Joseph Rogers.

Page not given. Robert Kae had a grant of 300 acres of land on the East side of the Third Swamp of Blackwater in the Lower Parish of Surry County, in Robert Flake's line to Arthur Allen's corner for the transportation of six persons with names in records beneath the patent, 12 7ber 1662.

Rec. teste: Nich. Spenser, Sec., 20 Apr. 1682. Hen. Chicheley. On the back of the patent, Robert Kae, Sr., and Robert Kae, Jr., of the Isle of Wight County assign to Jno. Pittford of Surry County this patent of 300 acres of land. 4 March 1683/4.
Richard Beighton, John Parson, John Parson, Jr.

Page 349. 4 March 1683/4. Luke Myzealle for himself and heirs assigns 50 acres at the head of Gray's Creek adjoining David Andrews to Mr. William Thompson's line, 50 acres part of a patent to Jno. Newsum 1 April 1644 and assigned by him to Luke Myzealle, deceased, father, being dated 18 Dec. 1647 now to Bartholomew Brittle.
Will Foreman, Joseph Malden.

Page 350. 7 9ber 1682. Ni. Witherington for 4000 lbs. tobacco sells to James Cane 75 acres of land bought to Robert Gilbert.

The following abstracts were made from the upside-down pages inserted in the back part of Book II.

Page 1. 8 6ber 1680. Augustine Hunnicutt, Jr., Roger Rawlings, John Peirce of Surry County, are bound to the court of Surry County for 40,000 lbs. of tobacco in consideration of an obligation that Augustine Hunnicutt, Jr., pay to Elizabeth, orphan of Jno. Cooper, deceased, her child's part of the goods and chattels of her late father, deceased, as shall appear upon record, when she comes to lawful age, she to be educated and taught the Christian religion, etc.
Wit.: Elizabeth Carter, Wm. Edwards.

Page 2. 1680. Wm. Carpinder, Wm. Simmons, and Henry Briggs bound to the Court for 40,000 lbs, of tobacco. Wm. Carpinder to pay to Robert, orphant of Robt. Cartwright, a child's part of the goods and chattels of his late father, when he is of age.
Wit.: Hannah Harrison, Thomas Cotton.

Page 3. Received of Wm. Edwards of Surry County several costs of admittance to probate.
    Mr. John Ruffin    for est. of Jno. Goring
    Rob. Randall    for est. of Ann Hoskin
    Eliza Newhouse    for est. of Thos. Newhouse
    Wm. Rowland    for est. of Daughter Baly
    Ni. Smith    for est. of Thos. King
    Katherine Cornell    for est. of Samuell Cornell
    Charles Williams    for est. of Mary Haydon
26 7ber 1680. Henry Hartwell, Clerke of Court.

Page 4. 30 8ber 1680. John Gotheridge, Sr., of Isle of Wight County, Wm. Newsum, and Roger Delke of Surry County are bound to the Court for 4000 lbs. of tobacco on the estate of Soll. Davis, deceased.
Wit.: John Case, Wm. Edwards.

Page 5. Augustine Hunnicutt, Jr., Wm. Seward, and William Freeman are bound to the Court for 4000 lbs. tob. Aug. Hunicutt to pay to the orphans of John Hodge, deceased, their part of their father's estate.
Wit.: John Barnes, Wm. Cockerham.

Page 6. 12 9ber 1680. John Case, Capt. Charles Barham, and Wm. Seward are bound to the Court. Jno. Case to pay to Edward, orphan of Edward Browne, deceased, his part of his father's estate.
Wit.: John Rutherford, Will. Foreman.

Page 7. Charles Williams, Thos. Edwards, Wm. Harris...to pay to Wm. Goard, orphan of Henry Goard, etc.
Wit.: Wm. Seward, Wm. Edwards.

Page 8. 2 9ber 1680. Thos. Busby, John Moring, Wm. Simmons; Thos. Busby to pay to Wm. Charleton his part of his father's est.
Wit.: Robt. Ruffin, Wm. Edwards.

Page 9. 2 9ber 1680. Geo. Foster and Stephen Allen. Stephen Allen to pay to John and Prudence, orphans of John Kindred, deceased, their part of their father's estate.

BOOK II, 1671-1684                                                125

Page 10.  2 9ber 1680.  Thos. Horton, Jno. Phillips, Sr., and John Price bound
to the Court for 10,000 lbs. tob.  Thos. Horton to pay Francis, orphan of
Edward Davis, deceased, her portion of her father's estate.
Wit.: Seaward, Thomas Edwards.

Page 11.  2 9ber 1680.  Katherine Cornell, Wm. Foreman, and Aug. Hunnicutt,
Jr., are bound to the Court for 40,000 lbs. tobacco.  Katherine Cornell,
admx. of her husband, Samuel Cornell.
Wit.: Wm. Seward, Wm. Cockerham.

Page 11.  1 March 1680.  Thos. Warren, Wm. Foreman, Ni. Sessums bound to the
Court for 40,000 lbs. tob.  Thos. Warren to pay to Allen, Robert, and William,
orphans of Mr. Thos. Warren, deceased, their part of their father's estate.
Wit.: Wm. Seward.

Page 12.  Mary Swann, Wm. Edwards are bound for 20,000 lbs. tob. for administration on the est. of Mary Norris.
Wit.: John Rodwell, Wm. Arnoll.
Signed: Mary Swann, Wm. Edwards.

Page 13.  18 June 1680.  Roger Pitter, Wm. Freeman, 20,000 lbs. tob.  Roger
Potter is admr. of Est. of Thos. Foxcroft, deceased.

Page 14.  5 July 1681.  Fra. Upchurch, Robert Reynolds.  Francis Upchurch granted administration on estate of Michael Upchurch, deceased.
Wit.: John Thompson, Wm. Seward.

Page 15.  May 1682.  Ann Sowerby, Ed. Bayley, to pay Margaret, orphan of James
Sowerby, deceased, a child's part of her father's estate.
Ar. Jordan, Wm. Edwards.

Page 15.  9 July 1681.  John Rutherford, Wm. Simmons, Ed. Petway.  John Rutherford admr. for Thos. Cockerham, son to Wm. Cockerham, deceased.
Wit.: John Thompson, David Arther?

Page 16.  Wm. Chambers, Wm. Newsum, Wm. Gray are bound to the Court.  Wm.
Chambers to pay to Mary, orphan of Wm. Chambers, deceased, her part of her
father's estate.
Wit.: Jno. Harris, Robt. Ruffin.

Page 17.  1 9ber 1681.  John Skelton, Joseph Malden, bound to the Court for
10,000 lbs. tob.  Whereas Prudence Kindred, orphan of John Kindred, by the
Court, appoints to John Skelton until she comes of age or is married.
Wit.: Robt. Ruffin, John Edwards.

Page 17.  8 April 1682.  Jno. Clarke, William Chambers, Roger Ralings to
deliver to James Hodge, orphant of Jno. Hidge, deceased, a child's part of
his father's estate.
Wit.: Thos. Edwards, Wm. Edwards.

Page 18.  4 May 1682.  Wm. Hunt, Maj. Arthur Allen, Benjamin Harrison, bound
to the Court for 60,000 lbs. tob.  William Hunt to pay to Richard Parker,
orphan son of Richard Parker, deceased, a child's part of his late mother,
Judith Parker's estate when he is of age.
Wit.: John Thompson, Wm. Edwards.

Page 19.  Samuell Thompson, Samuell Plow, Geo. Foster are bound for 500 lbs.
tob. to keep an Ordinary with no unlawful gains in house, yard, or orchard,
no servant on the Sabbath, Holy days, or during Divine Worship or Sermon
take the name of all lodgers, unless the persons are well known.  Sell Ale,
Beer, and Strong Drink lightly sealed, etc., provided for traveller good
dyett, Lodging, Housing, etc.

Page 19.  15 June 1681.  Thomas Bage, Robert House, are bound to the Court
Wm. Rogers, orphan of Richard Rogers, apprenticed to Thos. Bage.
Wit.: Wm. Simmons, Wm. Edwards.

Page 20. 16 July 1683. Wm. Newman, Math. Swann are bound to the Court for 10,000, 16 July 1681. Wm. Williams, orphan of Lewis Williams is bound to Wm. Newsum until he is 21 years old, 16 July 1683.
Wit.: Robert Ruffin, Wm. Edwards.

Page 21. John Dunsfield owes the Court. Richard Robinson, Orphan of Andrew Robinson, bound to John Dunfield untill he is 21 years old.
Wit.: Roger Potter, Samuell Thompson.
Signed: John Dunford.

Page 21. 12 July 1683. Sion Hill, Geo. Williams of Surry County, bound to the Court. Sion Hill to pay the orphan of Lewis Williams, deceased, the portion of her late father's estate when she is of age, and to teach her the Christian religion.

Page 22. 3 July 1683. John Targett, Geo. Foster of Surry County. Then to pay to Stephen Vahan, orphan of Walter Vahan, deceased, his part of his father's estate.
Wit.: Wm. Simmons, Wm. Edwards.

Page 23. David Andrews, Jr., Geo. Fisher, Thos. Ironmonger are bound for 60,000 lbs. tob. to pay to Geo. Hogwood, orphan of Francis Hogwood, deceased, his part of his father's estate.
Will. Evans, Wm. Edwards.

Page 23. 1 Sept. 1683. Thos. Tias, Wm. Simmons, Jas. Ellis are bound for 20,000 lbs. to pay to Walter Holdsworth what is due from his late father, deceased.
Wit.: John Sharp, Owen Mirick.

Page 24. 14 Sept. 1683. Edward Rowell, Wm. Foreman, Charles Williams, to pay to Samuell, Elizabeth, Mary, Susannah, orphans of Samuel Cornell, deceased, their part of their late father's est., when of age.
Wit.: Wm. Edwards.

Page 25. 8 June 1681. Will. Foreman, Lt. Coll. Wm. Browne, 10,000 lbs. of tob. Wm. Hare, orphant of Wm. Hare, is bound to Wm. Foreman; nine years bound out.
Wit.: Sam. Swann, Wm. Pollard.

Page 26. 2 7ber 1683. Thos. Sowerby, Wm. Foreman. Thos. Sowerby to teach Jno. Collier, orphant of John Collier, the Christian religion.
Wit.: Elias Osborne, Wm. Edwards.

Page 26. 26 8ber 1683. Wm. Gray, Wm. Edwards to deliver to Edward Amry, orphant of Thomas Amry, deceased, his part of his father's estate.

Page 26. Samuel Thompson, Wm. Edwards, Thos. Sowerby, admrs. of the estate of Wm. Dorch, deceased.
Wit.: Wm. Thompson, Wm. Malden.

THE END

INDEX

A name may appear more than once on a page. The reader is advised to check for variant spellings.

(?), Anthony, 10
(?), Elias, 36
(?), Francis, 51
(?), Coll. Geo., 76
(?), Harry, 27
(?), Hen., 14
(?), Henry, 71
(?), James, 44
(?), Jennet, 90
(?), Jno., 44, 63, 64
(?), Michael, 42
(?), Richard, 48
(?), Robt., 47
(?), Thos., 62
(?), Wm., 23

Abbott, Sam, 1, 30
Adams, Capt., 44
    Joshua, 54
    Peter, 9, 10, 31, 47, 62, 65, 86
    Thomas, 29, 43, 54, 57, 98, 100
    Capt. Thomas, 40, 44, 110
    William, 110
Adkins, Joane, 78
    Richard, 78
    Thos., 58
Adrian, Judith, 85
Agborowe, Mr., 20
    Wm., 6, 17
Albertson, Albert, 70, 96
Alder, John, 29
Allcocke, Thos., 38, 40, 43
Allecocke, Thos., 42
Allen, Dr., 87
    Mr., 103
    Mrs. Alice, 76
    Anthony, 36
    Anthonye, 73
    Ar., 49, 111
    Arthur, 9, 12, 14, 18, 36, 37, 38, 39, 50, 59, 62, 66, 68, 69, 70, 80, 83, 98,

(Allen, Arthur, cont'd.), 102, 103, 106, 110, 113, 115, 116, 117, 122, 123
    Capt. Arthur, 101, 108
    Maj. Arthur, 116, 119, 125
    Francis, 73
    Humphrey, 12, 50, 74,
    Julian, 105
    Katherine, 115, 117
    Margaret, 80, 100
    Stephen, 74, 80, 82, 83, 85, 86, 104, 124
    William, 21, 50, 116
Allerton, Joanna, 41
Allson, James, 71
Aloorson, Wm., 97
Alscope, James, 90
Alsoope, James, 99
Alsope, Mr., 102
    James, 95
    Judith, 95
Aman, Wm., 19
Amory, Charles, 86
    See also Amry.
Amry, Benj., 72
    Ch., 121
    Charles, 65, 84, 107, 112
    Ed, 68
    Edward, 67, 126
    Jno., 121
    Thomas, 53, 67, 126
    See also Amory.
Amy, Ann, 105
    John, 105
Andrewes, Thos., 15
Andrews, Ann, 28, 67, 78, 84, 98, 120, 124, 126
    Elizabeth, 98
    Richard, 110, 118, 121, 122
    Thomas, 27, 28, 29, 33, 34, 39, 41, 45, 46, 61, 81, 85, 120
Ann, Indian, 103

INDEX

Annam, Wm., 50
Antibas, John, 68
Antrobas, Joseph, 86
Antrobos, Joseph, 91
Antrobus, Joseph, 73, 74, 79, 81, 94
ap Thomas, Thomas, 8, 11, 16
Applewhaite, Henry, 59, 62, 75
Archer, Mary, 113
  Roger, 113
  Robert, 120
  Wm., 103, 112, 120
Armstrong, Hen., 121
Arnold, Ann, 121
  Edward, 121, 122
  Thomas, 121, 122
  Wm., 120
Arnoll, W., 97
  Wm., 73, 125
Arther, David, 125
Artillerye, Henry, 35
Ashton, John, 49
Aston, Stephen, 101, 105
  Watt, 44
Atkins, Richard, 80
  Robt., 13, 15
Atkinson, Francis, 60
  James, 61
  Jno., 115, 121
  Thos., 61
  Wm., 74, 87
Attkin, Richard, 51
Attkins, James, 54
  Richard, 7, 21
  Robert, 5, 38
  Wm., 38
Austin, Robert, 101
  Sarah, 101
Avery, Ann, 87
  Richard, 77, 79, 121
  Wm., 87
Averye, Mark, 17
Axleford, Tobias, 54
Aylett, Wm., 89
Ayman, (?), 50


B-(?), Richard, 56
Babb, Robert, 64, 72
  Roby, 63
Bacon, Col., 120
  Coll. Nathan, 110
Bage, Thomas, 125
Bageley, Job, 17
Bagg, Thomas, 99
Bagley, Hugh, 115
  Peter, 115
Baiden, Wm., 105
Bailey, Ar., 19
  Arthur, 18
  Henry, 98
Baison, John, 51
Baker, (?), 18, 64, 68

(Baker, cont'd)
  Capt., 111
  Mr., 14
  Chr., 2
  Eliza, 116
  Elizabeth, 100
  Henry, 66, 74, 86, 91, 99, 100, 104, 105, 112, 123
  Hin. (or Hen.), 118, 119
  John, 79, 100
  Lawrence, 5, 10, 12, 31, 42, 44, 45, 75, 79, 80, 87, 89, 93, 96, 100
  Capt. Lawrence, 47, 57, 58, 66, 68, 70, 73, 74, 77, 88, 89, 97, 100, 101, 105, 110, 116, 123
  Samuel, 10
  Tho., 79, 97
Balden, Elizabeth, 123
  Wm., 123
Baldwin, Elizabeth
  John, 20, 59
  William, 123
Baley, Edward, 120
Balie, John, 74
Ballard, Thomas, 60, 63
Baly, (?), 124
  Edward, 120, 121
Bancos, John, 34
Banks, John, 63
Bannister, Mr., 7, 13
  Clara, 13
  Eliza, 14, 20
  Hen., 6
  Henry, 6, 9, 30
  Jno., 17
Banton, Dr., 86
Barber, Mrs., 72
  John, 60, 76
  William, 91
Barbribb, Wm., 68
Barcroft, Charles, 13
Barecroft, Charles, 14
Barefoot, Geo., 16
Bardy, Jno., 97
Barham, Capt., 90, 101, 102
  Charles, 8, 38, 48, 49, 53, 56, 57, 60, 66, 68, 73, 74, 79, 82, 86, 89, 91, 93, 98, 100, 101, 111, 114
  Capt. Charles, 79, 83, 84, 89, 90, 92, 100, 106, 110, 124
  Coralul, 67
  Richard, 48
Barker, Mr., 57
  Ann, 86, 89, 109

(Barker, cont'd)
   James, 28
   Jethro, 109
   John, 7, 8, 28, 29,
      32, 35, 36, 38, 45,
      48, 84, 85, 86, 89,
      95, 109
   John, Jr., 97
   Joshua, 95
   Capt. Law., 39
   Letitia, 75
   Rich., 100
   Wm., 24
Barlow, (?), 59
   Eliza, 62
   Thomas, 62, 96, 98,
      100, 121
Barnes, Ann, 55
   Humph, 45
   Humphre, 55
   John, 53, 67, 78, 80,
      82, 84, 88, 89, 99,
      110, 112, 124
   Rich, 15
   Walter, 32
Barrett, Mr., 85
   Edward, 70
   James, 108
   Capt. William, 108
Barrlowe, Thos., 59
Barrott, Mr., 107
   James, 121
Barroughe, John, 29
Barrow, Mr., 2
   Jno., 2, 15
   Thos., 114
Bartlett, (?), 112
   Mr., 92
   Dorothy, 56
   Walter, 40, 49, 79,
      81, 86, 91, 92, 99,
      110, 112, 115
   William, 45
   Goody, 56
Bartley, Dorothy, 65
   Patrick, 57, 65, 68
Bartly, Goodman, 56
Barton, Jno., 112
Barwicke, Daniel, 5, 6
Basham, Elizabeth, 66
Baskwitz, Marmaduke, 51
Bason, John, 43
Basse, Xpher, 96
Bateman, Robert, 5
Bates, Henry, 108
Batick, Jno., 32
Batt, Jno., 12, 20
   M., 27
   Wm., 4, 5, 6, 7, 12,
      13, 14, 15, 18, 19,
      20, 30, 31, 33, 34,
      58
Battel, (?), 21
Battell, Ann, 33
   Jno., 119

(Battell, cont'd.)
   Math., 7
   Mathew, 8, 18, 33, 37,
      43
   Matthew, 20, 21, 33,
      34, 35, 36
Battle, Mason, 57
   Mat., 43
   Mathew, 48, 51
   Matthew, 41, 42, 54
Baugham, Charles, 42
Bavin, (?), 4
   Richard, 3, 4, 5, 12,
      45
Bavinn, Elizabeth, 33
Baxter, Jno., 113
Bayle, Henrye, 15
Bayley, Ed, 125
Baylie, Jno., 16, 67
   Thos., 15, 24
Baylor, James, 4
Bayneham, John, 121
Beale, John, 84, 85
Beaman, Joseph, 28
Beaseley, John
Beasley, John, 69
Beattie, John, 40
Beazley, Job, 17
Bechino, Edward, 74
Bechinoe, David, 40
Beck, Lancelett, 119
   Lancelot, 115
   Launcelett, 122
Beckett, Charles, 86
Beckwith, (?), 59
   Elizabeth, 98
   Grace, 98
   Marmaduke, 38, 59
Bedinfield, Theophilus, 37
Beighton, Richard, 123
Bemis, Thos., 52
Bendall, James, 85, 87
Bennett, (?), 45
   Jonas, 104
   Richard, 5, 6, 11
   Gov. Richard, 76
   Thomas, 29, 67
Benns, Thomas, 77
   See also Binns.
Bentley, Francis, 120
   Thos., 43, 45, 75, 99,
      102, 120, 121
Bentlie, Thomas, 108
Bently, Tho., 87
Benton, Jno., 11
Berkeley, (?), 3, 93
   Fra., 106
   William, 5, 31, 35,
      59, 64, 71, 79, 83,
      84, 96, 98
   Capt. William, 96
   Gov. William, 60, 94
   Sir William, 9, 12,
      19, 30, 38, 53, 65,
      90, 104, 109, 112

INDEX

Bernard, Col. William, 76
Berrye, Jno., 9
Bess, Indian, 112
Besse, Mr., 89
Beverly, Robert, 103
Bevin, Mrs., 3
Biddle, Rich., 32
Bidford, John, 61
Biggins, Laurence, 38
Biggs, Thos., 15
Bigton, Richard, 117
Bilbro, Thos., 60
Bilbrough, (?), 66
    Thos., 67
Bilde, Edward, 32
Billings, John, 41
Billingsley, Wm., 43
Billison, Jno., 8
Binam, John, 113
Bingham, John, 44
Bingley, James, 114
Binham, John, 44
Binnell, Hezekiah, 40
Binns, Mr., 64
    Martha, 13
    Thomas, 4, 6, 13, 20, 29, 33, 52, 61, 63, 64, 65, 111, 112
    See also Benns.
Binum, John, 119
Birchell, Jno., 47
Bird, Ann, 99, 104
    John, 61, 64, 80, 83, 99, 100, 104
    Thomas, 82, 84, 99, 115
    Wm., 73, 81, 115
Birde, Mr., 17
Bish., James, 106
Bishoff, Jno., 6
Bishop, Capt., 53
    John, 86, 92, 93, 94, 100, 121
Bishopp, Capt., 16
    Coll. Henerye, 19
    Jno., 4, 13, 15
Black, John, 58
Blackborne, Jane, 17
    John, 3, 4, 15, 17
    Wm., 121
Blackbourn, Wm., 123
Blackbourne, (?), 3
    John, 6, 12
Blackburn, John, 45
    William, 119
Blackburne, John, 12
    William, 102
Blake, Geo., 122
Bland, Mr., 62
    Edward, 1, 3, 8, 99, 109
    Giles, 99, 112
    Mrs. Jane, 8
    John, 1, 8, 99, 109, 112
    Richard, 1

(Bland, cont'd.)
    Sarah, 112
    Theo., 70
    Theodoric, 109
    Theodorick, 7, 8, 21, 109, 112
    Theodosia, 99
    See also Blande.
Blande, (?), 51
    Edward, 19
    Francis, 29
    John, 21, 29
    Theodorick, 19, 21, 29
    Thos., 19, 28
Blayton, John, 74
    Thos., 66, 72, 81, 100, 120
Blesley, Elizabeth, 102
Blisley, Elizabeth, 103
Blondmore, Richard, 50
Blow, George, 37, 40, 46, 49, 51, 61, 110, 113
    Margaret, 113
    Margery, 49
    Margritt, 51
    Richard, 108, 113, 115, 119, 121
Bloyse, Rob., 7
Blunt, Marye, 17
    Richard, 6, 10, 14, 17, 83, 107, 111
    Thomas, 107, 108, 111, 116
    Wm., 92, 101, 104, 105
Board, Jno., 6, 10
Boaz, Christopher, 7
Boez, Christopher, 7
    Xpo, 7
Bond, John, 13, 23
Booker, Roger, 23
Bookmaster, John, 50
Boone, Tompson, 55
Boswell, Tho., 79
Bothwell, Capt. William, 21
Boulding, Wm., 44
Bowles, Wm., 75
Braddie, John, 2
Braderton, Henry, 34, 42
Brady, Dorothy, 69
    Ellene, 48
    Ellenor, 48
    Jno., 2, 45, 48, 52, 54, 62, 72, 78
    Patrick, 69
Bradye, Johanna, 14
    John, 6, 10, 27, 30
Brains, Rich., 15
Bralye, Robert, 75
Brams, Humphrey, 44
Bramston, John, 71
    Mildred, 71
Branch, George, 106, 109, 123
    Susannah, 109, 123
Brasseur, John, 98

INDEX 131

Brassier, Richard, 100
Brasso, Christopher, 96
Brassure, (?), 1
Braxup, Nathanaell, 77
Brent, Giles, 13
Brereton, Thos., 30
Bresse, Wm., 14, 41
Bretton, Temperance, 13
    William, 13
Breweton, Thomas, 37
Brewster, Anthony Sackford, 13
    Eliza, 13, 40
    Sack, 5, 6, 7, 8, 9, 10
    Sackford, 12, 13, 15
    Sarah, 1
    Thomas, 12, 13
    Zach., 15
Briant, Jno., 6
Bricknel, Wm., 66
Bridgeman, Edward, 78
Bridger, Col., 112
    Jos., 58
    Col. Joseph, 97, 98, 110
Bridgers, Hezachiah, 41
Bridges, Anthony, 40
    Anthonye, 25
    William, 83
Bridgman, Edward, 72, 121
Brigge, Tim., 104
Briggs, Henry, 43, 45, 50, 53, 54, 60, 69, 97, 104, 107, 112, 116, 119, 120, 124
    Margery, 116
    Mary, 52, 107
    Rich., 55
    Richard, 69, 79, 86, 93, 111
Brigs, Henry, 51, 52, 57, 72, 74, 81
    Rich., 70
Briscoe, W., 116
Brittle, Bartholomew, 120, 124
Broaddrib, Wm., 119
Broadrib, (?), 119
    Wm., 121
Brock, Richard, 62
Brocke, Robt., 123
Brooks, Henry, 101
Broughton, John, 67
    Thos., 22
Brown, Coll., 39
    Ann, 42
    Baton, 61
    William, 21, 62, 63, 116
    Capt. Wm., 53
Browne, Capt., 11
    Col., 4, 39
    Maj., 93, 95, 96
    Ann, 5, 25, 37, 40
    Berkeley, 42
    Edward, 56, 111, 115, 124

(Browne, cont'd.)
    Elizabeth, 56
    Geo., 7
    Capt. Henerye, 10
    Henry, 34, 37
    Capt. Henry, 38
    Col. Henry, 5, 13, 14, 15, 25, 33, 42
    John, 62, 75, 93
    Mary, 120
    Thomas, 33
    William, 5, 12, 17, 25, 26, 34, 58, 63, 64, 68, 87, 92, 95, 104, 106, 116, 120, 123
    Capt. William, 45, 46, 60
    Col. William, 120
    Lt. Col. William, 77, 117, 126
    Maj. William, 96, 97, 106, 107
Bruster, Elizabeth, 68
Bruten, Jno., 34, 40, 42
Bruton, John, 4, 44, 67
Buckmaster, (?), 84
Buford, James, 72
Buirde, Thos., 97
Bull, John, 51
Bullock, Rich., 68
Bunell, Hez., 77
Bunhill, Joane, 118
Bunnell, Eskiah, 100
Bunnell, Henry, 120
    Hezekiah, 40, 61, 117, 118
Bunnoll, Hezekiah, 106, 123
Burchell, Ed., 54
    William, 10, 30
Burcher, George, 10, 37, 38, 43
    Jno., 38
    Mary, 37, 38
    Maurice, 38
    Morris, 37, 43, 58
Burches, Maurice, 51
Burges, John, 49, 74
Burgess, Ann, 108
    Job, 80
    John, 12, 45, 56, 58, 65
    Mary, 56
    Robert, 58, 66, 69, 70, 97, 99, 103, 108, 119
    Capt. Robert, 103
    Susannah, 65
Burke, Elizabeth, 13
Burshell, Ed., 58
    Sabian, 41
    William, 41
Burwell, Wm., 24
Busby, Mr., 104
    Mrs., 104

INDEX

(Busby, cont'd.)
  Grace, 73
  James, 36
  Janis, 91
  Joane, 82
  Susanna, 116
  Susannah, 115, 116
  Thomas, 20, 25, 31, 35,
    36, 45, 54, 55, 64,
    68, 70, 73, 74, 82,
    83, 84, 94, 95, 98,
    100, 103, 104, 112,
    115, 116, 120, 124
  Lt. Thos., 91
  William, 104
Bushell, Edward, 37, 44, 47,
  49, 50, 51, 52, 54,
  55, 57, 58, 59, 61,
  64, 65, 67, 69
  Mary, 52, 67
Bussey, George, 31
Butler, (?), 50
  Joyce, 60, 77
  William, 17, 18, 50,
    55, 60, 70, 74, 77,
    78, 82
  Maj. William, 12, 58,
    60, 74
Butte, William, 25
Butte, Henry, 25
  William, 25
Buttes, Wm., 14
Buttler, Wm., 32, 86, 97
Butts, Wm., 24
Bynam, John, 49, 109, 114,
  116
  Rosamond, 116
  Rose, 113
Bynham, John, 75
Bynum, John, 113


Candlis, Thomas, 62
Cane, Andrew, 15
  James, 124
  Thomas, 94
Cardinpaine, Cr., 121
Carker, John, 80
Carlisle, Rich., 100
Carpenter, Francis, 31
  William, 54, 67, 78
Carpinder, Wm., 101, 124
Carpinter, Wm., 87, 99, 114,
  115
Carr, John, 75, 107
Carter, (?), 1, 122
  Mr., 62, 63
  Mrs., 62
  Alice, 8, 13, 14
  Alyse, 61
  Aylse, 62
  Eliz., 14
  Elizabeth, 124
  George, 33, 42, 51, 61,
    62, 65, 74, 79, 85,
    123

(Carter, cont'd.)
  Jno., 32
  Mary, 85, 86
  Rich., 16
  Robert, 46
  William, 2, 8, 13, 14,
    15, 62
Carterage, Rob., 49
Cartright, Elizabeth, 77
  Robert, 77, 78
Cartwright, Ben., 16
  Robert, 49, 51, 54, 66,
    67, 96, 124
Cary, Jane, 67
  Jno., 55, 63, 66, 67,
    69, 75, 91, 101, 104,
    106, 110
  Miles, 61
  Col. Miles, 59
  Sam., 51
  Thos., 49, 51
Case, Isabel, 82
  Isabell, 80
  Isabella, 60
  John, 68, 111, 121, 124
  Judith, 101
  Richard, 21, 33, 34, 45,
    60, 61, 62, 80, 82,
    115
Casey, John, 57
Casse, John, 66
Castle, Robert, 51
Catton, Maid Servant, 42
Caufield, Lieut. Col., 36
  Mr., 90
  Dorcas, 9
  Eliza, 9, 118
  Rebecca, 67
  Robert, 9, 50, 59, 66,
    68, 70, 77, 78, 80,
    82, 83, 86, 88, 91,
    92, 93, 94, 100, 101,
    103, 106, 108, 110,
    112, 114, 117, 118,
    119
  Mrs. Robert, 101
  Wm., 9, 50, 59
  Lieut. William, 4
  Lieut. Col. Wm., 38
Causey, Jno., 95
Cawse, John, 2
Cawsey, John, 2
Chaddock, (?), 52
  Henry, 47
Chaddocke, Hen., 52
Chalker, John, 55
Challoner, Wm., 102
Chambers, (?), 65
  Margery, 86, 101
  Mary, 78, 121, 125
  William, 66, 70, 78, 84,
    101, 121, 125
Chamble, Wm., 105
Champion, John, 107
Charles I, King of England,
  35

# INDEX 133

Charles II, King of England, 35, 103
Charles, John, 45, 67
Charleton, Wm., 124
Cheeseman, Lieut. Col. John, 76
Chicheley, Hen., 123
Chichley, Henry, 117
Chickeley, Sir Henry, 114
Chickley, Henry, Deputy Gov., 110, 114
Chiffers, Thos., 34
Chiles, Walter, 1, 5, 15, 30, 42, 59
Chischester, Wm., 122
Chissell, James, 88
Chissett, James, 88
Chivers, Elizabeth, 49, 117, 123
    Thomas, 34, 49
    William, 117, 118, 122, 123
Christrin, Evaginus, 42
Churchman, Ann, 65
    Robert, 22
Claiborne, Gov. Wm., 11
Clarie, Judith, 36, 39
    Thomas, 34, 36, 39, 79
Clark, John, 29
    Thomas, 60
Clarke, (?), 1, 113
    Geo., 24
    Henerye, 26
    Henry, 53, 106, 112, 122
    John, 36, 56, 57, 58, 74, 81, 84, 94, 102, 115, 121, 122, 125
    Katherine, 56
    Mary, 60, 113
    Phillip, 69
    Richard, 10, 36, 41, 47, 84, 112, 119
    Thomas, 16, 32, 53, 54, 60, 66, 71, 73, 83, 87, 97, 121, 122
    William, 41, 72, 94, 119
Clary, John, 49
    Thomas, 48, 67, 110
Clarye, Thos., 35
Clay, Charles, 23
    Ezra, 67
    John, 24, 37, 38, 40, 42, 68, 113
    Thomas, 71, 88, 111, 114
Clayborne, Col. Wm., 76
Claye, Eliza, 111
    John, 11
    Thomas, 114
Clements, (?), 44
    Edward, 67
    Jeremiah, 30, 36
    John, 43, 104, 105

Clemmens, Jno., 46
Clemons, Capt., 119
Clemts., Jno., 101
Clough, John, 123
Clutterbuck, Mary, 108
Coates, Daniel, 7, 12
    Mrs. Daniel, 7
    Eliza, 11, 12
Coats, Ralph, 53
Cobb, Henry, 37
    Nicholas, 44
Cobcutt, Margaret, 80
    Robt., 80
Cobicutt, Rob., 39
Cock, William, 74, 106
Cocke, Mr., 16
    Samuel, 49
    Thomas, 96
    Wm., 22
Cocker, Eliza, 107
    John, 12
    William, 58, 107
Cockerham, (?), 56
    Bro., 9
    Capt., 71, 76, 79, 82, 114
    Lt. Col. Geo., 66
    Gulleham, 67
    John, 51
    Thomas, 65, 125
    William, 2, 9, 10, 21, 36, 42, 47, 48, 49, 50, 53, 60, 62, 65, 124, 125
    Capt. William, 37, 57, 59, 62, 65
Cockin, William, 57, 58, 66, 75, 79
Coffelder, Major, 79
    Robert, 79
Coffer, John, 54
Cogan, Jno., 7, 8, 20
Coghland, James, 66
Cogill, Wm., 51
Coker, John, 119
Colby, Ed., 62, 63
    Edwin, 33
Cole, Col. 120
    Thomas, 122
    Col. William, 110
Coleby, Rob., 119
Collier, Edward, 63
    John, 1, 40, 63, 77, 107, 108, 111, 126
    Joseph, 111
    Mary, 107, 108, 111
    Thomas, 111
Collins, Mr., 102
    John, 12, 104, 119
    William, 12
Colly, Ed., 63
Collyere, Jno., 99
Colner, Thos., 24
Colt, Richard, 1
    Thos., 57

Comes, Henerye, 30
Commes, Henerye, 20
Comos, Henry, 36
Compton, Ch., 22
    Charles, 22
Concent, Absatt, 25
Coneson, Thos., 43
Conquest, Edward, 56
Converse, Jno., 23
Cooke, Edward, 14
    George, 37
    Thomas, 32
    Tobias, 10
    Tobyas, 34
    William, 116
Cookin, Wm., 57
Cooper, Elizabeth, 106, 124
Cooper, John, 2, 3, 33, 34,
        103, 106, 124
    Margaret, 106
    Phillis, 2
Coote, Jere., 24
Copcutt, Robt., 15
Copeland, Wm., 54
Corbin, Gawin, 84
Corbyn, Henry, 70
Cordenpayne, Cornelius, 66,
    104
Cordipayne, Cornelius, 94
Corker, (?), 4
    Capt., 57, 106, 109
    Mr., 25, 29
    Mrs., 14
    Dorothe, 14
    Dorothye, 31
    John, 1, 2, 6, 7, 10,
        13, 14, 15, 16, 20,
        27, 28, 30, 33, 36,
        37, 38, 40, 41, 45,
        47, 51, 52, 54, 55,
        57, 63, 71, 72, 76
    Luch, 121
    Lucy, 111
    Susannah, 109
    William, 5, 12, 45, 49,
        52, 53, 54, 55, 57,
        63, 82, 85, 86, 91,
        109
    Capt. Wm., 39, 51, 52,
        58, 85, 109
Cornell, Elizabeth, 126
    Katherine, 124, 125
    Mary, 126
    Samuel(1), 21, 49, 88,
        124, 125, 126
    Susannah, 126
Cornish, Antho., 121
    Margrit, 66
Cornwall, Samuel, 59
Corpe, Gartrid, 91, 94
    Geo., 80, 87, 91, 92,
        94
Cosignat, Arnell, 71
Cotten, Thomas, 78
Cotton, Thomas, 119, 121,
    124

Countenance, Josephus, 32
Courtman, John, 4, 5, 15,
    27
Covington, Thomas, 9, 10
Cowle, Thomas, 122
Cox, John, 83
    Capt. Wm., 7
Crabb, Wm., 15
Craddocke, Wm., 15
Cradock, Henry, 36
Craford, Nich., 66
Crafton, Maj., 29
    Widdowe, 3
    Mary, 2
    Marye, 2, 3
    Thomas, 2, 3, 12
Creed, Widdow, 63
    Ralph, 26, 34, 39,
        45, 49, 51, 116
    Robert, 34
Creeds, Mary, 109
Crewes, Thos., 73
Crews, Thos., 73, 78, 94,
    97, 109
Cripps, Geo., 123
Crofton, Widdowe, 3
Crooketts, (?), 89
Crosbe, (?), 18
Crues, Tho., 93
Cruse, Joane, 60
    Thos., 60, 61, 82, 83
Cuddiford, Robert, 101
Cullmer, Thos., 44, 50
Culmer, Mr., 41
    Hannah, 42
    Thomas, 7, 8, 10, 14,
        20, 26, 35, 37, 42,
        43, 44
Culpeper, (?), 83
    Gov. Thomas, 114
Cuodifer, Robert, 102
Curry, Masum, 8
Curtis, Edward, 39, 50
    Sarah, 110
    Thomas, 2


Dame, Henry, 16
Danby, John, 79
    See also Daube.
Daniel, Adam, 13
Darby, Wm., 44
Daube, Izabell, 67
    John, 67, 120
    See also Danbe.
Davies, John, 79
    Mary, 78
    Rowland, 104
Davis, Ar., 121
    Arthur, 123
    Edward, 104, 109, 121,
        125
    Francis, 125
    Hugh, 120
    Jannet, 81
    John, 79

INDEX 135

(Davis, cont'd.)
   Mary, 79, 80, 111
   Richard, 52, 55
   Soll., 124
   Tho., 86
   William, 22, 26
Davison, Alexander, 100
Dawkes, John, 48, 87
Dawl, Benj., 33
Dawson, Anne, 42
   Hen., 71
Dearemon, Robert, 116
Deberry, Peter, 52
de Courtee, Lucas, 28
Deholl, (?), 99
de Jores, Aman, 15
Delk, Rebecca, 57, 92, 110
   Roger, 44, 45, 55, 57,
      88, 92, 95, 99,
      110
Delke, Mr., 30
   Rebecca, 45, 74, 81,
      110
   Roger, 34, 40, 45, 49
      74, 81, 92, 104,
      110, 124
Delonbatt, Lewys, 5
Delores, Amaro, 55
Denfield, John, 93
Denigon, George, 47
Denison, Charles, 121
Dennett, Robert, 15
Dennis, Anne, 46, 80, 114
   Richard, 16
   Robert, 46, 50, 52
   William, 41
deSores, Amaro, 19
Despard, Jno., 69
Dewe, Richard, 10
Deyney, Luke, 21
Dibdall, (?), 123
   John, 1, 3, 4, 8, 9,
      14, 16, 19, 34
   Richard, 3, 4, 8, 9,
      46
Dickinson, Griffin, 82
   Griffith, 16, 52
   Thomas, 57
Dickson, Griffith, 20
Die, John, 42
Digby, Robert, 7
Diggs, Madam, 120
   Edward, 11
Dimeage, Thos., 6
Dimmette, Thos., 14
Dinnis, Robert, 50, 51
Divall, (?), 57
Dobbe, Jno., 10
Dobbs, Jno., 4, 10
Dodd, Mr., 112
Dolly, Ben., 35
   Jno., 47
Dollye, John, 31
Dollyes, John, 52
Domingo(e), George, 83, 84

Dorch, Wm., 126
Dotson, Amara, 106
Dow, Edward, 32
Dowdeswell, Richard, 32
Dowing, Geo., 122
Dowinge, Wm., 69
Dowling, (?), 70
   William, 39, 60, 62
Doxwell, Robert, 62
Draper, Wm., 97
Drew, Faith, 111
   Johanna(h), 25
   John, 50
   Mabell, 61, 77, 111
   Richard, 35, 38, 42, 44,
      49, 50, 61, 63, 64,
      65, 66, 67, 68, 70,
      74, 77, 78, 79, 83,
      86, 107, 111
   Thomas, 24, 28, 107,
      111, 117
Drewery, Thos., 23
Drewry, John, 41
Drinker, Thos., 41
Drinkwater, P., 21
   Pet., 22
Drowe, Thos., 25
Drue, Thos., 23
Drummond, Sarah, 107
   William, 36, 39, 107
Drumond, Wm., 81
Dualos, Rich., 123
Due, John, 121
Duglas, Geo., 35
   Samuel, 41
Duke, William, 81, 98, 112
Dulmore, Thos., 33
Dun, John, 122
Dunfield, John, 126
Dunford, John, 78, 95, 111,
   126
Dunn, John, 101
   Joseph, 20
   Obedience, 101
   Thomas, 99
Dunnington, Thos., 15
Dunstan, Cecillye, 46
   Cecilye, 34
   Cecylia, 38
   Cicely, 39
   Hester, 36
   John, 32, 33, 34, 36,
      38, 39, 73, 74, 75,
      79, 82
   Peleg, 32, 33, 34, 39,
      46, 49, 56, 73, 76
   Pheleg, 38
   Ralph, 18, 32, 33, 34,
      36, 38, 39, 46, 53
   Sicelye, 73
Dunster, Robt., 2
Dunston, Cicely, 8
   Hester, 79
   John, 79, 94
   Peleg, 79

INDEX

(Dunston, cont'd.)
   Ralph, 79
Dunstone, Mr., 123
   Peleg, 105
Duthace, Diana, 79
   William, 79
Duthaco, Chas., 79
Dvais, Hannah, 73
   Jane, 73
Dye, Jno., 30, 40, 41


Easell, Timothy, 112
Easille, George, 112
Easton, Trystam, 58
Edloe, Mathew(e), 15, 41
Edward, Mr., 101
Edwards, Mrs., 111
   Gulielmi, 89
   John, 99, 105, 125
   Sam, 23
   Sarah, 5
   Thos., 112, 116, 118,
     124, 125
   William, 5, 6, 7, 15,
     17, 25, 27, 30, 31,
     33, 40, 44, 52, 64,
     73, 75, 77, 78, 79,
     81, 82, 83, 86, 87,
     89, 90, 91, 93, 95,
     96, 98, 99, 100,
     101, 105, 112, 113,
     116, 117, 118, 119,
     120, 124, 125, 126
Eliote, Elinor, 115
Elizabeth, negro, 55
Elliott, Elinor, 115
   Phillip, 20
Ellis, Edward, 15, 28, 30,
   54
   James, 111, 113, 126
   Jeremiah, 68, 72, 92,
     95, 102, 106, 108,
     112, 114, 117, 118,
     120
   Margaret, 83, 100
   Mary, 102
   Thos., 28
Ellison, Robert, 22
Else, Ellis, 41
Elson, James, 65, 66, 67
Elye, Robert, 24
Emerson, John, 67, 75
Emlin, Henry, 2
Emmerson, Jno., 87
Emmett, Mary, 53
Endicus, Da., 16
Endlow, (?), 76
Eneline, (?), 4
England, Fra., 12
   Francis, 52
Epes, John, 114
Epps, Capt., 16
   Capt. Francis, 76
   Maj. Francis, 119
   Capt. Jno., 56

Esell, Richard, 7
Esquire, John, 104
Essel, Tim, 106
Evans, Ab., 120
   Abraham, 114
   Anthony(e), 68, 69, 79,
     117
   Dorothy, 68
   Fra., 104
   Ro., 115
   Robt., 104, 109
   Thos., 56
   Will, 113, 119, 122
   William, 123, 126
Eveline, (?), 4
Evens, Antho., 78
   Robt., 16
Everett, John, 117
Everist, Francis, 105
Ewan, Mary, 34
Ewin, Mr., 34


Faris, B., 51
Farlow(e), Joseph, 107, 111
Farned, Edward, 113
Farrell, Herbert, 105
Faucett, Anthony, 15
Fawden, Maj. Geo., 12
Feild, Richardina, 6
Felton, Alice, 25, 36
   Thomas, 3, 35, 36
Fen, Edward, 48
Fenn, Anthony, 112
   Edward, 30
Fermer, Thomas, 122
fferringham, Tho., 82
Field, Peter, 114
Figgers, Bartholomew, 113,
   117, 119
Filmore, Mr., 12
Finlay, John, 103
Firth, Sam., 103
Fisher, George, 126
   John, 9, 10, 14, 15,
     18
   Joseph, 9, 32, 46
   Marye, 9
   William, 9, 26, 31, 32,
     33, 34, 39
   Capt. William, 120
ffitchett, Joshua, 90
Fitzgarrett, Edward, 16
Fitzharding, Lord, 89
Fiveash, Joyce, 118
Flake, Robert, 61, 123
Flere, Theophilus, 39
Fletcher, Hamball, 39
   Lance, 103
   Mary, 100, 101
Flood, Capt. 47, 49
   Col., 46, 57, 74
   Mr., 122
   Charles, 21
   James, 52
   Jane, 44, 48, 51, 52,

INDEX 137

(Flood, Jane, cont'd.)
    52, 67, 71, 74
    John, 3, 4, 12, 14, 17,
        18, 19, 21, 27, 30,
        31, 78, 100, 109,
        120
    Col. John, 15, 19 25,
        31, 52, 67, 71, 74,
        108
    Theophilus, 44
    Thomas, 25, 30, 31, 36,
        39, 45, 55, 63, 64,
        94, 122
    Capt. Thos., 44, 45, 47,
        51, 67, 75
    Walter, 66, 67, 71, 74,
        75, 77, 106, 118,
        119, 122
Flower, Jno., 23, 24
Flowers, Thomas, 62
Foanes, Rich., 56
Foard, Charles, 41
    Joseph, 111, 121, 123
Folliot, Edward, 10
Folliott, Edward, 14
Follis, Edward, 33
Folph, Humphry, 109
Fones, Joane, 50
Foord, Mary, 30
Forbes, James, 13, 104, 105
Forbesse, James, 106
Forbus, Isabelle, 96
    James, 111
Ford, Charles, 21, 24, 25,
    108
Forde, Charles, 15, 21, 25
Fordman, Wm., 116
Foreman, (?), 55
    Hester, 123
    John, 55
    William, 9, 40, 54, 73,
        77, 78, 83, 85, 86,
        113, 123, 124, 125,
        126
Forman, William, 92
Fortesque, Mr., 43
Foserraft, Thos., 111
Foster, Christopher, 87, 104,
    106, 120, 121
    Elizabeth, 93
    George, 46, 54, 63, 78,
        87, 91, 92, 93, 94,
        96, 120, 124, 125,
        126
Fowler, Mr., 11
    James, 73
ffowles, Wm., 81
Fox, Capt. Edward, 14
    Capt. John, 14
    Robert, 5, 18, 19
Foxcroft, Thos., 125
Frame, John, 6, 24
    Capt. John, 8
Francis, Henry, 59, 63, 65,
    85, 96, 99, 102,
    108, 109

Freebourne, John, 41
Freeman, Capt., 11
    Bridges, 15
    Capt. Bridges, 76
    Col. Bridges, 11
    Thomas, 54
    William, 53, 104, 124,
        125
Freestone, John, 73
French, Anthonye, 30
Frenett, Arthur, 28
ffrestone, John, 79
Freyett, Antho., 16
Friers, John, 22
Fripps, Jno., 22
Frizell, Andrew, 67
ffydion, Aylse, 81


Gaiffing, John, 113
Gaoin, Thos., 53
Gapin(g)(e), William, 10,
    16, 30, 53, 60
Gardiner, Martin, 55
Gardner, (?), 55
    Charles, 115
Garratt, Peter, 15
Garrett, Jacob, 55
Garvett, Jno., 104
Garye, Jno., 5, 16
Gasgoville, Mary, 105
Gates, Mr., 31
Gates, Thos., 31
Gavin, Wm., 60
Gawine, Wm., 36
Gear, Joane, 66
Gee, Col. John, 12
George, John, 25, 63, 72
Ghissett, James, 88
Gibbings, Jno., 4
Gibbond, Thomas, 102
Gibbons, Thos., 94, 96, 102,
    104
Gibbs, Edward, 23
    Jno., 24
Gibons, Thos., 101
Gibson, Geo., 15
    Thos., 100
Gilbert, Widow, 85
    El(l)inor, 48, 91
    Rober, 124
    Roger, 91, 119
Gilburt, Elinor, 90
    Mary, 90
Giles, John, 119
    Thos., 99
Gillowe, Fra., 18
Gittinge, John, 17
Gittings, John, 6, 12, 15,
    28, 29, 30, 35, 36,
    43, 45, 46, 50
    Richardina Field, 7
Goard, Henry, 68, 78, 106,
    107, 124
    William, 124
Golborn, Martin, 121

Goode, John, 68
Goodridge, James, 99
Goose, Samuel, 61
Gopeinge, Wm., 9
Gorange, John, 9
Goreing, John, 108
Goring, Mr., 88, 112
    James, 75
    John, 67, 69, 77, 92, 106, 107, 108, 109, 124
Goringe, John, 72
Gossage, Richard, 13
Gossall, Jno., 9
Gotheridge, John, 124
Gough, Mathew, 23
    Capt. Mathew, 23
Gower, Francis, 73
Granger, Jno., 32
Gransome, Elizabeth, 113, 114
    Jasper, 113
    Jeas, 113
Grant, Widdow, 24
Grantham, Edward, 121, 122
Grascome, John, 102
Grassome, Mr., 106
Graves, Jno., 17
Gray, (?), 17, 45, 99, 116
    Capt., 73
    Francis, 28, 36, 38, 43, 45, 56, 57, 60, 64, 78, 83, 111, 116, 119
    Capt. Francis, 38, 39
    Henry, 100, 111
    Jane, 31
    John, 82, 99, 104, 111, 123
    Mary, 78, 111
    Peter, 36
    Thomas, 2, 8, 15, 16, 21, 28, 29, 30, 31, 41, 57, 60, 80, 82, 83, 94, 104
    William, 51, 73, 74, 78, 86, 97, 101, 104, 111, 113, 116, 121, 125, 126
Green, Mr., 57
    Edward, 100
    Katherine, 64
    Peter, 64
    Richard, 104
Greene, Mrs., 42
    Edward, 97, 116
    John, 88, 110, 117
    Katherine, 64, 79
    Kathering, 57
    Katheryne, 55, 58
    Peater, 10
    Peter, 6, 13, 29, 38, 42, 55, 57, 58, 60, 64, 68, 79
    Richard, 99

(Greene, cont'd.)
    Thos., 64, 65
Greenfield, Christopher, 30, 36, 54
    Xpher, 15, 16
Greenwelt, Garrett, 54
Greenwood, Edward, 28, 92
    John, 73
Gregory, Alice, 45
    Charles, 39, 51
    John, 34, 45, 49, 56, 88
    Susannah, 49
Gregorye, Alice, 40
    Alse, 67
    Charles, 20, 30, 68
    John, 28, 36, 40, 66
    Capt. John, 59
Grewe, Thos., 104
Grey, Francis, 94
    Mary, 94
Griffin, Maj., 75
    James, 66, 95
Grimes, Eustice, 9
    Martyn, 49
Grimmett, Christian, 86
Griswold, James, 45, 55
Grove, Capt., 48
    Elizabeth, 71
    John, 19, 23, 61, 64, 66, 69, 70, 72
    Capt. John, 66, 70, 84
    Robert, 107
Groves, Capt., 83
Growe, Thos., 104
Grymes, Eustace, 12
Gualtney, Goody, 56
    Widdowe, 58
    Mary(e), 56, 58
    Thomas, 56, 57, 61
    William, 57
Gullett, Robert, 120
Gulley, Rob., 121
Gully, Thos., 76
Gunnell, Edward, 112
Gwaltney, Thos., 54, 61
    William, 58
Gyles, Robert, 81


Hacker, Ann, 86
    Joh., 86
Hacume, Josiah, 118
Hadlye, Thos., 4
Hagard, Thos., 117
Hagood, Henry, 66
Hainsworth, Dr., 120
Hall, Geo., 58
    Wm., 17, 19, 30, 119, 120
Halliot, Edward, 10
Ham, Jerome, 15
Hamblett, Richard, 24
Hameline, Jno., 112
    Stephen, 28

INDEX 139

Hamey, David, 2
Edward, 3
Hamleton, (?), 85
Hamlin, Robt., 33
    Stephen, 56
Hamline, Mr., 17
Hammond, Jane, 8
    John, 8
    Martin, 5, 8, 17, 32
    William, 8
Hamond, Maj. Gen. Manwaring, 56
    Martin, 31
Hanatt, Wm., 15
Hancock, Eliza, 110
    Jno., 47
    William, 88, 92, 110
Hancocke, Geo., 63, 51, 67, 110, 112, 113
Hancoke, Wm., 84
Hane, Tho., 82
Hanero, Segg, 16
Hanes, Samuel, 31
Hanett, W., 16
Hankins, Richard, 33
Harding, Geo., 123
Hardinge, Eliza, 9
Hardy, Elizabeth, 25
Hardye, Capt., 12
    Elizabet, 21
    Elizabeth, 21
    George, 23
    Capt. Geo., 13
    John, 54
    Mary, 74, 85
    William, 47, 54, 62, 74, 79, 84, 85, 92, 126
Harker, Fra., 43
    John, 43
    Thomas, 51
Harloe, John, 70, 71
Harlow, John, 61
Harman, Will, 10
Harnsford, Edward, 19
Harrell, Garrett, 15
    Hubert, 75
Harrington, Francis, 7
Harris, (?), 31, 61, 67
    Elizabeth, 28
    George, 104
    John, 86, 114, 125
    Mary, 111, 114, 122
    Richard, 12, 14, 44, 49, 61, 65, 66, 78, 83, 93, 107, 121
    Samuel, 62
    Thomas, 33, 58, 108, 114, 122
    William, 62, 64, 70, 108, 111, 114, 121, 122, 124
    Capt. Wm., 16
Harrison, Dr., 12
    Benjamin, 5, 14, 49, 51, 58, 63, 66, 67, 69, 71, 75, 78, 87, 91

(Harrison, Benjamin, cont'd)
    93, 97, 101, 104, 106, 107, 109, 111, 113, 116, 117, 118, 119, 120, 123, 125
    Genjamin (Benjamin?), 117
    George, 13, 40, 47
    Hannah, 124
    John, 120
    Lester, 5
    Peter, 42, 43
    William, 77, 107, 114
Harry, Jno., 15, 36
Hart, Henry, 118, 122
    Thos., 11, 40, 56
Harte, Robert, 93
    Thos., 47, 53, 93
Hartlye, Thos., 7
Hartt, Thos., 47
Hartwell, Henry, 120, 124
    Hn., 110
Harvey, Wm., 97
Harvie, John, 8
Harwood, Alexx., 22
    Geo., 22
    Capt. Thomas, 76
    William, 86
Harwyes, Wm., 67
Haslewood, Wm., 3
Hasty, (?), 17
Haswell, Samuel, 33
Hawkes, Wm., 34
Hawkins, Jno., 29
Hay, John, 63
    Thos., 120
Haydon, Mary, 124
    Samuel, 72
    Samuell, 88
Haye, Thomas, 62
Hayes, Jacob, 107
Hayes, Wm., 82
Haynes, Mr., 26
Hayward, John, 56
    Nicholas, 112
Heath, Adam, 91, 97
    William, 35, 36, 55, 65, 82, 83, 91, 99, 104
Hegynison, Humph., 112
Heith, Edward, 41
Heiward, (?), 2
    John, 4, 5
    Michael, 2
Hemlocke, Wm., 7
Hethe, Mr., 2
Hewitt, Wm., 69
Heyward, (?), 73
Hide, Jurah, 33
    Richard, 15, 29, 30, 54, 69, 72, 106, 119
Hie, William, 54
Higgenford, Capt., 33
Higginson, Col. Humph., 76
High, Thomas, 75, 96, 104, 112, 114

Higham, Indian, 13
Hill, (?), 64
  Col., 16, 44
  Maj., 12, 74
  Mr., 89
  Edward, 11, 37
  Col. Edward, 56
  George, 69
  Hannah, 19
  Harman, 77
  Harmon, 55
  Jane, 100
  Mary, 57
  Matthew, 19
  May, 79
  Nicholas, 12, 17, 57, 58, 64, 79
  Maj. Nicholas, 64
  Richard, 14, 19, 34, 64, 74, 95, 100, 105
  Robert, 14
  Sion, 78, 97, 103, 111, 113, 126
  William, 63, 73, 89, 94
Hillard, Thos., 50
Hilliard, (?), 60
  Jane, 50
  John, 49, 50
Hilyard, John, 49
Hilyars, (?), 57
Hitchcock, John, 4
Hix, John, 1
Hobourne, John, 61
Hobson, Mr., 119
  Mathew, 14
Hodge, James, 125
  Jno., 44, 105, 106, 125
  Mary, 103
Hoge, Thomas, 62
Hoggson, Mary, 38
  Matthew, 30, 37, 38, 43
  Maylon, 48
Hogwood, (?), 120
  Elizabeth, 98
  Francis, 15, 17, 49, 51, 52, 58, 64, 77, 87, 90, 97, 98, 99, 107, 126
  Frentris, 51
  George, 119, 126
  Richard, 107
  William, 77
Holburt, Anthonye, 31
Holden, Joseph, 107
Holdins, (?), 4
Holeman, Chris., 62
Holeway, Jeremie, 14
Holeman, Christo., 78
Holiman, Christopher, 79
Hollams, Andrew, 32
Holleman, Christopher, 71, 101
Hollingsworth, Henry, 69
Holmes, Thos., 90

Holmeswoods, Jno., 2
Holmewood, John, 1, 4
Holmwood, Mr., 12
  John, 4, 5, 7, 8, 14, 19, 56
  Will, 12
Holsworth, Walter, 126
Holt, Mr., 66
  Elizabeth, 70
  Randall, 8, 16, 53, 63, 69, 72, 79, 90, 91, 93, 98, 106, 121
  Thos., 70
  William, 122
Holte, Mr., 66, 88
  Rand., 57
Holton, Hannah, 115
  Thomas, 8
  Wm., 71
Hone, Thos., 83, 100, 105
Honicutt, Austin, 92
Hooe, Rice, 17, 68
Hooper, (?), 81
  Wm., 82
Hopewell, George, 64
Hopkins, Richard, 33, 34
Horsemans, War., 28
Horton, Thos., 125
Hosker, Wm., 28
Hoskin, Ann, 124
Hoskins, Barth., 23
  Nicholas, 114
Hotten, Roger, 2
Houby, Sarah, 44
Houlston, Ralph, 105
Houlsworth, Walter, 39, 50
House, Martha, 120
  Robert, 43, 44, 70, 101, 112, 115, 120, 125
Howard, Phill, 72
Howe, Thos., 115
Howell, Edmond, 4, 57, 97, 99, 105, 111, 121
  Edmund, 91, 93, 95, 99, 104
  Garrett, 17
  Rebecca, 99
  Thomas, 84, 85
Howes, Robert, 108
Howgood, Wm., 123
Howgoode, Francis, 4
Howse, Robert, 40
  Wm., 40
Howsmanden, Worsham, 36
Hoydon, Sam, 68
Hubbard, Robert, 12
Huby, Judah, 44
Hubye, Sam, 8, 12, 13, 18
Hudson, Jude, 110
  Rowland, 51, 110, 113
Hugate, James, 19, 29, 54
  Jasque, 29
Huguet, Jasque, 19
Hukins, Wm., 18
Hulin, Edward, 44

INDEX 141

Humphrey, Evan, 104
Humphrye, (?), 13
Hunicutt, Asters?, 84
    Austin, 21
Huniford, (?), 64
    Phil(l)ip, 63, 64, 78, 101
Hunnicutt, Augustine, 52, 70, 123, 124, 125
    Austin, 34, 38, 42, 44
    Austine, 6
    Hen., 105
    John, 72, 73, 97, 104
    Robert, 107
Hunniford, Jane, 64
    Phillip, 64, 74
Hunt, Fortune, 55
    Nathaniel, 22
    Robert, 35, 47
    Thomas, 20, 37, 43, 44, 46, 55, 80, 82, 89, 94, 96, 102, 109, 115
    William, 78, 113, 117, 118, 125
Huntley, Jno., 17
Hurd, Henery, 24
    Henerye, 24
Hurlston, Edward, 9
Hurlstone, Edward, 7
Hurt, Thos., 47
Husdon, Judah, 113
    Rowland, 113
Hutchesson, Edward, 75
Hutton, Daniel, 1, 2, 4, 8, 12, 14, 17, 79
    Elesabeth, 79
    Elizabeth, 14
    Jno., 22
    Rebeckah, 8
Hux, Goody, 102
    Eleanor, 120
    John, 2, 6, 15, 31, 33, 38, 40, 41, 70, 122
    Mary, 61, 70
    Thomas, 92, 101, 102, 117, 118, 123
    William, 75, 84, 99
Hy, Thos., 121
Hyard, Tho., 84


Inge, Vincent, 75
Ireland, Stephen, 59
Ironmonger, John, 123
    Thos., 78, 97, 99, 126
Irvin, Wm., 53
Issell, Timothye, 4
Ivey, John, 46
Ivy, John, 13, 15
Izard, Tim, 120


Jackson, Henerye, 22
    Henry, 22
    Robt., 22

(Jackson, cont'd.)
    Zachariah, 111
James, Abell, 59
    Edward, 110
    Margery, 48, 53, 76
    Richard, 48, 53, 76, 106
Jannsey, John, 53
Jarrard, Henrye, 20
Jarratt/Jarret(t)(e)/Jarrots/Jarrott.
    Charles, 86, 101
    Richard, 28, 42, 44, 55, 60, 64, 66, 67, 70, 74, 86, 101
Jarrell, Thos., 27, 80, 114, 122
Jarret. See Jarratt.
Jarrett. See Jarratt.
Jarrette. See Jarratt.
Jarroll, Thos., 68, 108, 122
Jarrots. See Jarratt.
Jarrott. See Jarratt.
Jauncey, James, 17
    Thos., 17
Jeames, Dorothye, 22
    William, 21, 22
Jeams, Wm., 22
Jeanes, Wm., 24
Jeffries, Herbert, 108
    Gov. Herbert, 105
Jenkins, James, 18
Jennings, Mr., 19
    Geo., 120
    John, 4, 6, 12, 19, 21, 23, 29, 33, 36, 46, 54, 58, 97
    Capt. John, 98
    Col. John, 21
    Thos., 99
    William, 15, 17, 20, 21, 24, 25, 29, 31, 36, 39, 41, 42
    Col. Wm., 21
Jerrell, Tho., 77
Jeweller, Pheebe, 96
Jnoson, Martin, 121
Joanes, (?), 4
    Richard, 71
Johnson, Geo., 63
    James, 104
    John, 6, 120
    Martin, 55, 72, 80
    Nicholas, 104, 105, 109, 121
    Samuel Wharton, 59
Jollye, Eliza, 13
Joly, Jeames, 5
Jones, (?), 105
    Mr., 51
    Abell, 59
    Alcie, 11
    Alice, 105
    Eliza, 40, 115
    Foulke, 1
    Frances, 2

## INDEX

(Jones, cont'd.)
Henry, 7
James, 90, 95, 116
Jane, 118
Jno., 121
Ralph, 26, 30
Richard, 15, 118
Robert, 103, 114
Susannah, 100, 105
Thomas, 16, 17, 20, 31, 66
William, 104
Jonson, Nicholas, 100
Jordan, Capt., 9, 37
Col., 51, 56, 65, 80, 89, 90, 93
Lt. Col., 81, 121
Arthur, 14, 17, 21, 23, 35, 41, 43, 44, 45, 46, 59, 67, 79, 82, 83, 93, 94, 106, 107, 119, 125
Elizabeth, 35
Francis, 46
George, 1, 3, 6, 10, 12, 14, 15, 17, 25, 27, 29, 32, 34, 35, 39, 40, 43, 47, 48, 50, 51, 52, 53, 54, 55, 58, 59, 60, 70, 73, 79, 80, 91, 93, 94, 106
Capt. George, 3, 5, 11, 17, 19, 37, 38
Col. George, 47, 71, 83, 87
Lt. Col. George, 45, 52, 66, 67, 74, 75, 89, 90, 96, 101, 105, 107, 119
James, 93
Jannit, 122
Richard, 101, 113, 119, 123
Capt. Roger, 119
Thomas, 77, 78, 87, 93, 108, 114, 117, 119, 121, 122, 123
William, 43, 53, 119
Jotham, Charles, 40
Judkins, Charles, 110
Lidia, 82
Robert, 104
Samuel, 62, 82, 104, 109
Will, 68
Judy, negro, 104

Kae, Mary, 110
Robert, 57, 74, 77, 99, 104, 109, 110, 113, 115, 121, 123
Katherine, servant, 42
Kay, Robert, 61
Kee, Robert, 74, 81

Kelle, Wm., 101
Kent, John, 7
Kersey, Ann, 100, 102
Jno., 100
Kew, Dorothy, 8
Kiah, negro, 90
Kie; negro, 80
Kigan, Karby, 9, 12
Karbye, 20
Karbrye, 6
Kiketan, molatto, 105
Kille, Wm., 66
Killo, Dorothy, 105
Killybreck, James, 67
Kilpatrick, James, 66, 67
John, 84
Kimpe, Barth., 1
Kindred, Betty, 81
John, 67, 68, 70, 71, 72, 74, 81, 84, 92, 105, 106, 124, 125
Mary, 106
Prudence, 124, 125
Richard, 60
King, (?), 31, 69
Jane, 29
John, 2, 6, 9, 15, 17, 18, 20, 21, 29, 31, 35, 44, 47, 60, 64, 65, 66, 70, 75, 77, 80, 83, 92, 93, 97, 100, 102, 108, 109, 111, 113, 120, 123
Nathaniel, 45
Robert, 25
Thomas, 47, 100, 104, 124
Kinge, John, 21, 69
Thos., 105
Kippin, John, 54
Kippinge, Andrew, 22
Kirkman, Francis, 43
Kirtland, Ebenezer, 96
Kite, William, 83
Kitto, William, 102, 105, 116, 121
Knight, Dr., 87
Geo., 80
Jeremiah, 107
John, 23
Nathaniel, 40, 52, 53, 57, 66, 74, 82, 83, 94, 97, 107, 108
Peter, 19
Knighton, Henry, 75
Knipe, Barth., 22
Knot, Sarah, 87
William, 87
Knott, Mary, 55
William, 87, 117, 118, 123
Knowles, John, 43
Konder, John, 55
Kyrtland, Eleanor, 96

INDEX 143

Lacey, Mary, 116
   Robert, 116
Lacy, Robert, 81, 88, 92
Lacye, Martin, 61
Laine, Hannah, 57
   John, 19
   Robert, 54, 57
   Thos., 72
Lancasheare, Robert, 1
Lane, Hannah, 42, 43
   Nicholas, 32
   Ri., 119
   Richard, 113, 119
   Robert, 42, 43
   Thos., 32, 40, 44, 47,
      78, 91, 92, 94,
      105
Largie, James, 111
Lasley, Anne, 79
   Patrick, 79
Lathacot, Robert, 39
Lathard, Hen., 20
Latyard, Henry, 52
Lawrence, Richard, 61, 62,
     76, 83, 101
   William, 50
Lawson, Christopher, 27, 39,
     40, 61
   Xpo, 7
Lawyer, Eliza, 13
Layce, Martin, 61
Lea, Alice, 35, 36, 54
   Alse, 35
   Henry, 33
   Jno., 35
   William, 5, 6, 8, 25,
     28, 30, 33, 35, 36,
     38, 41, 45, 46, 49,
     54, 55, 60
Leade, Jno., 19
Leake, Jno., 2, 4, 39, 45
   Wm., 42
Lear, Jno., 115
Leatherland, Robert, 25
Ledener, Dr., 86
Lee, (?), 5
   Dr., 106
   Mr., 100
   George, 68, 69, 72,
     74, 75
Lee, George, 89, 95, 100,
     101, 102, 103, 106,
     115, 120
   Dr. George, 92
   Richard, 110
   Robert, 64, 71, 86, 94,
     102, 109, 116, 117
   Wm., 39
Leech, Richard, 100
Leeke, John, 19, 45, 46, 48
LeGrade, John, 46
Legran, John, 114
Legrand, John, 59, 75, 85,
     96, 99, 114
LeGrande, John, 60, 80, 95

Lengor, Wm., 24
Lewen, Wm., 14
Lewis, Christopher, 39, 40,
     61, 62, 101
   Jane, 39, 40
   Jo., 86
   Kett, 85
   Septhen, 105
   Stephen, 102, 104, 105
   Tom, 93
   Wm., 33
   Xo., 90, 95
   Xpher, 33, 40, 55
Liat, John, 32
Liddiard, Jno., 107
Lidford, (?), 115
   John, 83
Lile, Judea, 113
   Wm., 113
Lillicrop, Thos., 49, 50, 64,
     73, 75, 79
Lillycrop, Thos., 42
Limbry, Phillip, 54
Lindford, Joh., 84
Linscott, Gyles, 55
Linsey, James, 95
Lissison, Thomas, 49
Litford, John, 82, 115
Little, Wm., 88, 110
Littleboy, Law., 8
Littleton, Nathaniel, 23
   Col. Nathaniel, 76
Lockett, Thos., 64
Loftis, Adam, 24
Loide, Cornelius, 23
London, Mr., 44
Long, (?), 102, 111
   Capt., 102
   Mr., 92, 102
   A., 42
   Arthur, 36, 39, 49, 52,
     62, 66, 79, 84, 92,
     102
   Capt. Arthur, 102
   George, 117
   Mary, 117
   Richard, 56
Longe, Arthur, 79
Longwoode, (?), 32
Looke, John, 41, 44, 45, 49,
     50, 54, 55, 57
   Rebecca, 55
   Samuel, 104
Lookell, John, 38
Lookes, John, 41
Lord, Fra., 67, 112
   Francis, 116
Lotte, Jno., 23
Loucringe, Thos., 22
Louder, Thomas, 12
Loudlow, Robert, 44
Loveday, Geo., 120
Lovejoy, James, 66
Loweden, Wm., 15
Lucas, Ann, 31

# INDEX

(Lucas, cont'd.)
  Henry, 73
  Rich., 121
  Wm., 31, 80, 108, 114
Ludlow, Col. Geo., 5
  Daniel, 14
  John, 15, 51
  Thomas, 89, 96
Ludwick, Left., 2
Luke, John, 41
  Thos., 12
Lupo, Rich., 83
Luther, Martha, 58
  Martin, 68, 74
Lyle, Judah, 114
  William, 113, 114, 120
Lynde, Mathew, 23, 24

Mabery, John, 64
Mabrick, Alex., 8
Macanne, Marshall, 64
Macko, Owen, 91
Mackrell, Peter, 7
Madmonker, Timothy, 34
Magett, Allen, 49
  Samuel, 61
Maggott, Sam., 120
Magnes, Mathew, 82
Magney, Charles, 7
Magnis, Mathew, 101
Magnus, Mayou, 104
Maive, Jno., 21
Major, James, 69
  Robt., 5
Malden, Joseph, 113, 116, 117, 119, 120, 124, 125
  Wm., 126
Mallaka, negro, 43
Malott, negro, 44
Manfield, Geo., 47
Mansell, David, 22
Mansfell, Maximilian, 109
Mansfield, Geo., 50, 52, 64
Marable, George, 101, 106, 120
  John, 33
Margaret, servant, 101
Markham, Jno., 8
Markina, Morbia, 55
Markins, Murrur, 106
Marrilow, Wm., 95
Marriott, Maj., 52, 72, 118, 120
  Master, 27
  Mr., 49
  Alice, 84, 104
  Jno., 91
  Martha, 99
  Mary, 122
  Mathais/Matthias, 53, 65, 70, 71, 72, 73, 80, 85, 97
  Mt., 121

(Marriott, cont'd.)
  William, 5, 6, 8, 9, 12, 13, 15, 17, 20, 21, 25, 27, 28, 31, 32, 33, 34, 37, 42, 43, 44, 49, 50, 52, 54, 57, 61, 64, 65, 69, 70, 71, 72, 85, 92, 120
  Capt. William, 38
  Maj. William, 39, 42, 51, 66, 69, 70, 87, 94, 122
Marritt, Mas., 92
Marsh, Thomas, 17
Marshall, Capt., 15, 16
  George, 31, 38, 48, 52, 86
  Thomas, 115
Marsten, Thomas, 46
Marston, Thomas, 46, 95
Mart, John, 32
Martin, (?), 22
  Wm., 19
Martine, John, 21, 22
Mary, Indian, 97
Masingale, Daniel, 14
Mason, Mr., 20, 27, 88, 94, 100, 107, 121
  Amos, 43
  Ann, 43
  Eliza, 13
  Francis, 36, 56, 59, 62, 77, 78, 90, 92, 98, 100, 101, 104, 105, 106, 111, 113, 114
  ffrancis, 81
  George, 101
  Jacob, 23
  James, 2, 4, 5, 9, 12, 13, 27, 31, 33, 40, 44, 47, 62, 91
  John, 32, 42, 43, 44
  Mary, 122
  Mathew, 51
  Nicholas, 122
  Peter, 41
  Robert, 4
  Thomas, 102
  William, 48
Masonn(e), Jacob, 23, 24
  James, 21, 26, 27, 28, 29, 38
  Thomas, 35
Massingale, Daniel, 7, 48
Master, Francis, 69
Mathas, Thomas, 118, 122
Mather, Thomas, 118
Mathew, Ja., 120
Mathewes, Edm., 2
Mathews, Sam., 26, 99, 104
  William, 45, 106
Mathyson, John, 113
Matthews, Samuel, 26, 30

(Matthews, cont'd.)
   Col. Samuel, 76
Maurice, Thomas, 29
May, Richard, 121
   William, 68
Maynes, Mayson, 75
Mayo, Fra., 18, 19
Mays, Will, 50, 73
Meadows, Henry, 21
Meare, John, 64
Meazelle, Luke, 124
Meazle, Lawrence, 104
   Luke, 113
Meddow, Henry, 44
Meddowes, Henry, 13, 26
Meddows, Dorothy, 58
   Henry, 5, 65, 68, 69
Medley, Robt., 15
Melton, Tho., 77
Meredith, John, 48, 53, 76
   Mary, 48, 53, 76
Meridale, Col. Richard, 13
Meriweather, Eliza, 103
   Fra., 89
   ffrances, 82
   Joan, 103
   Nicholas, 44, 56, 62,
     68, 80, 82, 99, 103,
     106, 108, 109
   No., 103
Meriwether, Fra., 87, 95
   Nicholas, 81, 93
Merrell, Wm., 12
Merriweather, Mrs., 120
   Nicholas, 12, 13
Merydale, Richard, 9
Mezel, Luke, 2
Micane, Michael, 82, 84
   Sarah, 82
Michael, negro, 34
Michard, Michaell, 73
Michell, (?), 73
   Christopher, 44, 54
   Peter, 118
   Wm., 29
Middleton, Edward, 67
   Sarah, 83
Midleton, Geo., 64, 83,
   94, 97
Midyett, Thos., 68
Miller, John, 115
   Kerper, 105
   Richard, 121
Mills, Mr., 42
   Fortune, 37, 38, 40,
     41, 52, 66, 67, 71
   Francis, 52
   James, 38, 40, 41, 43,
     44, 45, 51, 52, 53,
     56, 59
   William, 46
Minard, Jno., 110
Mines, John, 80
Miniard, Jno., 97
Minnister, Hampton, 26
Minter, Naomi, 36

Minyard, (?), 98
Mirick, Owen, 120, 126
Miro, Owen, 121
Mise, Owen, 112
Missill, Luke, 53
Mitchell, Chs., 2
   Xo., 91
Mitford, Robert, 104, 112
Mizell, Chris., 57
   Deborah, 87
   Law., 100
   Luke, 31, 48, 85, 87,
     92
Mizelle, Luke, 15, 33, 40,
   41, 56, 58
Mizle, Luke, 47
Modmore, John, 30, 48, 53,
   76
Mohun, John, 70, 84
Mont, John, 32
Montaigne, Edward, 112
Moonk, Richard, 123
Moore, Alex, 118, 119
   Mary, 119
   Thos., 79, 115
Mooreing, Mrs., 86
Mooring, John, 108
Mooringe, Jane, 82
More, Mr., 15
   Alexander, 118, 119
   Ellexander, 119
   John, 47
   Mary, 118
   Thos., 71, 84, 119
Morecock, John, 51
Morecocke, John, 28, 35,
   39, 41, 56
Morgaine, Thos., 35
Morgan, (?), 17
   Mr., 120
   Thos., 48
Morick, Owen, 93
Moring, John, 72, 77, 82,
   99, 103, 106, 107,
   120, 121, 124
Moringe, John, 84
Morley, Edward, 72
Morris, Nicholas, 32
   Rich., 68, 121
   Rive, 32
   Thomas, 29
   William, 71
Morrison, Nicholas, 73
   Thomas, 68
Morryson, Major, 26
Morse, John, 83
Morslay, Robert, 8, 15, 20
   William, 28
Morsley, Robt., 5
Morten, (?), 50
Morton, Wm., 50
Moryson, Charles, 112
   Francis, 69
Moseley, Robert, 36
Mosely, Robert, 13
Moss, Jno., 97

# INDEX

Mosse, Jno., 94
Moulson, Foulk, 31, 53
Moulsworth, Col., 15, 16
Moyer, John, 112
Mudgett, Thos., 51, 95
Muggett, Ann, 61
 H., 55
Muggott, Allen, 42
Muilley, Charles, 39
Munger, John, 80
Murray, Francis, 54
 James, 28, 63, 78, 110
Murrell, Wm., 2, 4, 6
Murrey, James, 84
Murry, Ja., 121
Myles, Wm., 71
Myrick, Mary, 113
 Owen, 113, 115, 119
Myzealle, Luke, 124

Nance, William, 63, 78, 81, 95, 97, 100
Napkin, Ed., 69
Neady, John, 103
Netherland, Robert, 112
Newell, Jonathan, 5
 Jno., 28
 Richard, 44
Newett, Wm., 108
Newhouse, Eliza, 124
 Thomas, 46, 100, 124
Newitt, Wm., 104, 121
Newman, John, 52
 Richard, 51
 William, 70, 126
Newper, Ja., 121
Newsham, Dr., 121
Newsom, Francis, 45
 Wm., 80, 81
Newsome, Wm., 23, 65
Newsum, (?), 69
 Mr., 74
 Ann, 68, 115
 Jno., 124
 Thos., 64
 Wm., 30, 65, 68, 76, 77, 78, 82, 84, 90, 91, 93, 100, 108, 111, 114, 115, 117, 122, 124, 125
Newton, (?), 33
 Francis, 34, 70
 Mrs. Francis, 33
 Nicholas, 34
Nicholas, 40
Nicholls, Jno., 121
 Roger, 121
Nicholson, Geo., 123
 Roger, 8
Norman, James, 58
Norris, Mary, 125
North, Edward, 41
 Jno., 44
Norton, Francis, 3

Norwell, Geo., 120
Norwood, Chas., 11
 Edward, 115
 William, 43, 45, 47, 51, 54, 107
Nuis, Thomas, 80
Nusam, Wm., 62

Oakham, John, 37
Oberry, Philip, 66
Ogborne, Wm., 15
Ogbournes, (?), 2
Okeham, Henry, 70
 John, 20, 46
Oldis, William, 65, 66, 85, 86
Oliver, Edward, 36, 60, 71, 95, 98
Orchard, Jno., 4, 20, 67, 97, 101, 102
 Mary, 101
Osborne, Mr., 109
 Elias, 45, 63, 73, 74, 95, 102, 105, 106, 109, 113, 114, 115, 116, 119, 120, 122, 126
 John, 69
 Rich., 70
Osbourne, Elias, 119
 John, 69
Owen, Bartholomew, 30, 34, 35, 37, 38, 39, 40, 41, 47, 48, 49, 51, 56, 60, 72, 97, 101, 103, 106, 107, 123
 David, 96
 Hugh, 103
 Jane, 106
 Joane, 123
 Johannah, 72
 Col. John, 84
 Katherine, 101
Owens, Mr., 86
Owles, Cornelius, 68

Pace, Richard, 103, 120
Packer, Samuel, 106
Paine, Nicholas, 96
 Samuel, 15, 25
Pall, Col., 120
Pallmer, Robert, 85
Palmer, Robert, 4, 75, 83
Pamoast, Edward, 118
Pamplin, Jane, 17
Parke, Capt., 24
 Alice, 24, 31, 32, 33, 46, 123
 Ann, 18, 19
 Aylce, 123
 Aylse, 65
 Lt. Col. Daniel, 110
 Giles, 32
 Capt. Giles, 33

INDEX    147

(Parke, cont'd.)
   Robert, 43, 98, 113
   Wm., 18, 19
Parker, Mr., 51
   Widow, 106
   Joseph, 12
   Judah, 78
   Judith, 125
   Richard, 97, 125
   Samuel, 106
   Tho., 83, 84
   Wm., 85
Parnell, David, 14
Parolye, Dr., 21
Parrocke, John, 108
Parry, Wm., 24, 66
Parsons, James, 59
   Jo., 22
   Jonathan, 15, 22
Patmore, Katherine, 68
Paul, Parton, 107
Pauley, Jo., 23
Peach, Mathais, 77
Peacock, Wm., 27
Pearse, Capt. Wm., 39
Peck, Eliza, 87
Peebles, Capt., 16
Peed, John, 49

Peekweeke, John, 67
Peel, Rich., 69
Peeters, Geo., 88, 110
   Mabell, 110
   Thomas, 15
Pegler, William, 9
Pegraff, Dorothy, 110
Peirce, John, 124
   Thos., 26
   Wm., 26
   Capt. Wm., 26
Pender, John, 80
Penn, Wm., 19
Penny, Robert, 104, 113, 119
Perkings, Thomas, 59
Perry, B., 121
   Capt. Henry, 26, 30
   Nicholas, 9, 14, 15, 20, 23, 79
   Wm., 24
Perrye, Nicholas, 5, 6, 7, 28
Person, John, 123
Peter, negro, 14
Petro, John, 60
Pettaway, Edward, 13, 14
Pettway, (?), 47
   Mr., 123
   Edward, 29, 31, 38, 44, 52, 87, 91, 92, 101, 104, 105, 118
   Wm., 101, 104
Pettus, Coll. Thomas, 11, 76
Petway, Edw., 9, 40, 47, 53, 54, 61, 62, 63, 65, 73, 74, 125
   Elizabeth, 61, 62, 63

(Petway, cont'd.)
   Wm., 118
Peyton, Henry, 64
Pharlow, Joseph, 111
Phibbs, Jo., 4
Philips, Edward, 32
Phillips, David, 109
   Jno., 44, 47, 62, 78, 92, 97, 104, 105, 109, 111, 125
   Wm., 42, 45, 53, 113
Phillips, Elizabeth, 81
   John, 81
Phipps, John, 28
Pickerell, Hannah, 105
   Wm., 104, 120
Piddenton, Thos., 116, 117, 118
Piddinton, Thos., 118
Pilkinton, Wm., 43
Pinhorne, Ann, 45
Pipken, John, 61
Pitkin, John, 76
Pitman, Mary, 65
   Thos., 57, 61, 62, 65, 82
   Capt. Thos., 58, 80
   Wm., 119
Pitt, Mr., 8
   Elizabeth, 58
   Mary, 58
   Robert, 23
Pittford, Jno., 115
   Sarah, 115
Pittman, Capt., 2, 100, 102
   Francis, 39
   Thomas, 1, 2, 13, 15, 28, 29, 31, 35, 39, 49, 76, 78, 94, 96, 101, 104, 105, 107, 110, 113, 114
   Capt. Thos., 45, 52, 121
   Wm., 114
Pittway, (?), 37
   Mr., 36
   Ed., 28
Place, Mr., 89
   Roland, 92
   Rowland, 52, 68, 73
Plau, Mary, 64
   Samuel, 64, 125
Playce, Rowland, 50
Ploie, Wm., 99
Plough, John, 106
Plow, Jane, 92
   Samuel, 33, 52, 78, 80, 93
Plowe, Samuel, 33, 85, 104
Plunt, Thos., 30
Pollard, Wm., 117, 121, 126
Ponderton, Richard, 48
Poole, Ralph, 17, 20, 119, 120
Pope, Mary, 66
Popham, Rebecca, 50

(Porter, cont'd.)
  Elizabeth, 61, 64
  William, 61, 63, 64
Porteus, John, 111
Poter, (?), 29
Potin, Edmond, 5
Potter, (?), 30
  Capt., 120, 121
  Cuthbert, 56
  Doll, 29
  Jno., 23, 24
  Ned, 29
  Robert, 98
  Roger, 15, 21, 29, 37, 38, 41, 45, 46, 55, 57, 58, 73, 74, 77, 78, 92, 94, 99, 110, 111, 123, 125, 126
  Capt. Roger, 110, 120
Pottypole, Wm., 51
Powell, Clare, 39
  George, 5, 18, 19, 39, 69
  Mary, 8
  Marye, 5, 8
  Richard, 8
  William, 18, 19
  Capt. William, 18, 19
Powis, Robert, 24
Powsum, Wm., 105
Preassure, John, 63
Presson, Henry, 120
Preston, Geo., 24
  Roger, 51
Price, Maj., 120
  Mr., 9
  Jno., 6, 7, 72, 78, 84, 90, 91, 92, 93, 98, 100, 101, 102, 105, 120, 125
  Mary, 100, 102, 105
  Walter, 63
Pride, Wm., 63
Prime, Edmond, 99, 100
  George, 93
  Richard, 105
Prince, George, 93
  Jno., 121
  Rich., 121
Procter, Geo., 75
Proctor, (?), 89, 98
  Mr., 89
  Geo., 63, 72, 77, 81, 82, 83, 85, 87, 91, 92, 94, 96, 97, 98, 99, 101, 102, 104, 108, 109, 120, 121
  Mary, 33
Proser, Wm., 91
Prosser, Wm., 110, 112
Pryce, Howell, 7, 57
Pryse, Hoel, 28, 46
  Howell, 16
  John, 82, 84

Pugh, Daniel, 117
Pulestone, Roger, 122
Pulystone, Jno., 104
Purify, Edward, 54
Purnell, Wm., 22


Quarrell, Wm., 24, 25
Quelse, Martin, 72
Quilsian, Evaginus, 42


Race, Richard, 103
Radway, Wm., 15, 16
Raines, Jno., 6
Ralings, Roger, 125
Ramsey, Edward, 100
Rand, Sp., 40
Randall, Robert, 110, 124
Randolph, Hen., 6, 7
  Henerye, 7
  Henry, 20, 64, 66, 95
  Judith, 97
  Philip, 122
  Wm., 95
Raply, Thos., 120
Ratchelle, Ralph, 100
Rawlin, Jno., 3
Rawling, Jno., 119
Rawlings, (?), 21, 69
  Alse, 68
  Eleanor, 46
  Gregory(e), 4, 5, 15, 41, 44, 69
  John, 2, 28, 38, 39, 41, 43, 44, 45, 46, 48, 49, 50, 51, 53, 56, 58, 60, 61, 69, 70, 73, 75, 77, 81, 92, 108, 109, 110, 111, 121
  Mary, 92
  Roger, 37, 38, 42, 56, 68, 80, 81, 99, 102, 116, 121, 124
Rawlinson, Wm., 56
Raymond, Geo., 7
Read, Abraham, 23
Reade, Capt., 18
  Wm., 77, 120
Reading, Tho., 86
Reaves, Jno., 15
Reddick, James, 49, 66, 67, 68, 74, 79, 86, 111
  Mary, 74
  Robert, 75
Reddicke, James, 75
Redick, Mary, 79
Redwood, Anthony(e), 21, 27, 29
Reedwood, Anthony, 21
Reenes, Wm., 53
Regan, Daniel(l), 59, 61, 62, 81
  Eliza, 59
Reinolds, Thomas, 10

Renals, Francis, 49
Rennells, Francis, 45
    Nicholas, 45
    Robert, 45
Rennolds, Mr., 46
    Nicholas, 7, 24, 49
    Thos., 27
    Dr. Thos., 25
Renolds, Robt., 74
Rewliston, Jno., 109
Reynolds, Dr., 52
    Mr., 17
    Jane, 52
    Nathan, 102
    Nicholas, 9
    Robert, 74, 92, 125
    Thomas, 10, 52
Richards, Mr., 16
    Edw., 17
    Henery, 30
    Henry, 15, 16, 20, 38, 43, 47
    John, 5, 15, 16, 17, 18, 20, 21, 24, 26, 30, 31, 37, 38, 44, 47
    Lott, 53, 69, 103
    Ralph, 60
Richardson, Samuel, 83
Richman, Francis, 43
Rickett, Wm., 9
Ricketts, Lott, 64
Riddock, James, 64, 93
Riggan, Kirbye, 5
Ripley, Elizabeth, 49
Rix, Rich., 15
Roans, Dan, 77
Robbinson, Andrew, 8, 38, 46
    Susannah, 46
Roberts, Nat., 120
    Robert, 6
    Thomas, 55
Robertson, Andrew, 73
Robinson, Andrew, 33, 38, 40, 42, 48, 49, 53, 56, 64, 82, 113, 126
    Ann, 38, 56
    Cotton, 81
    Richard, 126
    Susanna, 73
    Thos., 47
Robley, Thos., 113, 121
Rochell, Elizabeth, 113
    Ralph, 66, 87
Rodwell, Jno., 116, 125
Rogane, Daniel, 116
Rogant, Daniel, 62
    Eliza, 62
    John, 75, 87, 105, 116, 117, 118, 120, 121, 122
    Joseph, 63, 69, 71, 73, 78, 102, 103, 105, 114, 123

(Rogers, cont'd.)
    Mary, 118, 121, 122
    Richard, 15, 63, 125
    Wm., 16, 125
Roland, Wm., 95
Rolfe, Mr., 107
    Thomas, 36, 91, 107
Rollinson, Wm., 36, 85
Rolph, (?), 57
Rome, Daniel, 120
Rookeings, Wm., 93, 95
Rookin, Willyam, 21
Rooking, Wm., 74
Rookinge, Wm., 95, 97
Rookings, (?), 67, 102
    Eliza, 2
    Jane, 95
    Wm., 52, 66, 68, 73, 78, 80, 94, 95, 98, 100, 103, 105, 111, 113
Rookins, Wm., 42
Room, Daniel(1), 57, 60, 69, 115
Roome, Daniel, 87, 122
    Margarett, 122
    Mary, 69
Roomis, Dan, 91
Roopo, Anthony, 60
Rose, Ann, 56, 106
    Jane, 56, 106
    Mary, 56, 106
    Maurice, 83
    Morris, 3
    William, 3, 4, 8, 15, 29, 33, 34, 45, 56, 61, 64, 75, 106, 118
Ross, Mr., 2
    Wm., 81
Rossey, Anthony, 61
Rouse, Harry, 73
    Walter, 15
Rowell, Edward, 126
    James, 13
Rowland, Fra., 110
    Wm., 121, 124
Rowles, James, 111
Rowse, Abraham, 85
Royes, Rich., 97
Rudder, Edward, 24
Rudds, John, 106
Ruffin, Eliza, 99
    John, 124
    Richard, 113
    Robert, 77, 78, 90, 9 99, 100, 105, 108, 111, 114, 116, 119, 120, 121, 122, 124, 125, 126
    Wm., 99
Rugherford, John, 125
Rumball, Mr., 119
Rumsey, Ed., 69
Rutherford(e), John, 15, 98, 99, 105, 121, 124, 125

INDEX

Sadler, Jno., 17
   Rowland, 23
Saines, John, 9
Sallway, John, 63, 92,
   107
Salter, Thos., 49, 58
Salway, Mr., 87, 91, 97,
   100
   Eliza, 85
   John, 58, 60, 61,
      64, 68, 70, 73, 74,
      75, 79, 82, 83, 85,
      86, 87, 89, 92, 94,
      95, 97, 99, 102,
      105
   Mary, 74
Samberton, Deliverance, 41
Samsell, Wm., 31
Samson, James, 73
Sanders, Jno., 15, 20
Sanderson, Edward, 47
   Montagne, 7
Sandes, Wm., 17
Sands, Henry, 53
Sapcoate, Abraham, 87
Sappington, John, 66, 68
Savage, William, 9
Sawyer, Eliza, 13
   John, 33
Saynes, Jno., 2, 7
Scarboro, Wm., 46
Scarbrough, Wm., 29, 30, 50
Scarbrow, Wm., 48, 63, 72
Scott, Harme, 7
   John, 56, 79
   Wm., 30
Seaborn, Geo., 13
Seale, Jos., 110
Seaward, (?), 125
   Wm., 54
Seely, Geo., 66
Seesam, Nicholas, 113
Selway, John, 79, 81
Senderson, Edward, 7
Senior, Jno., 2, 24, 62,
   63, 105
   Thos., 77, 91, 97,
      101, 102, 104, 105,
      109, 114, 121
Senod, Wm., 116
Sessoms, Nicholas, 113
Sessums, Nicholas, 76, 118,
   122, 125
Seward, (?), 98
   Mr., 101
   Elizabeth, 56
   William, 56, 66, 68, 69,
      70, 75, 77, 82, 84,
      103, 110, 114, 124,
      125
Sewell, John, 10, 13
Sharp, John, 126
Sharpe, Richard, 20
   Thos., 69
Shaw, Robert, 68, 72, 75

Sheapard, Ann, 10
   Elizabeth, 10
   John, 10
   Priscilla, 10
   Robert, 10
   Maj. Robert, 10
   Susan, 10
   William, 10
Sheares, Abraham, 14
   Elizabeth, 14
Shears, Abraham, 29, 30
Shelley, Philip, 118
Shelly, Phillip, 114
   Wm., 114
Shelton, John, 104
Shepard, Maj., 38
   Jno., 122
   Robt., 4
   Capt. Ro., 11
   Wm., 6
Sheperd, Maj. Robert, 44
Shepheard, John, 109
Shepherd, Eliza, 9
Sheppard, Alex, 103
   Francis, 24
   Jno., 88, 93
   Robert, 68
   Capt. Robert, 69
Shepperd, John, 47
Sherbourne, James, 69
Sherwood, (?), 108
   Mr., 81, 89, 95
   Ratchell, 114
   Will, 65, 68, 71, 72,
      73, 74, 75, 78, 79,
      80, 81, 82, 83, 84,
      85, 86, 88, 89, 90,
      91, 94, 95, 98, 114,
      115, 120
Shines, John, 73
Shipham, Jno., 70
Shipman, Edmund, 30
Shivers, Elizabeth, 122
   William, 115, 116
Shogh, Wm., 17
Shohocings, Jno., 86
Short, Elizabeth, 31, 40,
   45
   William, 97, 115
Shorte, Elizabeth, 64, 83
   Mary, 84
   Thomas, 44, 64
   William, 15, 63, 64,
      65, 73, 83, 84
Shortland, Ann, 33
   Ralph, 33
   Richard, 6, 8
Shrewsbury, Francis, 106
Shrewsby, Thomas, 105
Shrimpton, Sam'l, 95
Sidway, Capt, 16
   Benjamin, 1, 15, 16,
      18, 19, 24, 26, 27,
      30, 36
   Capt. Benjamin, 5, 14,
      21

(Sidway, cont'd.)
   Mary, 21
   Thos., 10, 122
Sidwaye, Ben., 7
Sidwell, Ann, 38, 39
   John, 38, 39
Silvester, Nathaniel, 30
Simbry, Phillip, 63
Simmons, (?), 60
   Elizabeth, 114
   Fra., 72
   Mary, 109
   Wm., 9, 18, 21, 40,
      64, 108, 109, 114,
      124, 125, 126
Simonds, Mr., 85
Simons, Mr., 49, 82
   Simon, 51
   William, 77, 80, 99,
      103, 120
Simpson, (?), 1
   Ann, 56
   Eliza, 7
Sine, Goodman, 29
Sizer, Ann, 100
Skelton, Edward, 33
   John, 101, 125
Skiner, Mary, 80
   Richard, 43, 67, 74
Skinner, Anthony, 54
   Jason, 112
   John, 66, 90, 97, 104
   Mary, 65, 90, 110
   Richard, 14, 34, 52,
      55, 65, 80, 99
   Lt. Richard, 95
   William, 54
Slaughter, Francis, 12, 13,
   14
   Jno., 10
   Ralph, 11
Smiley, Chris., 66
   John, 67
Smith, (?), 104
   Christopher, 68, 103,
      110, 122
   Deborah, 87
   Maj. George, 70
   Isabell, 101
   John, 47, 60, 82, 87,
      92, 105, 113, 114,
      117, 118, 119, 121
   Mary, 114, 118
   Nich., 113, 114, 118,
      124
   Richard, 34, 49, 91
   Thomas, 25, 47, 48, 53,
      67, 76, 111, 123
   Wm., 73, 79, 85, 94
Sneade, Robert, 20
   Samuel, 22
Soane, Mr., 26
   Hen., 29
Somers, Mr., 64
Sorrell, Robert, 26

Sorsby, An., 120
   Catrina, 120
   Francis, 61, 62, 81
   Katherine, 61
Soulcott, Otho, 68
Southerland, Robert, 25
Sowerby, Ann, 125
   Francis, 33, 34, 54,
      59, 77, 95, 115, 121
   James, 3, 31, 33, 34,
      48, 101, 125
   Margaret, 125
   Thomas, 48, 54, 87, 97,
      107, 108, 109, 120,
      121, 126
Sowerbye, Francis, 21
   James, 20
   Thomas, 20, 21
Sowers, Jas., 120
Sparks, Capt., 21
   Sarah, 46
Sparrow, Charles, 16, 38
   Dorothy, 50
   Mary, 50
   Sarah, 50
   Selby, 45
Sparrowe, Ch., 17
   Charles, 28
Spencer/Spenser/Sponsor
   (?), 47, 80
   Capt., 90, 121
   Alex., 104, 105, 119,
      121
   Ann, 74
   George, 116
   Joane, 111
   John, 62
   Nicholas, 29, 59, 60,
      62, 123
   Robert, 2, 5, 13, 29,
      30, 31, 33, 35, 36,
      37, 40, 42, 43, 44,
      46, 47, 48, 51, 52,
      53, 58, 59, 62, 65,
      71, 72, 73, 74, 75,
      80, 81, 84, 87, 90,
      93, 96, 105, 109,
      111
   Capt. Robert, 88, 89,
      91, 97, 101, 105,
      106
   Lt. Col. Ro., 42
   William, 26, 59
Spenser. See Spencer.
Sponsor. See Spencer.
Spilltimber, (?), 25, 27,
   51, 87
   Anthony(e), 27, 35, 41,
      45, 48, 60, 61
   Aug., 53
   John, 14, 15, 27, 78
   Mary, 48
Spilltimbere, (?), 57
Spiltimber, Anthony, 49,
   120

(Spiltimber, cont'd.)
  John, 2, 5, 10
  Martha, 120
Spragan, Rudolph, 22
Spring, Wm., 43, 73, 97,
  100, 121
Springer, William, 120
Stagg, Capt., 18
Stagge, Thos., 12
Stanford, Mr., 71
  Anthony, 70, 84
Stanhard, Susannah, 33
Stanly, Ann, 25
Stanton, Mr., 29, 42
  Mrs., 28
  Dorothy, 112
  Mary, 28, 46
  Nathan(iel), 37,
    39, 44, 46, 47, 51,
    53, 55, 58, 59, 60
  Richard, 45
  Robert, 1, 2, 3, 4, 5,
    6, 7, 9, 10, 12, 14,
    15, 16, 17, 20, 21,
    26, 27, 28, 30, 32,
    33, 34, 35, 36, 38,
    39, 43, 44, 45, 46,
    47, 53, 76
  Wm., 46, 112
Steephen, Tho., 32
Steephens, Mr., 41
  George, 33
  Tho., 32
Steevens, John, 57
  Richard, 38, 39, 44
  Sam'll, 41
  Thos., 70
  Wm., 15
Steevenson, Thos., 16, 25
Stento, Wm., 112
Stepham, Edmunde, 75
Stephens, Geo., 6, 23, 58,
  59, 63
  James, 58, 59
  Susannah, 23
Steven, Mr., 74
Stevens, Rich., 8
Stevenson, John, 74
  Tho., 80
Steventon, Tho., 89
Steveton, Tho., 80
Stinger, Jno., 23
Stinton, Wm., 116
Stock, Aylee, 103
  Jno., 103
Stocke, John, 83, 97
Stone, James, 24
Stoner, Thos., 67
Storeman, Steph., 55
Story, Robert, 33
Stradling, James, 72
Stratford, Anthony, 32
Stratton, Dr., 121
Strinfellow, James, 109
Strong, Thos., 21

(Strong, cont'd.)
  Wm., 37, 43, 47, 50, 53
Sturdivant, Daniel, 47, 54
Sugar, Jno., 114
Sugg, Edward, 49
  Geo., 26
  John, 62
Suggs, Jno., 34
Suklemoe, Sam., 91
Summer, Fra., 89
Sumner, Fran., 94, 99
  ffran., 91
Swaine, Sam., 27
  Seth, 15
Swan, Mathew, 92
Swann, (?), 83, 98
  Capt., 108
  Col., 29, 52, 61, 75,
    82, 88, 93, 100,
    104, 106, 109
  Lieut. Col., 25
  Maj., 117, 121
  Mary, 116, 117, 120,
    123, 125
  Mathew, 84, 88, 94,
    109, 121, 126
  Samuel, 27, 28, 43, 71,
    73, 77, 100, 110,
    116, 117, 123, 126
  Capt. Samuel, 92, 106,
    107, 114
  Maj. Samuel, 114, 115,
    116, 119, 120
  Sarah, 115, 116, 117,
    120, 123
  Susannah, 34
  Thos., 15, 17, 18, 19,
    23, 25, 37, 46, 56,
    58, 83, 84, 89,
    104, 116, 123
  Capt. Thomas, 34, 45
  Col. Thomas, 1, 9, 13,
    14, 17, 26, 34, 38,
    42, 43, 45, 47, 55,
    73, 83, 84, 85, 89,
    94, 95, 96, 97, 98,
    117
  Lt. Col., 6, 9, 12, 26
  Tobias, 10
Swans, Col., 103
Swett, Wm., 62, 94, 115, 121
Sykes, Bernard, 112
Symmondes, Mr., 14
Symonds, Mrs., 97


Tabb, Thomas, 60
Taberer, Thos., 14, 80
Talbot, John, 81
  Thomas, 81
Talbott, Peter, 23
Tamor, Ed., 66
Tanner, Daniel, 23
  Edward, 76, 99, 112
  Thomas, 112

# INDEX

Tapley, Adam, 100
Targett, John, 126
Tatem, Eliza, 69
   Isaac, 29, 59, 80
   James, 33
   John, 44, 45, 56, 69, 70
Tatum, Chris., 122
   Issac, 52
Tayler, Dr., 87
   Francis, 89, 113, 121
   James, 12
   Jno., 17
   Sarah, 102
   Walter, 103, 111
   Col. Wm., 11
Taylor, Dr., 86
   Francis, 67, 88, 91, 100, 109
   Dr. Francis, 95
   James, 37, 75
   John, 58, 63, 67
   Mary, 83
   Richard, 63
   Sam, 6
   Thos., 57, 67, 80, 92
   Walter, 83, 117
   Maj. Wm., 76
Tench, Richard, 20
Tennis, Francis, 48
Thom, Francis, 93
Thomas, (?), 15
   John, 66, 67, 82, 91
   Margaret, 103
   Martin, 107
   Thomas, 67
   William, 1, 5, 6, 15, 16, 18, 20, 25, 36, 50, 60, 69
   Capt. Wm., 16
Thompson, (?), 72
   Mr., 98, 111
   Mrs. 63, 101, 102
   Benjamin, 96
   Catherine, 81
   John, 41, 54, 60, 76, 78, 119, 125
   Katherine, 62, 106, 119
   Samuel, 116, 118, 119, 120, 123, 125, 126
   Walter, 60
   William, 44, 48, 50, 51, 53, 54, 56, 62, 77, 86, 94, 98, 105, 106, 115, 119, 120, 122, 124, 126
Thomson, Mr., 83, 93
   John, 41
   Katherine, 81, 85
   Samuel, 81
   Sarah, 41
   William, 45, 81, 82, 84, 85, 89, 90, 91, 94, 101
Thorn, Martin, 109

Thorne, Dorothy, 66
   Dorothy, 66
   Martin, 103, 121
   Wm., 62
Thornton, Katherine, 99
Thropp, Thomas, 123
Tias, Richard, 8, 13, 28, 43, 48, 85, 87, 91, 97, 103, 107
   Thos., 48, 83, 85, 126
Tichner, Stephen, 23
Tillary, Henry, 49
Tilnor, Mary, 68
Tine, Thos., 99
Tirrey, Dorothy, 112
   John, 112, 113
Tius, Richard, 48
Tombs, Francis, 44
Tompson, Sam, 122
Tony, Capt. Nich., 69
Tooke, Jno., 43, 48
   Rebekah, 48
   Wm., 82, 88
Tooker, Widow, 99
Townes, Matthew, 123
Townsend, Wm., 75
Trafton, Joseph, 45
Travis, Edward, 65, 107
   Elizabeth, 107
Trenett, Arthur, 28
Triuett, Anthony, 7
Triuette, Anthony, 6
Troy, Jno., 93
Truett, Anthony, 6, 7
Tucker, Daniel, 62
   Jane, 64
   Joseph, 62
   Samuel, 64
Tuke, Wm., 37, 42
Tulley, Capt., 18
Tully, Jno., 22
Turner, Wm., 5
Turpin, Robt., 69
Twy, (?), 85
Tyas, Richard, 81, 107, 109
   Capt. Richard, 28

Underhill, Elizabeth, 90
Underwood, Thomas, 45, 59
   Wm., 24
Upchurch, Edward, 49
   Fra., 125
   Michael, 43, 88, 125
   Michaell, 34
   Michell, 80
Upsheau, Daniel, 53
Upshure, Michael, 43
   Michaell, 34

Vahan, Christopher, 45, 47, 71
   George, 109
   Stephen, 109, 126

(Vahan, cont'd.)
   Walter, 100, 104, 121, 126
   Xpher., 47
   Xpo., 7
Vantor, Ellis, 53, 54, 63, 64
Vantore, Thos., 62
Varnam, Geo., 16
Varnell, Thos., 24
Vaughan, Christopher, 51, 58
   William, 1
Vause, Robt., 24
Vawhan, Walter, 109
Veale, Daniel, 20
Vessell, Janneys, 2
Vicars, Wm., 101
Vigore, Jos., 22
Vincent, John, 77, 116
   Wm., 22
Vinsent, John, 109, 115
Vinson, Jas., 107
   John, 56, 105


Wade, Daniel, 109, 111
   Tho., 87
Waitley, Charles, 40
Walabacke, Richard, 98
Waldan, Christopher, 36
Walker, Geo., 66
   John, 55
   Timothy, 84, 100, 104, 105
Wall, John, 23
   Joseph, 57, 74, 78, 101, 118, 121
   Susan, 101
   Thomas, 49, 51, 87, 90
Waller, Mary, 119
   Thos., 119, 121
Wallett, Corn., 55
Wallis, Abraham, 102
   John, 68
   Thos., 115
Walls, Thos., 19
Walters, Thos., 23
Walthall, Wm., 16
Walton, John, 55
Walward, Wm., 79
Warburton, (?), 97
Ward, Thos., 58, 116
   Wm., 21
Warde, Anis, 3
Ware, Frances, 5
   Thos., 63, 91
Waringe, Thos., 5
Warner, John, 104
   Richard, 13
Warren, (?), 120
   Mr., 57
   Allen, 125
   Aylse, 62, 71
   David, 23, 50

(Warren, cont'd.)
   Edward, 54, 62, 69, 78, 87, 94, 98, 100
   Elizabeth, 72, 73
   Grace, 98
   James, 112
   Jane, 71, 72, 73
   John, 64, 66, 77, 78, 92, 93, 95, 112, 115, 120, 123
   Mary, 93
   Mawdlin, 115
   Robert, 6, 13, 21, 64, 95, 107, 111, 125
   Sarah, 21
   Thos., 10, 16, 25, 27, 38, 39, 40, 45, 47, 51, 63, 65, 66, 71, 72, 73, 85, 107, 118, 125
   Wm., 71, 72, 125
Warrendine, James, 17
Warrener, Richard, 13
Warrilow, Susanna, 71
   Wm., 71, 99
Warrine, Thos., 54
Warriner, Mathew, 15
Warring, John, 109
Warringe, Thos., 2, 5, 6
Warrings, John, 64
   Thos., 10
Warrolow, Wm., 47
Warwell, Tho., 83, 86
Washington, Francis, 68
   Jno., 30
   Richard, 108
Waterhouse, Sam., 15
Waters, Comm. Capt. Richard, 5
Watkin, Elias, 70
   Elizabeth, 91
   G., 65
   George, 45, 47, 50, 52, 53, 54, 55, 57, 58, 59, 60, 62, 63, 65, 66, 68, 69, 70, 72, 73, 74, 75
   Capt. Geo., 73, 95
   Gertrude, 62, 63, 66, 72
   James, 62, 70
   Jane, 53, 76
   Richard, 53, 76
Watkins, Mr., 68, 81, 89
   Mrs., 89
   Benjamin, 34
   Elizabeth, 12, 13, 90
   G., 123
   George, 31, 41, 42, 44, 50, 51, 56, 79, 80, 82, 83, 85, 100
   Capt. Geo., 83, 90, 91, 97
   Henry, 78, 97, 105
   James, 77, 97

# INDEX 155

(Watkins, cont'd.)
  Jane, 48
  John, 5, 13, 78, 97,
    99, 108, 109, 116,
    119
  Richard, 48, 80
  Xo., 90, 91
Watson, Isaih, 75
  James, 62
  Thomas, 104
Watterhouse, Samuel, 20
Wattkins, Geo., 43
  James, 16
  John, 5, 9, 39, 40
  Nich., 22
Watts, Ann, 30
Wattson, Thos., 42
Weaver, John, 108
Webb, Edward, 53
  Robert, 14, 20, 25, 31,
    32, 39
  Steephen, 32, 39
  Stephen, 14, 32
  Thos., 21, 23
  Wm., 14, 15, 17, 32,
    64, 69, 116
Webbs, Mr., 11
Webster, Capt., 63
  Daniel, 34
  Rich'd, 91
  Capt. Richard, 14
  Thomas, 43, 51, 54
Webward, Wm., 82
Weekes, Mary, 106
  Stephen, 106
Welbanks, Edward, 80
Welbeck, (?), 80
  Mr., 64
  Richard, 65, 72, 73,
    81, 82, 97
  Robert, 104
Welbecke, Richard, 68, 87,
  89, 95
Welch, Thos., 7
Wells, Wm., 82
Welluck, Rich., 79
Wenters, Mr., 89
West, Richard, 92, 95, 100
Westhorpe, Maj. John, 16
Westophen, Indian, 31
Westorpe, Jno., 15
Westropes, (?), 20
Wetherall, Ro., 23
Wheeler, Nevitte, 103
Whitthowe, Tho., 38
Whiddon, John, 108
Whitaker, William, 22
Whitbey, Jose, 25
  Mary, 25
White, Eliza, 86, 109
  Henry, 13, 15
  John, 11, 18, 19, 75,
    77, 108, 111
  Mary, 86, 87, 109, 111,
    114
  Robt., 108

(White, cont'd.)
  Thos., 118
  Wm., 59, 68, 106
  Maj. William, 108
Whitehorn, Conway, 64
Whitman, Anthony, 29
Whitmell, Joseph, 15, 26
Whitmoald, Joseph, 31
Whitney, John, 108
Whitson, John, 74, 81, 82,
  83, 85
  Martha, 74
Whitt, Eliza, 55
Whittle, Robt., 35
Whittye, Capt., 5
  Capt. Jno., 6
Wiggin, Mr., 12
Wiggins, Capt., 121
  Thos., 115
Wilbeck, Mr., 67
  Rich., 99
Wilbecke, Rich., 62
Wilde, Robert, 64
Wilham, Tho., 87
Wilkerson, John, 15, 120
Wilkins, Edmund, 34
  Edward, 52
Wilkinson, Mr., 11
  Jno., 16
  Math., 84
  Thomas, 82
Willcox, (?), 21
Willes, Chas., 81
Willett, (?), 85
Williams, Mrs., 111
  Charles 78, 124, 126
  Daniel(1), 13, 60, 66,
    70, 73, 97
  David, 48, 76, 82, 84,
    96, 121
  Donell, 95
  Geo., 78, 104, 126
  Lewis, 105, 109, 111,
    126
  Martha, 100
  Mary, 111, 115, 119
  Maurice, 37
  Morris, 37, 43
  Nicholas, 15, 27, 111
  Paul, 120
  Rice, 14
  Roger, 62, 75, 115,
    116, 119
  Roy, 85
  Samuel, 74
  Wm., 126
Williamson, Mr., 61
  Robert, 59, 62
Willis, Col., 70
  Henry, 113
Willson, Jno., 15, 113
  Ni., 111, 113
  Wm., 20
Willyams, David, 29
  John, 37
Wilson, Nich., 109

INDEX

(Wilson, cont'd.)
    Robt., 24
Wimberly, John, 67
Winchester, Margaret, 72
Winclos, Richard, 123
Winder, Rich., 119
Winecaster, Margaret, 59
Winn, Anthony, 68
Winne, Capt. Robert, 56
Winter, Thos., 70
Wise, Thos., 34
Witherington, Katherine, 104
    Nicholas, 99, 105, 119, 124
Witnell, Joseph, 20
Wombwell, Capt., 12
Wood, Mr., 15
    Ab., 7
    Jno., 12
    Wm., 17
Woodford, Robert, 4
Woodhouse, Goodman, 5
    Thomas, 1, 2, 4, 6, 8, 12, 15, 44, 45, 68, 93
Woods, (?), 57
Woodward, Enoch, 108
    Geo., 18
    Richard, 25
    Capt. Wm., 72
Worgan, William, 103
Worlick, Wm., 4
Wormeley, Ra., 110
Worrin, Thomas, 4
Worwell, Thos., 89, 90
Wright, Jno., 81

(Wright, cont'd.)
    Thos., 28
Wyat, Capt. Nicholas, 113
Wyatt, Capt., 119
    Mr., 16
    Antho., 28, 56
    Edward, 56
    N., 80, 114
    Capt. Ni., 78
    Robert, 116
Wynne, Thos., 47
Wyrick, Owen, 104
Wytell, Robt., 49


Yar..., Col. Argall, 76
Yardly, Col., 12
Yarrett, Mr., 12
Yates, (?), 51
    Mathew, 48
    Matthew, 38
    Steeven, 5
    Stephen, 2
Yeoman, Thos., 23
Young, Anthony, 60
    Edward, 15


Zaines, John, 9, 26, 30, 45
    Thos., 45
    Wm., 26, 30
Zanes, Wm., 26
Zaynes, John, 8

www.ingramcontent.com/pod-product-compliance
Lightning Source LLC
Chambersburg PA
CBHW071848230426
43671CB00012B/2112